Contents

CONTENTS

Acknowledgements

We would like to register our thanks formally to the following people, without whom it would not have been possible to conduct this research.

Jane and Roger Lindsay and the interviewers of North East Market Surveys conducted the follow-on survey field-work on this project. We are also grateful to Nick Clay and Marc Cowling of the Small and Medium-sized Enterprises (SME) Centre, Warwick for conducting additional follow-on interviews and to Adam Strange for questionnaire design and management in the early phase of the project.

The assistance of Sue Cooke and Yvonne Cobbold in identifying the status and location of Science Park firms initially interviewed in 1986 was much appreciated.

Tracy Webster and Glenda Hall at the SME Centre provided excellent secretarial and typing services throughout the research.

KPMG Peat Marwick provided vital support in this study. KPMG acted as both a sponsor and contractor, undertaking a large number of the business interviews. Andrew Newland, head of the research and technology practice, directed KPMG's involvement and represented the firm as sponsor of the study. KPMG's research team was led by Charles Hammond and consisted of full-time researchers, Raphäelle Mazenc and Heike Schlappa, as well as staff from many KPMG offices throughout the UK. KPMG provided valuable input to both the design and implementation of the study and gave an important commercial focus to the work undertaken.

We would also like to thank the sponsors of this research for their interest, commitment and comments and, in addition, the Department of Trade and Industry (Irene Brunskill, Brett Grant, Bill Lunny, Martin Nonhebel and Brian Parsons), National Westminster Bank (Peter Ives) and the United Kingdom Science Park Association (Derek Burr, Peter Russell and John Turner). In particular the many insightful comments of David Rowe, chairman of the steering committee, were above and beyond the call of duty. The opinions expressed in the report, of course, are those of the authors alone and not necessarily those of any of the above sponsoring organisations.

Finally, we would like to record our gratitude to all the firms interviewed in this research for giving up their valuable time.

P. Westhead
D. J. Storey

SME Centre, University of Warwick

February 1994

List of Abbreviations

ACOST	Advisory Committee on Science and Technology
HEI	Higher Educational Institution
KPMG	Klynveld Peat Marwick Goerdeler
NTBF	New Technology-based Firms
QSE	Qualified Scientists and Engineers
R&D	Research and Development
SMART	Small Firms Merit Award in Research Technology
SME	Small and Medium-Sized Enterprises
TEC	Training and Enterprise Council
UKSPA	United Kingdom Science Parks Association
USM	Unlisted Securities Market
VAT	Value Added Tax

Chapter 1

Introduction

"Over recent years, continuous increases in the number of science parks (SPs) have been observed without any corresponding progress in the theoretical analysis of their existence" (Maggioni, 1992, p 12).

1.1 Background During the past few decades it has been appreciated by national and local governments, universities and private industry that technological innovation has a key role to play in revitalising economically deprived localities. As a result policy makers throughout Europe and North America have been increasingly concerned with the creation of small NTBF's (Rothwell and Zegveld, 1982; Oakey, 1985, 1991a, 1991b; Amin and Goddard, 1986; Simmie and James, 1986; Breheny and McQuaid, 1987; Aydalot and Keeble, 1988; Oakey and Cooper, 1989; Donckels and Segers, 1990; Henneberry, 1992). This effort has been particularly notable in the United Kingdom with the promotion of NTBF start-ups in a variety of property-led "incubator" environment clusters (for a detailed summary see Grayson, 1993).

> "The local university would act as a growth pole, being a locus of high technology information to established industrial firms and, at the same time, being a source of new technology-based firms" (van Dierdonck et al., 1991, p 111).

However, as early as 1985, the Science Park movement in the United Kingdom was criticised by Oakey (1985, p 59) who questioned the presumed "role models" of American university developments being transferred to a British university setting. For example, Oakey (1985) warned:

> "...without the generation of production to create the critical mass of technical production skills, the new science parks are unlikely to reach a stage where the full critical mass of research and development and production economies allow the self-sustained growth of the development. A degree of 'ivory towerism' is inherent in the superficial social responsibility apparent in the setting up of science parks" (p 64).

He went on further to argue:

> "The current eagerness of university bodies to establish science parks is less based on a thorough understanding of how they might best create and nurture high technology industrial production, and more on a pragmatic attempt to come to terms with the current political climate" (p 66).

Supporting the latter view it has been argued by Shachar and Felsenstein (1992) that:

> "...despite individual case-studies that might show the opposite (Smilor et al., 1988), empirical evidence does not support the contention that the science park performs a growth pole function in the urban context or that it can act as a catalyst for further high technology development. There is no doubt, however, that successful science parks or technology agglomerations do have some form of amenity role to play. Their utility probably lies in their 'signalling' function (Appold, 1991). In an environment of locational uncertainty, they unconsciously transmit signals to

other firms engaged in the decision–choice process and in this way a local reputation is established. As such, they act more as local agents for economic development and less as an initial triggering factor or an on-going stimulus for urban economic development" (p 824).

However, it has been asserted by UKSPA that:

"It is a truism among the science park community that no two science parks are alike...[and it] is not possible to judge the success or otherwise of a single science park without taking account of its age, location and characteristics and it is unwise to generalise on the success or otherwise of the science park movement by considering one or two examples, however famous or prestigious they may be" (Grayson, 1993, p 119).

Also, it was appreciated by Monck et al. (1988) that:

"A full understanding of the growth of Science Parks, and in particular those established in the 1980s, can only be achieved through an understanding of the firms on the parks. It is important to know the extent to which they are in sectors which can genuinely be regarded as 'high-tech'. The performance of these businesses is also of great interest since they are often portrayed as major sources of new wealth. The key issue as far as Science Parks are concerned, however, is the extent to which the park adds value to a business" (p 101).

In order to gain an informed view of the benefits of a Science Park location detailed empirical evidence was collected through a questionnaire survey of firms located in 1986 on Science Parks in the United Kingdom. This 1986 survey study adopted the UKSPA's definition of a Science Park as a property-based initiative which includes the following features (Monck et al., 1988, p 64):

— formal and operational links with a university, other higher education institution or research centre

— encourages the formation and growth of knowledge based businesses and other associated organisations normally resident on site

— a management function which is actively engaged in the transfer of technology and business skills between the organisations on site and the HEI.

From the outset it was also appreciated that a survey of all firms located on Science Parks:

"...alone would not provide a clear indication of the added value of a park, since there would be nothing with which to compare the responses. Hence it was decided that similar questions should be asked of a group of otherwise similar firms not located on a park" (Monck et al., 1988, pp 101–102).

The use of "matched samples" has become widely appreciated in the small firms and the entrepreneurship research field (see Peck, 1985; MacGregor et al., 1986; Hitchens and O'Farrell, 1987; Storey et al., 1987a; O'Farrell and Hitchens, 1988; Birley and Westhead, 1992).

In total, 284 direct face-to-face interviews were conducted in 1986 (most frequently with the owner-managers of surveyed businesses), of which 183 were conducted with Science Park businesses and 101 were with off-Park businesses. This constituted 53 per cent of all tenants on United Kingdom Science Parks at the time of the survey, with Heriot Watt being the only significant location omitted. Monck et al. (1988) argued:

> "...that the firms in this survey do provide an adequate sample of Britain's new high technology industries, providing adequate geographical, technological, sectoral and ownership coverage" (p 110–11).

Even so, the off-Park firms were somewhat older, and less likely to be legally independent, than Park firms. Conversely, Science Park firms were generally younger, geographically more concentrated in the less prosperous parts of the United Kingdom and, in 1986, were smaller in employment size than their off-Park counterparts (Massey et al., 1992, p 55). Nevertheless, there was a broad similarity in the groups of firms, enabling valid comparisons to be undertaken.

The researchers then examined a number of different aspects of the two groups of firms, viz. the personal characteristics of the founders of these businesses, the technological characteristics of the firms, aspects relating to the property management of Science Parks, their financing and management and, finally, their performance and their economic contribution to the community.

Based on the 1986 survey results Monck et al. (1988) made a number of recommendations to policy makers, small business owners, the universities and Science Park managers, in order to foster high technology firm survival and growth. For the firms themselves their recommendations were as follows (pp 210–11):

- to move quickly to establish distribution channels to reach the markets and thereby maximise the returns available in a fast changing market-place

- to develop a constant flow of new products to offer in the market-place – one- or two-product companies are high risk

- to avoid an overemphasis on technology and ensure that the products developed serve a market need, and to develop a clear understanding of who will buy and why

- to build a management team and to recognise that marketing and business skills are essential for long-term growth

- to evolve towards more structured organisational and operational arrangements and to institute business planning.

In 1990 a follow-up pilot study of 35 firms from the original 183 Science Park tenants, together with a review (using UKSPA data bases) of the other 148 firms, was conducted by Storey and Strange (1992a). This pilot longitudinal study did not attempt any contact with the off-Park "control" group sample of high technology firms. Storey and Strange (1992a) found:

> "... that of the 183 firms located on a Science Park, and which were interviewed in 1986, 63% continued in 1990 to occupy some premises within the same Science Park. Of those 68 firms which have moved off, just over half (37 firms) continue to operate in some form, although possibly under a different owner. Of the remainder it is probably justifiable to regard the vast bulk as not trading in any identifiable form, and hence as failures" (p 18).

Based on this empirical evidence Storey and Strange (1992a) tentatively concluded that,

> "...the failure rate of firms on Science Parks is below that of UK businesses in general" (p 18).

1.2 Research objectives of the current study

Part I of the current study reports empirical evidence from a second and much more extensive longitudinal follow-on survey of firms located on and off Science Parks in 1986. Data were collected from surveyed firms during late 1992 and early 1993. As in earlier studies (Autio and Kauranen, 1992), the objective was to assess the current performance of surveyed businesses originally interviewed in 1986, as well as to identify over a six-year period the extent to which a Science Park location had "added value" to these firms. The following new empirical evidence surrounding the performance of surveyed firms located on Science Parks in 1986 has important implications for policy makers, small business owners, the universities and for the Science Park managers. Specifically, the research objectives of the longitudinal study were to answer the following questions:

- Do Science Park firms have different "closure" rates from their off-Park counterparts?

- Over the six-year period have surveyed Science Park firms changed their ownership type? Have surveyed Science Park firms been more subject to take-over, especially by foreign firms?

- Have young high technology Science Park firms moved away from "soft" customised services and consultancy towards "hard" standardised manufacture?

- Do Science Park firms have a different research thrust and commitment to R & D compared with their off-Park counterparts?

- Have links with the local university, polytechnic or other HEI become more formalised over the six-year period? What are the most important links with the HEI? Are links with the HEI desirable? How successful has the Science Park management team been in developing links between surveyed Science Park firms and local HEIs?

- Are there differences in the financing of Science Park and off-Park firms? Has this influenced their performance?

- Do Science Park firms have particular reasons for contacting external organisations and individuals for information, advice and assistance?

- What facilities on a Science Park have been made most use of since Science Park firms were surveyed six years ago?

- What has been the perceived role played by the Science Park manager in the development of surveyed Science Park firms? Has a Science Park location been an important factor in the operation of surveyed Science Park firms? What are the most important perceived benefits as well as disbenefits from being located on a Science Park?

- Do Science Park firms spin off more new firm founders than their off-Park counterparts?

- Has a Science Park location added value to the performance of independent single-plant Science Park firms in terms of increased job generation and wealth creation compared with off-Park firms? Specifically, do independent single-plant firms located on a Science Park in 1986 record more rapid employment growth than their independent off-Park counterparts?

- Are independent single-plant firms located on a Science Park in 1986 more ambitious than off-Park firms?

It must be appreciated from the outset that this study was initiated by UKSPA as part of its own research to provide feedback to its members in order to assist them and their parent universities and local authorities in the further development of their projects. Further, we acknowledge the view held by some commentators that:

> "The effect of science parks on the emergence of new high-growth companies can realistically be evaluated only after another 10 years at the earliest" (Autio and Kauranen, 1992, p 24).

Nevertheless, the following assessment of firms located on United Kingdom Science Parks is based on detailed direct questionnaire interviews with a subsample of the 148 (out of the original 183) – the remainder having been included in the 1990 pilot survey – Science Park firms which participated in the Monck et al. (1988) survey in 1986. Similarly, attempts have been made to contact the 101 off-Park firms originally interviewed by Monck et al. As in previous studies, the questionnaire was generally presented through direct interviews with the most senior person in selected firms.

Part II of this study reports empirical evidence from a new questionnaire survey of 71 firms which located on Science Parks in the United Kingdom during the post-1986 period. This "new sample" survey adopted the UKSPA's revised Science Park membership definition. To ascertain the "added value" of a Science Park location during the post-1986 period it was again decided to present similar questions to a group of "matched" firms not located on Science Parks in 1992. The new Science Park sample of 71 firms was "matched" with the new off-Park sample with regard to industrial activity, age of the business, organisation ownership type and the location of the surveyed business. Data from the "new sample" survey will be compared with the 1986 survey data in order to identify any temporal changes. As in the follow-on survey (Part I) the objective of the "new sample" evaluation is to assess the current performance of surveyed businesses, and to evaluate the extent to which a Science Park location has added value to those firms during the post-1986 period.

Part III explores in greater detail the follow-on and "new sample" data sets in relation to a series of cross-cutting issues:

- technological sophistication of surveyed firms on and off Science Parks

- inputs to R & D, including links with HEIs

- technology diffusion associated with R & D outputs

- financing the high technology-based independent firm

- the impact of the management function on surveyed Science Park firms located on "managed" Parks

- employment growth in independent single-plant firms.

1.3 Assumptions of the study

To understand fully the conclusions of this study it is important to be aware of the following key assumptions/limitations:

- To assess the benefits of a Science Park location random samples of Park firms (in 1986 and in 1992) were matched with similar samples of off-Park firms on the basis of four criteria (ownership, age, sector and geography). It must be emphasised here that samples (in 1986 and 1992) of off-Park firms were not identified and then matched with comparable Science Park firms on the basis of four criteria. The results from the latter matching procedure could have produced results different from those already presented in 1986 (Monck et al., 1988) and those detailed in Chapters 5 and 6 of the present study. As a result the following random samples of Science Park organisations may include markedly more young firms and organisations located in the government designated "assisted" areas. Consequently, the important question of whether Science Parks are, in fact, becoming the major focus for high technology businesses in the "northern" and "assisted" areas cannot be tested by this study.

- The "matching" methodology employed in this assessment of the role of organisations located on Science Parks has been criticised by some commentators. For example, it has been argued by Gibb (1992, p 133) that matching firms in policy-orientated research projects is nothing more than "pseudo-scientific sampling". We reject this view.

  The reason for matching firms was to make a genuine comparison between on- and off-Park firms. The choice of matching criteria was influenced by previous empirical work which indicated that organisation survival and growth is particularly associated with ownership, age, sector and geographical factors (Storey, 1994; Westhead and Birley, 1994). We, therefore, explicitly held these factors constant in the assessment. Organisations were not matched on the basis of employment or sales turnover because these two variables were used as performance measures.

- Science Park organisations are easier to track over a six-year period (Chapter 2). Generally, the quality of information surrounding the status of off-Park firms was weaker than that for Science Park firms. Deriving a definition of "closure" which validly compared Science Park businesses with the off-Park firms proved to be difficult. Nevertheless, we are confident that the wide definition of "closure" used in the study ensured that both groups of firms were treated comparably.

- Due to time and resource constraints the wide range of factors associated with business closure (Chapter 2) and absolute employment growth in surviving firms (Chapter 16) were not explored in detail. More in-depth additional multivariate analysis of the factors associated with organisation closure and employment growth in surviving organisations could usefully be undertaken.

- The results presented in Section 4.3 surrounding merger/take-over activity in the follow-on survey must be viewed with some caution due the small sample size. Further in-depth study should gather complementary information from a wider number of organisations located on and off Science Parks.

- In Chapter 8 the founders of independent high technology organisations are compared with founders of firms in more conventional sectors in the county of Cleveland. It can be argued that the differences between founders in the high technology samples and the Cleveland samples may, in part, be influenced by the fact that Cleveland has been designated an "assisted" area by Government, whilst a number of Science Park founders are also located in "non-assisted" areas.

- Due to the relatively small size of the "follow-on" and "new" samples it was decided to combine the two samples in order to undertake additional analysis by "assisted" area location, age of the business, NTBFs and "managed" Science Parks. However, we acknowledge that the "combined samples" of Science Park and off-Park firms presented in Part III of this study cannot be taken as a representative sample of high technology firms in the United Kingdom.

- Finally, the results presented in Section 16.4 surrounding the characteristics of fast employment growing independent single-plant firms must again be viewed with some caution due to the small number of cases available for analysis.

Part I

Where Are They Now?
Tracing a Cohort of
High Technology Firms,
1986–92

Chapter 2

The Survival and Closure of High Technology Firms 1986–92

2.1 Definition of organisation closure

This study uses the following definition of organisation closure. **An independent business is regarded as a closure if, in 1992, it is no longer identifiable as a trading business. An independent business which moves locations but continues as a trading business is not regarded as a closure. If the business is a subsidiary or a branch plant then it is regarded as having ceased if it no longer trades at its previous location.**

A similar definition was utilised by Cambridgeshire County Council and by Garnsey and Cannon-Brookes (1992, p 8 and p 9) in their longitudinal study of high technology businesses associated with the Cambridge Phenomenon.

This is a more wide-ranging definition than that which has been used by UKSPA who have used the following definition: **A business is defined as a closure where it goes into receivership or liquidation at the time at which it ceases to trade on or off the Science Park.**

Two differences between our definition and that of UKSPA emerge. The first is that we specifically include, as closures, businesses moving off the Science Park to an alternative location at which they ceased to trade. UKSPA, in principle, include these firms but its tracking procedures have less precision once the firm has left the Park. Such firms would not then normally be included in the UKSPA list of closures.

The second difference is that UKSPA do not classify as a closure the cessation of operations of a subsidiary or branch plant. The reason for this is that UKSPA note that the parent company continues to trade and therefore the business is not a closure. UKSPA also make the point that it is a feature of Science Parks to attract project teams, who often take the form of a subsidiary, to a Park for a period in order to accomplish an R & D task. The team is then relocated back to its parent organisation once the task is completed. This is regarded by UKSPA as a normal activity. For our part we include such cases as a closure on the grounds that our purpose is to identify establishment rather than enterprise closures. Since, in 1986, one-quarter of surveyed establishments on Science Parks were subsidiaries (compared with 9 per cent of off-Park firms), the difference in this assumption is of considerable significance.

However, the key justification for our definition relates to the purpose of this study. Our objective is to be able to track and compare over a six-year period the on-Park firms interviewed in 1986 with the off-Park firms. A definition of closure needs to be chosen which enables a valid and direct comparison to be made between the two groups of firms. It also needs to recognise that the quality of information about the off-Park firms is weaker than that for Science Park firms. A definition therefore has to be employed which the researchers can be confident ensures that both groups of firms are treated comparably.

The wider definition of closure employed here yields rates which are considerably higher than those UKSPA has quoted in its own statistics. This is quite understandable since this reflects the definition of closure which we have chosen to employ. It does not imply that the UKSPA data are "wrong", but merely that theirs is a narrower definition than we employ for the purposes of this study. It also does not imply that the definition (see Scott and Lewis, 1984) we have used is generally more appropriate for defining high technology business closure, or that UKSPA need alter its own definition.

The justification for our definition is primarily the pragmatic one that it alone provides a valid comparison between on- and off-Park firms. The basic data on changes over the past six years in Science Park and off-Park tenants interviewed in 1986 are shown in Table 2.1. This table shows that of the 148 firms interviewed in 1986 which located on a Science Park, 90 firms (61 per cent) remained in business in 1992 (but, of these, nine firms had subsequently moved off a Science Park).

Table 2.1   Surveyed Organisations in 1986: Where Are They Now?

	Science Park sample (b)			Off-Park sample		
	Total	Ind	Sub	Total	Ind	Sub
1. Survived – interview completed	59	49	10	50	44	6
2. Survived – either original or new address	31	26	5	19	18	1
3. Confirmed organisation/ branch ceased to trade	46	25	21	21	19	2
4. No telephone listing/ not recorded in telephone book or local trade directory	12	12	0	11	11	0
Total valid follow-on sample	148			101		
Valid response rate	66%			72%		

Excluded sample of 35 organisations selected for interview in 1990.

5. Survived – either original or new address, 1992.	24	17	7
6. Confirmed business/branch ceased to trade	11	6	5

Total sample closure rate (including no telephone listings) (c)	= 69/183 × 100 = 38%	32/101 × 100 = 32%
Total independent organisation closure rate (including no telephone listings) (d)	= 43/135 × 100 = 32%	30/92 × 100 = 33%
Total subsidiary organisation closure rate	= 26/48 × 100 = 54%	2/9 × 100 = 22%

Notes: (a) The "tracking" of Science Park organisations was more successfully achieved because information was more extensive from Science Park managers surrounding organisation name changes and/or business relocations. Note only 7 per cent of Science Park organisations could not be traced compared with 11 per cent of off-Park organisations.

(b) Nine surveyed firms located on a Science Park in 1986 have subsequently survived and moved to an off-Park location.

(c) Excluding those organisations with no telephone listing in the closure rate denominator, the more conservatively defined total sample closure rate is 33 per cent (57/171 × 100) for the Science Park sample compared with 23 per cent (21/90 × 100) for the off-Park sample.

(d) Excluding those independent organisations with no telephone listing in the independent organisation closure rate denominator the more conservatively defined closure rate is 25 per cent (31/123 × 100) for the Science Park sample compared with 23 per cent (19/81 × 100) for the off-Park sample.

(Ind)   Independent organisation in 1986
(Sub)   Subsidiary organisation in 1986

2   THE SURVIVAL AND CLOSURE OF HIGH TECHNOLOGY FIRMS 1986–92

2.2 Closure rates Row three in Table 2.1 indicates that 46 firms were confirmed as business or branch closures, whilst a further 12 firms (7 per cent) did not appear to be trading in any identifiable form (even after extensive searches through telephone and local trade directories as well as through the Companies House register) (row four). Row six of the table shows that 11 out of the sample of 35 firms approached in 1990 were also confirmed as closures so that the total number of closures was 69. With regard to the off-Park sample, 69 firms (68 per cent) survived, 21 firms (21 per cent) were confirmed to be either business or branch closures and a further 11 firms (11 per cent) could not be traced. Hence 69 (38 per cent) Science Park firms closed compared with only 31 (32 per cent) off-Park firms[1].

It is very difficult to compare these findings with any official statistics on the survival of United Kingdom businesses in general, since the basis of the comparison is imperfect. Perhaps the nearest comparison is with the percentage of businesses deregistering for Value Added Tax (VAT) which generally shows that between 1980 and 1990 about 11 per cent of listed firms deregistered each year (Daly, 1991, p 580). Based on an annual 11 per cent deregistration rate over this six-year period we would "expect", if their age distribution was identical to that of VAT-registered firms, that 92 Science Park firms would have closed, compared with 51 off-Park firms. The "observed" number of businesses closing on Science Parks was 23 firms fewer than that "expected" (69 "observed" closures compared with 92 "expected" closures). This suggested that, subject to important provisos,[2] the closure rate of firms on Science Parks was lower than that recorded of United Kingdom businesses in general. This latter result confirms the earlier findings presented by Storey and Strange (1992a, p 18).

Twenty fewer than "expected" off-Park sample firms had actually closed over this six-year period (31 "observed" closures compared with 51 "expected" closures). At this point, it must be appreciated that the off-Park sample in 1986 was slightly more "mature" (in terms of age of surveyed firms) than the Science Park sample, and consequently more off-Park firms had already surmounted initial obstacles to new firm survival in 1986. As originally noted by Monck et al. (1988):

> "... generally the off-Science Park sample tends to be rather older and better established than those of the Science Parks" (p 106)[3].

Three ways of estimating closure rates for the two samples are presented in the final section of Table 2.1. This table indicates that the total sample closure rate (including organisations with no telephone listings) is higher for the Science Park sample of 183 organisations interviewed in 1986 (38 per cent) than for the 101 organisations interviewed in 1986 off-Park (32 per cent).

However, this aggregate closure measure masks a significant difference between the two samples. Table 2.1 shows that, whilst the independent organisation closure rates for the samples are comparable (32 per cent and 33 per cent for the Science Park and off-Park samples, respectively), the subsidiary organisation closure rate is markedly higher in the Science Park sample (54 per cent compared with 22 per cent). The higher rates of subsidiary organisation closure recorded on Science Parks may be the result of two factors. First, Science Parks present subsidiary organisations with "flexible" lease terms and, during recessionary times, these organisations may find it cheaper to close their Science Park sites, rather than those elsewhere. Second, many subsidiary organisations locate on Science Parks for "fixed-length" projects and, when projects come to an end, the subsidiary activity may cease on the Science Park with the staff generally being reabsorbed into the parent organisation.

The closure data was also analysed for assisted areas only. Table 2.2 shows that, with respect to the aggregate total sample closure measure, 39 Science Park establishments (37 per cent) located in government-designated "assisted" areas for regional development assistance (Martin, 1985, p 382; Damesick, 1987, p 58) have closed, which is virtually double that recorded in the off-Park sample (nine closures: 19 per cent). It can also be inferred from this table that the organisation closure rates for the Science Park sample are markedly higher than for the off-Park sample with regard to independent firms (30 per cent and 20 per cent for the Science Park and off-Park "assisted" area samples, respectively) as well as subsidiary establishments. In fact, with regard to the latter the Park subsidiary organisation closure rate is virtually three times higher than that recorded by the off-Park sample (57 per cent compared with 17 per cent).

Table 2.2 Surveyed Organisations in 1986 Located in "Assisted" Areas: Where Are They Now?

	Science Park			Off-Park		
	Total	Ind	Sub	Total	Ind	Sub
1. Survived – interview completed	35	30	5	26	22	4
2. Survived – either original or new address	15	13	2	12	11	1
3. Confirmed organisation/ branch ceased to trade	27	13	14	4	3	1
4. No telephone listing/ not recorded in telephone book or local trade directory	7	7	0	5	5	0

Excluded sample of 21 organisations selected for interview in 1990

5. Survived – either original or new address 1992.	16	11	5			
6. Confirmed business/branch ceased to trade	5	3	2			

Total sample closure rate (including no telephone listings) (c)	= 39/105 = 37%	9/47 = 19%	
Total independent organisation closure rate (including no telephone listings) (d)	= 23/77 = 30%	8/41 = 20%	
Total subsidiary organisation closure rate	= 16/28 = 57%	1/6 = 17%	

Notes: (Ind)   Independent organisation in 1986
            (Sub)   Subsidiary organisation in 1986

The closure rates of establishments located on and off Science Parks in "non-assisted" areas are presented in Table 2.3. This table shows, with respect to the aggregate total closure measure, that only 30 Science Park establishments (38 per cent) have closed compared with 23 (43 per cent) off-Park firms. However, this aggregate closure measure masks a significant difference between the two "non-assisted" samples. It can be inferred from Table 2.3 that, whilst the independent organisation closure rate for the Science Park sample is lower than for the off-Park sample (34 per cent compared with 43 per cent) the Park subsidiary organisation closure rate is markedly higher than that recorded by the off-Park sample (50 per cent compared with 33 per cent).

A comparison of the evidence presented in Tables 2.2 and 2.3 indicates that the aggregate total sample closure level for Science Park organisations in "assisted" areas (37 per cent) is comparable to that recorded by Park firms in the "non-assisted" areas (38 per cent). Also, virtually a third of independent Science Park organisations in both areas have closed. However, a slightly higher level of subsidiary organisation closure was recorded in the "assisted" areas (57 per cent and 50 per cent for Science Park firms located in "assisted" and "non-assisted" areas, respectively).

The above results are in line with those presented in a longitudinal panel study of independent small firms in eight manufacturing sectors in London over the 1979–89 period. North et al. (1992, p 14) found that 42 per cent of the firms in the 1979 panel were no longer in existence by the end of 1989. Sectoral variations in survivability were apparent with the highest levels being recorded in those sectors recording a high investment in new product development and/or improved production technology. North et al. (1992) also presented empirical evidence which suggests that new firms are particularly prone to "infant mortality" and:

> "...that firms generally need up to 10 years to become firmly established and that the age of the firm after this period tends to become less significant" (p 15).

Table 2.3   Surveyed Organisations in 1986 Located in Non-assisted Areas: Where Are They Now?

	Science Park			Off-Park		
	Total	Ind	Sub	Total	Ind	Sub
1. Survived-interview completed	24	19	5	24	22	2
2. Survived – either original or new address	16	13	3	7	7	0
3. Confirmed organisation/ branch ceased to trade	19	12	7	17	16	1
4. No telephone listing/ not recorded in telephone book or local trade directory	5	5	0	6	6	0

Excluded sample of 14 organisations selected for interview in 1990

5. Survived – either original or new address 1992.	8	6	2			
6. Confirmed business/branch ceased to trade	6	3	3			

Total sample closure rate (including no telephone listings) (c)	= 30/78 = 38%			23/54 = 43%		
Total independent organisation closure rate (including no telephone listings) (d)	= 20/58 = 34%			22/51 = 43%		
Total subsidiary organisation closure rate	= 10/20 = 50%			1/3 = 33%		

Notes: (Ind)   Independent organisation in 1986
         (Sub)   Subsidiary organisation in 1986

Of even greater interest, North et al. (1992) found:

> "...that the ownership of freehold property can help determine whether or not a firm survives. It was certainly the opinion of managers of surviving businesses in freehold property that ownership of their premises had been a key factor contributing to their survival either by holding down fixed costs (especially in marginal businesses...or by providing collateral for borrowing....In contrast, firms in rented property sometimes had to

withstand significant rent increases, and, in some instances, to suffer displacement to make way for redevelopment schemes" (pp 17–18).

Mahmood (1992, p 203), using a longitudinal data base of over 12,000 newly established manufacturing plants in the United States, found that survival rates of plants in high tech industries were higher than those recorded in low tech industries. Interestingly, Mahmood (1992) concluded that exposure to risk could be reduced by increasing the initial start-up size of firms (for a similar conclusion see Mounfield et al., 1985, p 784 and p 788) and that:

> "Start-up size tends to be important in reducing the hazard rate in both low and high-tech industries" (Mahmood, 1992, p 206).

Moreover, Garnsey and Cannon-Brookes (1992) in their longitudinal study of high technology companies associated with the Cambridge Phenomenon concluded:

> "Data available for the period since 1990 suggest a 10% fall in the number of active high technology companies in Cambridgeshire.... The average annual failure rate increased from 1.5% per year in the early 1980s to 3.7% in the latter half of the decade. Since 1990, the available figures suggest that closures and moves have outnumbered start-ups by 3 to 1" (p 26).

Several criticisms may be made of this comparison of the closure rates of Science Park and off-Park firms. The first is that there were eight interviews with firms on the Bolton Science Park in 1986, and only two of these firms co-operated with us again in 1992. Bolton Science Park, however, currently is not a part of UKSPA and, it could be argued, should be excluded. Our view, however, is that the 1986 survey was deemed to include a representative sample of firms located on United Kingdom Science Parks at that time. We do not therefore see any reason to exclude firms surveyed in 1986 at this later stage.

A second criticism is that some of the firms which were included in the 1986 survey were either not high technology firms (for example, there are typing and secretarial services firms located on some Science Parks) or were semi-dormant businesses (seeking to trade, but having yet to make their first sale) or university-run businesses which perhaps were not wholly commercial concerns. In the 1986 survey there were about ten firms of this type, and it has been suggested to us that these should also have been excluded. We see no justification for such exclusions. It is clear that they were on Science Parks in 1986, even if some were not what may be regarded as "high technology", and in addition the study matched on- and off-Park samples according to sector.

The central criticism, however, is that the definition of closure which we have employed fails to recognise, in full, the contribution which a Science Park makes to technical and economic development. For example, where a business ceased to trade, even in the form of liquidation, the technology may still be developed by another business, and the Science Park may claim some "credit" for enabling that technology to become commercially tested. The implied assumption of our closure measure is that all is lost in these cases.

We have some sympathy with this point of view since, in some instances, it is clearly valid. However, it can be argued that this issue is equally likely to arise in the case of the off-Park firms. To resolve this matter a much more intensive verification of the implications of closures would have to be conducted than is possible here.

To repeat, our purpose was to ensure that a valid comparison was made between two groups of surveyed firms, given that information about one (the Science Park sample) is more extensive than that about the other (the off-Park firms). Since we have access to very much better information about Science Park than off-Park firms there is a real risk of bias in favour of Parks. This is because with their greater knowledge, Science Park managers can point to, for example, changes of name which could not be identified through directory, or even Companies House information, sources. Hence, businesses which in an off-Park location might be classified as closures could, with greater knowledge, have been classified as continuing businesses.

Our definitions were designed to minimise sampling differences of the type discussed above. Given these definitions our results show that aggregate closure rates are higher for Science Park firms than for off-Park firms. This is because the Science Park sample contained a higher proportion of subsidiary operations than the off-Park sample, and because the subsidiary plants had higher closure rates on the Park than independents. Taking the independent firms only, there was no difference in the closure rates. Given that the Science Park firms were significantly younger than the off-Park firms in 1986 this is a positive finding.

Our second key finding is that, insofar as we can make a comparison, it appears that high technology businesses in this sample have lower closure rates than is the "norm" (calculated from numbers of businesses deregistering for VAT).

2.3 Summary and conclusions

1. Deriving a definition of "closures" which validly compares the Science Park with the off-Park firms is difficult.

2. Nevertheless, using our chosen definition we found:

   (a) The sample overall (i.e. Science Park and off-Park firms) had a lower closure rate than would have been expected from comparing those firms with VAT registered businesses which cover (virtually) all sectors of the economy.

   (b) Science Park establishments had a higher closure rate than off-Park establishments, but independent establishments on Science Parks had a virtually identical closure rate to independent establishments located off-Park.

   (c) The overall higher closure rate of Science Park establishments emerged because subsidiaries, of which there are more in the Science Park sample, had higher closure rates on-Park than in off-Park locations.

   (d) Analysis at a finer geographical level revealed that Science Park organisations located in "assisted" areas closed at a rate which is virtually double that recorded by their off-Park counterparts. Both independent and subsidiary organisation closure rates were markedly higher for Science Park organisations in "assisted" areas.

   (e) The aggregate total closure rate recorded by Science Park organisations was found to be lower than that recorded by the off-Park group in the "non-assisted" areas. Also, the Park subsidiary organisation closure rate in the "non-assisted" areas was found to be markedly higher than that recorded by off-Park establishments. However, the independent organisation closure rate was lower for the Science Park than for the off-Park group.

(f) Overall, the aggregate total sample closure level for Science Park organisations in "assisted" areas was comparable to that recorded by Park organisations located elsewhere. However, at a finer level of analysis it was found that the Park subsidiary organisation closure rate was higher in the "assisted" rather than the "non-assisted", areas.

Chapter 3

The Characteristics of the Survivors

3.1 Introduction
Table 2.1 indicates that 109 follow-on interviews have been conducted, of which 59 were with firms originally located on a Science Park in 1986 and a further 50 were with off-Park firms. No surveyed off-Park firms in 1986 had subsequently relocated their primary operational premises to a Science Park location. As in the earlier study by Monck et al. (1988), it was not possible to gain complete information from all firms and so subsequent tables provide responses from less than the full 109 cases. As Monck et al. (1988) concluded:

> "...we have no reason to believe that, where there are cases missing, this leads to significant biases and so to misleading results" (p 105).

3.2 Geographical coverage
In terms of the geographical coverage of follow-on Science Park interviews they are broadly in line with those conducted in 1986. Table 3.1 indicates that three parks – Aston, Bradford and Cambridge – accounted for 34 per cent of interviews in 1986 and that in 1992–93 these three parks accounted for 36 per cent of total interviews.

Table 3.1   Science Park Locations Defined in 1986: 1992 Follow-on Survey

Science Park Location		Number interviewed in 1986	%	Number interviewed in 1992	%
1. Aston	(a)	22	12.0	6	10.2
2. Birmingham		4	2.2	3	5.1
3. Bolton		8	4.4	2	3.4
4. Bradford	(b)	16	8.7	7	11.9
5. Brunel		3	1.6	1	1.7
6. Cambridge		24	13.1	8	13.6
7. Clwyd		3	1.6	3	5.1
8. Durham		4	2.2	4	6.8
9. East Anglia		1	0.5	0	0.0
10. Glasgow		6	3.3	0	0.0
11. Hull		9	4.9	1	1.7
12. Leeds	(c)	5	2.7	2	3.4
13. Liverpool	(d)	7	3.8	5	8.5
14. Loughborough	(e)	7	3.8	3	5.1
15. Manchester		6	3.3	1	1.7
16. Nottingham		12	6.6	5	8.5
17. South Bank		16	8.7	2	3.4
18. Southampton	(f)	5	2.7	1	1.7
19. Surrey		5	2.7	2	3.4
20. Swansea		4	2.2	0	0.0
21. Warwick	(g)	16	8.7	3	5.1
Total		183	99.7	59	100.3

Notes:
(a)   1 firm surveyed in 1986 moved off the Park.
(b)   2 firms surveyed in 1986 moved off the Park.
(c)   1 firm surveyed in 1986 moved off the Park.
(d)   1 firm surveyed in 1986 moved off the Park.
(e)   1 firm surveyed in 1986 moved off the Park.
(f)   1 firm surveyed in 1986 moved off the Park.
(g)   2 firms surveyed in 1986 moved off the Park.

A similar pattern is apparent in the spatial distribution of off-Park interviews (Table 3.2). In 1986, the north and south-west of England standard regions accounted for 48 per cent of interviews; in 1992–93 they accounted for just over 40 per cent of follow-on interviews.

Table 3.2   Off-Park Locations Defined in 1986: 1992 Follow-on Survey

Standard Region	Number interviewed in 1986	%	Number interviewed in 1992	%
1. East Anglia	0	0.0	0	0.0
2. East Midlands	13	12.9	4	8.0
3. North	23	22.8	10	20.0
4. North West	3	3.0	0	0.0
5. South East	12	11.9	8	16.0
6. South West	25	24.8	10	20.0
7. Yorkshire and Humberside	11	10.9	9	18.0
8. West Midlands	0	0.0	0	0.0
9. Northern Ireland	0	0.0	0	0.0
10. Scotland	0	0.0	0	0.0
11. Wales	14	13.9	9	18.0
Total	101	100.2	50	100.0

The initial study conducted by Monck et al. (1988, p 218) also compared firms located in the "north" and "south" of the United Kingdom. The "south" was defined as those areas "...south of a line from the Wash to Bristol". A similar definition was used by Massey et al. (1992, pp 15–16) in their study of Science Parks in the United Kingdom and by Birley and Westhead (1990a, p 30) in their analysis of the performance of small firms in the United Kingdom. Basically, the "south" incorporates the most pressurised and affluent standard regions of East Anglia, the south-east and the south-west of England.

Table 3.3 shows that the current sample of Science Park firms included even more firms from the "north" (70.5 per cent and 76.3 per cent in 1986 and 1992, respectively). However, with regard to the off-Park sample the current sample continues to have just over 63 per cent of firms located in the "north" (Table 3.4).

Table 3.3   North/South Location: 1992 Follow-on Science Park Firms

Location	Number interviewed in 1986	%	Number interviewed in 1992	%
North	129	70.5	45	76.3
South	54	29.5	14	23.7
Total	183	100.0	59	100.0

Table 3.4   North/South Location: 1992 Follow-on Off-Park Firms

Location	Number interviewed in 1986	%	Number interviewed in 1992	%
North	64	63.4	32	64.0
South	37	36.6	18	36.0
Total	101	100.0	50	100.0

3.3 Ownership characteristics

Approximately, three-quarters of the 1986 Science Park sample comprised independent firms (Table 3.5). A further quarter classified themselves as subsidiaries. Over this six-year period the proportion of surveyed Science Park firms classed as subsidiaries increased by 4 per cent. As in the Science Park sample the majority of firms in the follow-on off-Park sample continued to be independent firms. Here the proportion of surveyed subsidiary firms rose from 9 per cent to 20 per cent.

Table 3.5   Ownership Characteristics of Firms: 1992 Follow-on Survey

| Ownership characteristics | Science Park | | | | Off-Park | | | |
| | 1986 Survey | | 1992 Survey | | 1986 Survey | | 1992 Survey | |
	No.	%	No.	%	No.	%	No.	%
1. Independent	135	73.8	41	69.5	92	91.0	40	80.0
2. Subsidiary	48	26.2	18	30.5	9	9.0	10	20.0
Total	183	100.0	59	100.0	101	100.0	50	100.0

3.4 Age of surveyed businesses

In 1986 information on the age of all businesses was gathered for only 239 firms. Sixty-three per cent of Science Park firms in 1986 stated they were less than ten years of age. Similarly, the current sample of Science Park firms drew heavily upon this younger age cohort of firms.

Roberts (1990) suggested that in high technology firms the early years of a firm's life are when changes are most likely, and so the current Science Park sample has a high concentration of firms amenable to change. Table 3.6 shows that 79 per cent of follow-on interviews were conducted with Science Park businesses which were less than ten years old in 1986. Also, the off-Park follow-on sample contains relatively few firms that indicated they were 26 or more years of age in 1986. (This cohort of firms may have been more likely to cease to trade due to family ownership succession problems rather than commercial pressures.) Nevertheless, the current off-Park follow-on sample contained relatively more firms from the 10–25 year age cohort than in the Science Park sample in 1986.

Table 3.6   Age of Firms: 1992 Follow-on Survey

| Age of surveyed firms in 1986 (years) | Science Park | | | | Off-Park | | | |
| | 1986 Survey | | 1992 Survey | | 1986 Survey | | 1992 Survey | |
	No.	%	No.	%	No.	%	No.	%
< 4	45	27.6	18	41.9	12	15.8	6	18.8
4–9	57	35.0	16	37.2	14	18.4	12	37.5
10–25	43	26.4	7	16.3	29	38.2	13	40.6
26–50	11	6.7	2	4.7	14	18.4	1	3.1
> 50	7	4.3	0	0.0	7	9.2	0	0.0
Total	163	100.0	43	100.1	76	100.0	32	100.0

3.5 Sectoral coverage and functions

The sectoral functions of surveyed high technology firms are presented in Table 3.7, with the figures referring to frequency of findings.

Consequently, as previously noted by Monck et al. (1988):

"The classifications in the table should, then, only be taken as broadly indicative of the functions of the surveyed firms" (p 109).

Table 3.7   Industrial Activities of Firms: 1992 Follow-on Survey (number of mentions)

Industrial activities	Science Park		Off-Park	
	1986 Survey %	1992 Survey %	1986 Survey %	1992 Survey %
1. Hardware and systems	26.2	22.2	16.8	34.8
2. Software	15.3	17.8	11.9	11.0
3. Microelectronics	9.8	8.1	24.8	8.4
4. Instrumentation	2.7	5.9	5.9	8.4
5. Automation	3.8	3.0	6.9	5.2
6. Electrical equipment	1.1	0.7	3.0	5.2
7. Medical	3.3	5.2	1.0	2.6
8. Pharmaceutical	2.7	0.7	4.0	0.0
9. Fine chemicals	0.5	1.5	0.0	1.9
10. Biotechnology	3.3	0.7	5.0	2.6
11. Mechanical	0.5	0.7	1.0	6.5
12. Environmental	3.8	3.7	6.9	1.9
13. Other manufacturing	0.5	0.0	1.0	0.6
14. Design and development	3.8	6.7	5.0	2.6
15. Analysis and testing/ other technical services	17.5	15.6	5.0	5.2
16. Financial and business service	4.9	7.4	2.0	3.2
Total	99.7	99.9	100.2	100.1

Over this six-year time period three industrial activities continued to account for over 55 per cent of all mentions in Science Park firms: hardware and systems, analysis testing/other technical services and software. In marked contrast, the frequency of industrial activities recorded by off-Park firms has not remained consistent to the same level as that recorded by Science Park firms (where it must be noted that production of products is restricted or discouraged on site or in some cases not allowed). The current off-Park sample contains relatively more firms engaged in hardware and systems as well as instrumentation, automation, electrical equipment and mechanical activities. In this subsample there has been a marked reduction in the number of firms mentioning microelectronics. It is interesting to note here that Garnsey and Cannon-Brookes (1992) in their longitudinal study of high technology companies established in Cambridge in 1985 found that the:

> "...electronics sector...[made] the most substantial loss of ground over the 5 year period" (p 16).

These researchers also noted that the Phenomenon was becoming:

> "...increasingly service based" (p 27).

Drawing upon North American literature on young high technology companies it has been asserted by Bullock (1983) that the typical firm will record substantial change with increasing age (particularly within academically owned companies). Most notably, Bullock (1983) suggested that:

> "This pattern of development can be described as a hardening process, starting with a 'soft' company, selling highly analysed technical solutions for specific problems, and ending with fully 'hard' companies, selling standardized and relatively simplified products to a general market" (p 12).

3   THE CHARACTERISTICS OF THE SURVIVORS

Bullock suggested the formation of "soft" companies by academic entrepreneurs engaged in providing services, writing software or providing consultancy has a number of advantages during the early development of a firm. First, it was low risk, since investment in capital equipment was minimal. Second, it provided an ideal opportunity for the individual to assess the existence of a market and possibly to decide whether he or she liked the idea of being in business. Over time, when a market was identified, it may have been deemed necessary to make some form of investment with, as a second stage, the provision of a customised product or service. At this point the decision may have been made by the academic entrepreneur to become fully involved in the business on a full-time basis, thereby again raising his/her personal risk. The final stage occurred when the business moved towards the production of a product, with this perhaps involving the installation of manufacturing capacity.

Empirical evidence to support this transition (or switch) from the "soft" to the "hard" has been presented by Roberts (1990) in his study of 114 high technology-based firms within the Greater Boston area, USA. From survey evidence he found:

> "...evolution over the first several years after founding toward more product-orientated businesses and away from consulting and R&D contracting..." (p 274).

The evidence is not wholly convincing because his data suggests that five to seven years later, two-thirds of surveyed firms appeared to be in the same "soft"/"hard" category as they had been when the business began. Furthermore, 10 per cent appeared to have softened rather than hardened. Virtually four firms out of five did not therefore appear to have hardened (Storey and Strange, 1992a, p 17).

To test this "soft" to "hard" hypothesis, surveyed firms in 1990 were asked about their sources of income since the business had been established:

> "From the responses it was difficult to observe any consistent pattern suggestive of a move in any consistent direction between 'hard' and 'soft'" (Storey and Strange, 1992a, p 21).

Similarly, during this follow-on study both samples of firms were asked to mention industrial activities from which they currently earned income. Consequently responses to this question can be compared for two points separated by real time. It is also important to appreciate here that during the 1986 survey it was noted that:

> "Off-park firms are twice as likely to be involved in manufacture on site as park firms, which is a predictable result, given the restrictions that many parks place on manufacture" (Monck et al., 1988, p 133).

Table 3.8 compares the responses to this question by the 183 firms surveyed in 1986 with the 59 Science Park firms surveyed in the 1990 study. (This transition is discussed in greater detail in Section 4.4.) The follow-on Science Park sample shows a sharp reduction in those firms mentioning income earned from contract design work (down from 21 per cent to 5 per cent). In contrast, there was an increase in income earned from software (up from 4 per cent to 24 per cent), consultancy work (up from 5 per cent to 23 per cent) and training (up from 4 per cent to 10 per cent). Within the current Science Park sample there is no evidence from this table that firms have made a transition from "soft" services to "hard" manufacturing.

Table 3.8 Industrial Activities from which Firms Currently Earn Income: 1992 Follow-on Survey (number of mentions)

Industrial activities from which income is earned	Science Park		Off-Park	
	1986 Survey %	1992 Survey %	1986 Survey %	1992 Survey %
1. Manufactured products	14	10	27	23
2. Sub-contract production work	6	2	6	6
3. Contract design work	21	5	14	7
4. Contract research	6	10	5	7
5. Testing/analysis	5	5	7	6
6. Consultancy work	5	23	5	14
7. Training	4	10	2	6
8. Software	4	24	1	22
9. Others	35	11	33	9
Total	100	100	100	100

Note (a) Firms surveyed in 1986 engaged either in 'leading edge' or 'high-tech' activities.

A similar pattern was recorded in the off-Park sample with no noticeable transition from "soft" to "hard". It can also be inferred from Table 3.8 that there was a similar increase in software and consultancy work by off-Park firms at the expense of contract design work and manufactured products. These results confirm the conclusion made in the 1986 survey that:

> "'Softer' activities are in general increasing.... Overall, there is little evidence of any shift from 'soft' to 'hard' activities" (Monck et al., 1988, p 139).

In their longitudinal study of companies associated with the Cambridge Phenomenon, Garnsey and Cannon-Brookes (1992) reached a similar conclusion. They found a:

> "...lack of evidence of 'hard' manufacturing firms from 'soft' consultancy style start-ups..." (p 5).

Moreover, they suggest that:

> "Among Cambridge firms there is reason to believe that those companies which start in service activities remain in them. Those founders who aim to produce a product usually do so from the inception. There are considerable difficulties in funding manufacture on the back of service activities; consultancy and R and D for clients seldom generate sufficient resources for manufacture and can divert founders from developing their own product" (p 20).

3.6 Summary and conclusions

This chapter compared the characteristics of the 109 firms which were interviewed in both 1986 and 1992 with the 284 firms originally interviewed in 1986. We conclude:

1. The geographical distribution of the two samples is similar.

2. There has been an increase in the proportion of firms, both on and off-Park, which are subsidiaries.

3. The 1992 sample, by definition, is older, but many of the older firms interviewed in 1986 have disappeared.

4. Sectoral composition of the firms has only slightly changed. There is no evidence of a movement from "soft" to "hard", but there is evidence of a move away from microelectronics. However, there is also evidence to suggest that more Science Park firms are moving into software, consultancy work and training.

Chapter 4

Changes in the Survivors, 1986–92

4.1 Introduction

Table 2.1 showed that 59 follow-on interviews were conducted with firms located on Science parks in 1986 (a valid response rate of 66 per cent), whilst a further 50 interviews were completed with off-Park firms (a valid response rate of 72 per cent). Over 88 per cent of interviews were conducted with male respondents (Table 4.1) and in over 52 per cent of cases in both subsamples the respondent was one of the original founders of the surveyed firm (Table 4.2). Consequently, there remains helpful continuity in both samples with regard to the person interviewed.

Table 4.1   Gender of Respondent: 1992 Follow-on Survey

Gender	Science Park		Off-Park		Total	
	No.	%	No.	%	No.	%
1. Female	7	11.9	5	10.0	12	11.0
2. Male	52	88.1	45	90.0	97	89.0
Total	59	100.0	50	100.0	109	100.0

$X^2 = 0.00$, d.f. = 1, significance level = 0.9978, accept H_0.

Table 4.2   Respondent Founder of the Firm: 1992 Follow-on Survey

Founder of the Firm	Science Park		Off-Park		Total	
	No.	%	No.	%	No.	%
1. Yes	31	52.5	33	66.0	58.7	64.0
2. No	28	47.5	17	34.0	45	41.3
Total	59	100.0	50	100.0	109	100.0

$X^2 = 1.50$, d.f. = 1, significance level = 0.2199, accept H_0.

This chapter will discuss the key differences and similarities between firms interviewed in 1992 and those surveyed in 1986. Businesses included in the on- and off-Park follow-on samples will be analysed with regard to demographics, geographical coverage, ownership and legal status, merger/take-over activity and characteristics, sectoral coverage and functions, and the performance of independent single-plant firms (in terms of job and wealth creation).

4.2 Firm demographics– geographical coverage, ownership and legal status

No statistically significant differences were recorded between the geographical coverage of surveyed firms in 1986 and 1992 (see Tables 3.3 and 3.4) ($X^2 = 1.42$, d.f. = 1, significance level = 0.2337, accept H_0). About two-thirds of firms in both subsamples were located in the "north". Further, it can now be inferred from Table 4.3 that there was also no difference in the geographical coverage of surveyed firms on and off Science Parks in 1992 with regard to being located in a government-designated "assisted" area. In fact, over 51 per cent of surveyed firms in both subsamples were located in an "assisted" area in 1992 (57.6 per cent compared with 52.0 per cent).

Table 4.3   Government Designated "Assisted" Area Location of Firms: 1992
            Follow-on Survey

Location	Science Park		Off-Park		Total	
	No.	%	No.	%	No.	%
1. Non-assisted	25	42.4	24	48.0	49	45.0
1. Assisted	34	57.6	26	52.0	60	55.0
Total	59	100.0	50	100.0	109	100.0

χ^2 = 0.16, d.f. = 1, significance level = 0.6926, accept H_0.

Similarly, there was no bias with regard to ownership characteristics (see Table 3.5). Whilst the Science Park follow-on sample contained a larger proportion of subsidiary firms (30.5 per cent and 20.0 per cent of firms at Science Park and off-Park locations, respectively) this difference was not in a statistically significant direction (χ^2 = 1.06, d.f. = 1, significance level = 0.3024, accept H_0). Consequently, it is to be expected that Science Park firms are more likely to have other sites in the United Kingdom (44.1 per cent and 24.5 per cent of firms on Science Park and off-Park locations, respectively), although not in a statistically significant direction (Table 4.4). Detailed ownership characteristics of surveyed Science Park firms are presented in Table 4.5.

Table 4.4   Firm Having Other Sites in the United Kingdom: 1992
            Follow-on Survey

Other sites	Science Park		Off-Park		Total	
	No.	%	No.	%	No.	%
1. Non-assisted	26	44.1	12	24.5	38	35.2
1. Assisted	33	55.9	37	75.5	70	64.8
Total	59	100.0	49	100.0	108	100.0

χ^2 = 3.68, d.f. = 1, significance level = 0.0550, accept H_0.

However, as in the 1986 study, firms in the off-Park sample were significantly older. Table 4.6 indicates that the current mean age of off-Park firms was 15.5 years compared with 12.3 years for Science Park firms. With regard to the legal status of surveyed firms, Table 4.7 shows that over 76 per cent of surveyed firms in both subsamples were private limited companies. A larger proportion of Science Park firms were quoted public companies (10.2 per cent compared with 2.0 per cent).

Table 4.5   Ownership in 1992 of Science Park Firms: 1992 Follow-on Survey
Coverage

Firm	Independent or subsidiary	Other branches	Where is head office	Business status
1.	Independent	None	n/a	Partnership
2.	Subsidiary	Yes = 1	UK	Non-quoted public co.
3.	Subsidiary	Yes = 1	UK	Private ltd co.
4.	Subsidiary	Yes = 6	UK	Public company quoted in the UK
5.	Independent	Yes = 4	UK	Partnership
6.	Subsidiary	None	n/a	Part of university
7.	Independent	None	n/a	Private ltd co.
8.	Subsidiary	None	n/a	Private ltd co.
9.	Subsidiary	Yes = 9	USA	Private ltd co.
10.	Independent	None	n/a	Public company quoted in the UK
11.	Independent	None	n/a	Public company quoted in the UK
12.	Independent	Yes = 3	UK	Private ltd co.
13.	Subsidiary	Yes = 1	UK	Private ltd co.
14.	Subsidiary	Yes = 1	Sweden	Public company quoted abroad
15.	Independent	None	n/a	Sole proprietorship
16.	Subsidiary	None	n/a	Private ltd co.
17.	Independent	Yes = 1	UK	Private ltd co.
18.	Independent	Yes = 1	UK	Private ltd co.
19.	Independent	Yes = 1	UK	Non-quoted public company
20.	Independent	None	n/a	Private ltd co.
21.	Subsidiary	None	Not known	Private ltd co.
22.	Independent	None	n/a	Private ltd co.
23.	Independent	None	n/a	Private ltd co.
24.	Independent	None	n/a	Private ltd co.
25.	Independent	Yes = 2	UK	Private ltd co.
26.	Independent	None	n/a	Private ltd co.
27.	Subsidiary	Yes = 1	UK	Private ltd co.
28.	Independent	Yes = 1	UK	Private ltd co.
29.	Independent	Yes = 1	UK	Private ltd co.
30.	Subsidiary	Yes = 1	UK	Private ltd co.
31.	Independent	None	n/a	Private ltd co.
32.	Independent	Yes = 1	UK	Private ltd co.
33.	Independent	None	n/a	Private ltd co.
34.	Independent	None	n/a	Private ltd co.
35.	Independent	None	n/a	Private ltd co.
36.	Subsidiary	Yes = 1	UK	Private ltd co.
37.	Independent	None	n/a	Private ltd co.
38.	Independent	None	n/a	Private ltd co.
39.	Subsidiary	Yes = 4	UK	Private ltd co.
40.	Independent	Yes = 1	UK	Private ltd co.
41.	Independent	Yes = 4	UK	Private ltd co.
42.	Subsidiary	Not known	Not known	Private ltd co.
43.	Subsidiary	Yes = 1	USA	Public company quoted abroad
44.	Independent	None	n/a	Private ltd co.
45.	Independent	None	n/a	Private ltd co.
46.	Independent	None	n/a	Private ltd co.
47.	Subsidiary	Yes = 2	UK	Private ltd co.
48.	Independent	None	n/a	Private ltd co.
49.	Independent	None	n/a	Private ltd co.
50.	Independent	None	n/a	Partnership
51.	Independent	None	n/a	Sole proprietorship
52.	Independent	None	n/a	Private ltd co.
53.	Independent	None	n/a	Private ltd co.
54.	Subsidiary	Yes = 2	UK	Public company quoted in the UK
55.	Independent	Yes = 1	UK	Private ltd co.
56.	Independent	None	n/a	Private ltd co.
57.	Independent	None	n/a	Private ltd co.
58.	Independent	None	n/a	Private ltd co.
59.	Independent	None	n/a	Private ltd co.

Note: n/a = not applicable

Table 4.6   Age of Firms: 1992 Follow-on Survey

Age of surveyed firms (years)	Science Park		Off-Park		Total	
	No.	%	No.	%	No.	%
1. 6–9	18	41.9	6	18.8	24	32.0
2. 10–15	16	37.2	12	37.5	28	37.3
3. 16–31	7	16.3	13	40.6	20	26.7
4. ≥ 32	2	4.7	1	3.3	3	4.0
Total	43	100.1	32	100.2	75	100.0
Mean	12.3		15.5		13.7	
Median	10.0		14.0		11.0	

"t" = –2.03, d.f = 73, significance level = 0.047, reject H_0.

Table 4.7   Legal Status of Businesses: 1992 Follow-on Survey

Age of surveyed firms (years)	Science Park		Off-Park		Total	
	No.	%	No.	%	No.	%
1. A public company quoted in the UK	4	6.8	1	2.0	5	4.6
2. A public company quoted abroad	2	3.4	0	0.0	2	1.8
3. A non-quoted public company	2	3.4	2	4.0	4	3.7
4. A private limited company	45	76.3	44	88.0	89	81.7
5. A partnership	3	5.1	1	2.0	4	3.7
6. A sole proprietorship	2	3.4	2	4.0	4	3.7
7. Part of the university	1	1.7	0	0.0	1	0.9
Total	59	100.1	50	100.0	109	100.1

4.3 Merger/take-over activity

Garnsey and Cannon-Brookes (1992, p 22) indicated that the proportion of independent companies associated with the Cambridge Phenomenon had fallen from three-quarters to two-thirds. They argued that:

> "This suggests a considerable increase in outside influence over the development of the Phenomenon...and public companies were not only attempting to diversify during this period, but were also looking to improve the quality and breadth of their R & D activities" (p 23).

With regard to the Science Park study no statistically significant differences were recorded between firms in the two subsamples with regard to the frequency and form of merger/take-over activity since 1986. In both subsamples approximately 20 per cent of surveyed firms indicated they had been engaged over the six-year period in some form of merger/take-over activity (12 Science Park firms compared with 10 off-Park firms) (Table 4.8). Over 58 per cent of merger/take-over activity amongst Science Park firms had occurred during 1989 and 1990, whilst the off-Park sample indicated a more even pattern of activity over the six-year period (Table 4.9). For both subsamples, over 49 per cent of firms indicated the merger had taken the form of an acquisition by a UK-owned firm, although a slightly larger proportion of Science Park firms indicated a merger between two similar sized firms (25.0 per cent compared with 11.1 per cent) or acquisition by foreign-owned firms (25.0 per cent compared with 11.1 per cent) (Table 4.10).

Table 4.8   Firms Engaged in a Merger/Take-over: 1992 Follow-on Survey

Engaged in a merger/take-over	Science Park		Off-Park		Total	
	No.	%	No.	%	No.	%
1. Yes	12	20.0	10	20.0	22	20.0

Table 4.9   Year Merger/Take-over Occurred: 1992 Follow-on Survey

Year	Science Park		Off-Park		Total	
	No.	%	No.	%	No.	%
1987	1	8.3	2	22.2	3	14.3
1988	1	8.3	1	11.1	2	9.5
1989	4	33.3	1	11.1	5	23.8
1990	3	25.0	2	22.2	5	23.8
1991	1	8.3	1	11.1	2	9.5
1992	2	16.7	2	22.2	4	19.0
Total	12	99.9	9	99.9	21	99.9

Table 4.10   Merger/Take-over Form Type: 1992 Follow-on Survey

From	Science Park		Off-Park		Total	
	No.	%	No.	%	No.	%
1. Merger between two similar sized firms	2	25.0	1	11.1	3	17.6
2. Acquisition by UK-owned firm	4	50.0	7	77.8	11	64.7
3. Acquisition by foreign-owned firm	2	25.0	1	11.1	3	17.6
Total	8	100.0	9	100.0	17	99.9

Table 4.11   Why Did the Merger/Take-over Occur (Number of Mentions): 1992

Why did it occur?	Science Park		Off-Park		Total	
	No.	%	No.	%	No.	%
1. Poor financial results	1	5.6	3	27.3	4	13.8
2. Retirement of founders	1	5.6	0	0.0	1	3.4
3. To access wider markets	6	33.3	3	27.3	9	31.0
4. Need for finance to redevelop products/ services	2	11.1	0	0.0	2	6.9
5. Need for new expertise to redevelop products/ services	2	11.1	0	0.0	2	6.9
6. Need for finance to increase existing product/service sales	0	0.0	2	18.2	2	6.9
7. Need for new expertise to increase existing product/service sales	3	16.7	1	9.1	4	13.8
8. To combine with a major competitor to increase presence in market	3	16.7	0	0.0	3	10.3
9. Other	0	0.0	2	18.2	2	6.9
Total	18	100.1	11	100.1	29	99.9

Table 4.11 shows that over a quarter of firms in both subsamples indicated the motivation for the merger/take-over was to gain access to wider markets. Science Park firms indicated a more diverse range of

reasons for merger/take-over than off-Park firms. Whilst the latter stressed it was due to poor financial results or a need for finance to increase existing product/service sales, Science Park firms additionally suggested a need for finance to redevelop products/services, a need for new expertise to increase existing product/service sales and the need to combine with a major competitor to increase presence in market. Not surprisingly, over 45 per cent of merger/take-over activity in both subsamples was initiated by the purchasing firm with only a third of firms in both follow-on groups suggesting they themselves had initiated it (Table 4.12).

Table 4.12   Which Party Initiated the Merger/Takeover: 1992 Follow-on Survey

Party that initiated the merger/take-over	Science Park		Off-Park		Total	
	No.	%	No.	%	No.	%
1. Selves/own firm	4	36.4	3	30.0	7	33.3
2. Purchasing firm	5	45.5	7	70.0	12	57.1
3. Other	2	18.2	0	0.0	2	9.5
Total	11	100.1	10	100.0	21	99.9

Table 4.13 indicates that when a Science Park firm was acquired the acquirer stressed the importance of gaining access to an enhanced "existing range of products/services". On the other hand, the acquisition of off-Park firms "resulted in introduction of new products/services" for the purchasing firm.

Table 4.13   Technology of the Original Firm Incorporated into the Purchasing Company's Portfolio of Products and Services: 1992 Follow-on Survey

Technology of the original firm incorporated	Science Park		Off-Park		Total	
	No.	%	No.	%	No.	%
1. Added to/enhanced existing range of products/services	7	63.6	2	28.6	9	50.0
2. Resulted in introduction of new products/ services	3	27.3	4	57.1	7	38.9
3. Technology not exploited by purchasing company	0	0.0	1	14.3	1	5.6
4. Other	1	9.1	0	0.0	1	5.6
Total	11	100.0	7	100.0	18	100.1

Nevertheless, over 79 per cent of firms in both samples indicated that the effects of the merger/take-over had been favourable, with the purchasing company increasing its market share by using the technology/skills of the purchased firm (Table 4.14). Thirty-six per cent of Science Park firms suggested that managerial expertise proved to be the single most important asset of the purchased firm to the purchaser, compared with 25 per cent for off-Park firms; the latter suggesting the most valuable asset was the technology (18.2 per cent compared with 37.5 per cent) (Table 4.15). However, the very small number of cases here make it unwise to attempt to draw definitive conclusions.

Table 4.14   Purchasing Company Increased its Market Share by Using the Technology/Skills of the Purchased Firm: 1992 Follow-on Survey

Innovative capacity increased its market share	Science Park		Off-Park		Total	
	No.	%	No.	%	No.	%
1. Yes	9	90.0	4	80.0	13	86.7
2. No	1	10.0	1	20.0	2	13.3
Total	10	100.0	5	100.0	15	100.0

Table 4.15   What Proved to be the Single Most Valuable Asset of the Purchased Firm to the Purchaser?: 1992 Follow-on Survey

Most valuable asset to the purchaser	Science Park		Off-Park		Total	
	No.	%	No.	%	No.	%
1. Technology	2	18.2	3	37.5	5	26.3
2. Markets	2	18.2	1	12.5	3	15.8
3. Managerial expertise	4	36.4	2	25.0	6	31.6
4. Location	1	9.1	1	12.5	2	10.5
5. Company name	1	9.1	0	0.0	1	5.3
6. Finance	1	9.1	0	0.0	1	5.3
9. Other	0	0.0	1	12.5	1	5.3
Total	11	100.1	8	100.0	19	100.1

Finally, whilst 80 per cent of responding off-Park firms indicated that the merger/acquisition had led to the introduction of new key areas of innovation in the original firm, this was the case for only 50 per cent of surveyed Science Park firms (Table 4.16), but again the number of cases is very small. In Science Park firms the other leading trend was for the previous areas of innovation in the original firm to be only maintained (37.5 per cent of firms).

Table 4.16   Innovative Capacity of the Original Firm Changed Since Acquisition: 1992 Follow-on Survey

Innovative capacity of original firm changed	Science Park		Off-Park		Total	
	No.	%	No.	%	No.	%
1. Reduction in key areas of innovation	1	12.5	0	0.0	1	7.7
2. Previous key areas of innovation maintained	3	37.5	1	20.0	4	30.8
3. Introduction of new key areas of innovation	4	50.0	4	80.0	8	61.5
Total	8	100.0	5	100.0	13	100.0

The facts that the main benefit to the acquirer was not always the technology, and that acquisition did not always lead to new products for the acquired, may suggest Science Park firms were somewhat less "leading edge" than might have been expected. Since the numbers are very small the answers given to these questions on merger/acquisition suggest the need to better investigate this topic with a larger sample of firms.

4.4 Sectoral coverage and functions

In 1986, firms were asked to indicate the industrial activity which they were principally engaged in and it was found that:

> "Off-park firms tend to be more involved in microelectronics, and less in computer hardware and systems, compared to Science Park firms...the latter being...far more heavily involved in analysis and testing. Amongst the sectors with lower populations, off-park firms are more likely to be found in instrumentation, automation, electrical equipment, biotechnology and environmental sectors. Science Park firms predominate in business services" (Monck et al., 1988, p 132).

Although the current survey did not ask precisely the same question, the patterns apparent in 1986 continued to be present six years later. Because of the difficulties in identifying a single main function, respondents were asked to mention the range of activities in which the firm was engaged.

Table 4.17   Surveyed Firms Engaged in the Following Industrial Activities (Number of Mentions): 1992 Follow-on Survey Coverage

Industrial activities	Science Park		Off-Park		Total	
	No.	%	No.	%	No.	%
1. Computer hardware	10	7.4	19	12.3	29	10.0
2. Computer-aided design products and services	4	3.0	6	3.9	10	3.4
3. Computer peripherals	4	3.0	12	7.7	16	5.5
4. Computer services including repair	12	8.9	17	11.0	29	10.0
5. Computer software	24	17.8	17	11.0	41	14.1
6. Electronic components incl. semi-conductors	1	0.7	1	0.6	2	0.7
7. Microprocessor application projects	6	4.4	1	0.6	7	2.4
8. Lasers	1	0.7	1	0.6	2	0.7
9. Fibre optics	2	1.5	4	2.6	6	2.1
10. Analytical and scientific instruments	6	4.4	9	5.8	15	5.2
11. Other electronic and communications-related equipment	4	3.0	11	7.1	15	5.2
12. Genetic/monoclonal products	2	1.5	0	0.0	2	0.7
13. Pharmaceutical and fine chemicals	1	0.7	0	0.0	1	0.3
14. Medical equipment and instrumentation	1	0.7	3	1.9	4	1.4
15. Other health products	4	3.0	1	0.6	5	1.7
16. Biotechnology products and services (non-medical)	1	0.7	4	2.6	5	1.7
17. Coal, gas and oil equipment and machinery	1	0.7	5	3.2	6	2.1
18. Geological, marine and other environmental products and services	4	3.0	1	0.6	5	1.7
19. Energy conservation equipment	1	0.7	2	1.3	3	1.0
20. Chemicals and allied products	2	1.5	3	1.9	5	1.7
21. Process controls, automation and robotics	3	2.2	7	4.5	10	3.4
22. Mechanical equipment and machinery	0	0.0	5	3.2	5	1.7
23. Electrical equipment and machinery	1	0.7	8	5.3	9	3.1
24. Other products for retail and consumer markets	0	0.0	1	0.6	1	0.3

4   CHANGES IN THE SURVIVORS, 1986–92

Industrial activities	Science Park		Off-Park		Total	
	No.	%	No.	%	No.	%
25. Finance and business services	10	7.4	5	3.2	15	5.2
26. Technical and consulting services	21	15.6	8	5.2	29	10.0
27. Design and development services	9	6.7	4	2.6	13	4.5
Total	135	99.9	155	99.8	290	99.8

The functions undertaken by firms are presented in Table 4.17. Science Park firms were more likely to mention involvement in "soft" activities such as computer software (17.8 per cent), technical and consulting services (15.6 per cent), finance and business services (7.4 per cent) and design and development services (6.7 per cent). Less than 8 per cent of Science Park firms mentioned they were engaged in computer hardware, electronic components including semi-conductors, microprocessor application projects, analytical and scientific instruments, process controls, automation and robotics, and mechanical and electrical equipment and machinery. In marked contrast, as found in 1986, off-Park firms were more likely to be engaged in the manufacture of "hard" products such a computer hardware (12.3 per cent); other electronic and communications equipment (7.1 per cent); and electrical equipment and machinery (5.2 per cent). This supports the conclusion of Massey et al. (1992) that these industrial activities:

> "...as a whole do not fit in with the popular conception of high-technology enterprises as IT-based" (p 44).

This research does not, however, identify the sectors in which surveyed firms currently earn income. Firms were asked to mention the industrial activities from which they currently earn income and the empirical evidence presented in Table 4.18 again supports the 1986 survey conclusion that:

> "Off-park firms are twice as likely to be involved in manufacture on site as park firms, which is a predictable result, given the restrictions that many parks place on manufacture. Science Park firms are more involved in design and development on site, and are usually marginally more involved in software development and production" (Monck et al., 1988, p 133).

Table 4.18   Industrial Activities from which Firms Currently Earn Income (Number of Mentions): 1992 Follow-on Survey

Industrial activities from which income is earned	Science Parks No.	%	Off-Park No.	%	Total No.	%
1. Manufactured products	18	10.2	33	23.1	51	16.0
2. Software (software packages)	25	14.2	18	12.6	43	13.5
3. Bespoke software	17	9.7	13	9.1	30	9.4
4. Consultancy work	40	22.7	20	14.0	60	18.8
5. Contract research	17	9.7	10	7.0	27	8.5
6. Contract design work	9	5.1	10	7.0	19	6.0
7. Sub-contract production work	4	2.3	9	6.3	13	4.1
8. Testing / analysis	9	5.1	9	6.3	18	5.6
9. Licence income	10	5.7	6	4.2	16	5.0
10. Training	18	10.2	9	6.3	27	8.5
11. Other	9	5.1	6	4.2	15	4.7
Total	176	100.0	143	100.1	319	100.1

It can be inferred from this table that twice as many off-Park firms (33 firms: 66 per cent) currently earn income from manufactured products than their Science Park counterparts (18 firms: 31 per cent). Conversely, a larger proportion of Science Park firms indicated they earned income from "soft" activities such as consultancy work and training. These differences magnify when respondents were asked to indicate the single most important activity as a current source of income (Table 4.19). Fifty per cent of off-Park firms indicated it was a manufactured product, compared with only 25 per cent of Science Park firms ($\chi_2 = 9.85$, d.f. = 3, reject H_0 at the 0.05 level of significance). In addition to manufactured products a larger proportion of Science Park firms indicated that consultancy work (20.3 per cent); software (standard packages) (18.6 per cent) and contract research (8.5 per cent) were principal sources of income.

Table 4.19   Single Most Important Activity as a Current Source of Income: 1992 Follow-on Survey

Main source of income is	Science Parks No.	%	Off-Park No.	%	Total No.	%
1. Manufactured products	15	25.4	25	50.0	40	36.7
2. Software (software packages)	11	18.6	2	4.0	13	11.9
3. Bespoke software	2	3.4	2	4.0	4	3.7
4. Consultancy work	12	20.3	8	16.0	20	18.3
5. Contract research	5	8.5	2	4.0	7	6.4
6. Contract design work	2	3.4	0	0.0	2	1.8
7. Sub-contract production work	0	0.0	3	6.0	3	2.8
8. Testing / analysis	3	5.1	3	6.0	6	5.5
9. Licence income	1	1.7	1	2.0	2	1.8
10. Training	2	3.4	0	0.0	2	1.8
11. Other	6	10.2	4	8.0	10	9.2
Total	59	100.0	50	100.0	109	99.9

Longitudinal analysis also indicates that, perhaps contrary to expectation, there has been no significant movement from "soft" to "hard" amongst surveyed Science Park firms. In fact, a sizeable proportion of firms appear to have made the strategic decision to focus upon a wider range of "soft" service-orientated activities (see Table 4.20). The table identifies 11 sources of possible income. Where the firm identified the source of income as being of some importance to the firm in the 1986 survey, this is shown as "+", and where this is identified as a source of income in the 1992 survey it is shown as "#".

Table 4.20 Source of Income in 1986 and 1992 of Science Park Firms

Firm	Manufactured products		Software (standard packages)		Bespoke software		Consultancy work		Contract research	
1.	#	+					#			
2.		+								
3.	#	+	#	+	#	+		+		
4.		+	#				#			
5.							#	+		
6.							#	+	#	+
7.		+	#	+	#	+	#	+		
8.							#	+	#	
9.	#	+				+	#	+		
10.	#	+				+		+	#	+
11.		+	#	+	#	+		+		+
12.	#	+	#							
13.							#	+		
14.		+				+	#	+		
15.							#			
16.			#	+	#	+	#	+	#	+
17.	#	+	#	+	#	+	#	+		
18.	#		#				#			+
19.	#	+				+		+		
20.			#		#	+	#			
21.			#	+		+	#	+	#	
22.							#	+		+
23.							#			
24.							#			
25.							#	+		+
26.		+	#	+		+	#			
27.	#	+	#	+	#	+	#			
28.		+	#	+		+				+
29.			#		#		#	+	#	+
30.								•	#	+
31.	#	+				+		+		
32.								+	#	+
33.	#	+	#				#			
34.		+				+	#	+	#	
35.	#									
36.							#	+		+
37.			#	+	#			+		
38.		+	#		#		#	+		
39.	#	+				+		+		
40.								+		
41.	#					+	#	+	#	
42.					#		#			
43.							#	+	#	+
44.	#	+								
45.	#	+	#	+				+		+
46.		+	#	+			#	+		
47.		+					#	+		
48.							#	+	#	+
49.		+	#	+	#	+		+		
50.							#	+		+
51.							#	+		
52.							#	+	#	
53.			#	+	#	+	#	+	#	+
54.		+	#	+	#	+	#	+		+
55.							#	+	#	
56.	#	+	#	+	#	+		+		
57.	#	+							#	+
58.			#	+	#	+	#		#	
59.			#	+	#	+	#	+		

Firm	Contract design work	Subcontract production work	Testing analysis	Licence income	Training	Other
1.	#	#				
2.					# +	+
3.					#	
4.				#	#	# +
5.						#
6.			# +		#	
7.	+		+	# +		
8.	#		# +		# +	
9.				# +	#	+
10.	+			+		
11.	+			+	+	#
12.						
13.						
14.						+
15.					#	+
16.	#			# +	# +	
17.				+	+	
18.	+				#	
19.		+	# +		#	#
20.	#	#	+			
21.				# +		
22.				#		
23.	#		+			
24.			#			* (1986)
25.					+	# +
26.						#
27.		#			+	
28.				+	+	
29.			+			
30.						
31.				+		
32.	+		+			
33.						
34.				+	+	#
35.						
36.	+		+	+	+	#
37.						
38.			+			
39.	#	#		+	+	+
40.			+			# +
41.			# +	# +	+	
42.			# +			
43.			#			
44.						
45.	+				#	
46.	+				+	
47.						
48.	+		# +			
49.				#	#	
50.	#	+			+	
51.	+					
52.	#			#	+	
53.	+		#		#	
54.	#	+	+	# +	# +	
55.						
56.	+				+	
57.				#		
58.				#	# +	
59.						

1992 = source of income
+   1986 = source of income
*   1986 = no income

In the 1986 survey a total of 172 sources of income were derived for the 59 follow-on Science Park sample firms, whereas, in 1992, 207 sources were identified. Table 4.20 shows that 103 sources of income

4   CHANGES IN THE SURVIVORS, 1986–92

(60 per cent) were identified by the same firms in both 1986 and 1992, indicating both the validity of the questioning and the stability of firms over the six-year time period. The stability of sources of income over the time period is in fact the most striking feature of the table. Nevertheless, this table also indicates that 13 surveyed Science Park firms (22 per cent) have subsequently stopped earning income from manufactured products. To compensate for this, only three Science Park firms (5 per cent) are now currently earning income for the first time from manufactured products. We conclude again that within the current younger Science Park subsample there is little evidence of any transition from "soft" services to "hard" manufacturing.

4.5 Performance of surveyed firms

From the outset it has been assumed that the high technology sector offers a major source of new wealth and employment opportunities. Analysis of the 1986 survey results revealed that:

> "...the small independent firm in the high technology sector exhibits significantly faster employment and sales turnover growth than a firm of a comparable age in the more conventional sectors" (Monck et al., 1988, p 223).

For example, Monck et al. (1988) revealed impressive employment growth in surveyed firms:

> "Among the firms surveyed, employment increased between 1985 and 1986 by 80 per cent among the firms on Science Parks and by 28 per cent among off-park firms" (p 208).

This section explores the performance of surviving surveyed firms located on and off Science Parks. In the analysis, "performance" will be examined under five headings: ability to spin-off new firms; employment creation; value of sales turnover; profitability; and anticipated future growth. A further measure of performance has already been detailed in Table 2.1 and discussed above surrounding the ability of firms surveyed in 1986 to survive to the end of 1992.

The discussion will distinguish between independent single-plant firms on and off Science Parks in an effort to identify any element of added value which the Park provides for the firms. As in the earlier study (Monck et al., 1988) if it is:

> "...shown that the firms located on a park grew significantly faster than those located elsewhere, this would be important supportive evidence – provided the two groups of firms were approximately matched – of the added value of a park location" (p 216).

Earlier, Table 3.5 showed that the Science Park sample contained about 30 per cent of firms which were not independent owner-managed firms:

> "In order to make valid comparisons between this study and others, and to make comparisons between firms within the survey, only single-plant independent firms are included (29 Science Park firms compared to 31 off park firms). This is because this group is much more likely to be affected by the environment which the park provides, rather than, for example, a subsidiary unit, the performance of which will be affected by decisions taken at head office" (Monck et al., 1988, p 213).

Spin-off rates, however, relate to all surveyed subsidiary, as well as independent, firms.

Approximately, one-third of firms in both subsamples indicated that employees had left the surveyed firm to establish their own business (33.3 per cent and 37.5 per cent of firms on Science Park and off-Park locations, respectively) (Table 4.21).

Table 4.21   Employees Left Firm to Establish Their Own Business: 1992 Follow-on Survey

Establishing own business	Science Parks		Off-Park		Total	
	No.	%	No.	%	No.	%
1. Yes	19	33.3	18	37.5	37	35.2
2. No	38	66.7	30	62.5	68	64.8
Total	57	100.0	48	100.0	105	100.0

$\chi^2 = 0.06$, d.f. = 1, significance level = 0.8102, accept H_0.

Over 83 per cent of the individuals in both groups who had left their former employer to establish a new business had done so during the last three years (Table 4.22).

Table 4.22   How Many Employees in the Last Three Years Have Left Surveyed Firms to Establish their Own Business?: 1992 Follow-on Survey

Same sector	Science Parks		Off-Park		Total	
	No.	%	No.	%	No.	%
0	3	15.8	3	16.7	6	16.2
1	10	52.6	6	33.3	16	43.2
2	4	21.1	5	27.8	9	24.3
3	2	10.5	4	22.2	6	16.2
Total	19	100.0	18	100.0	37	99.9

$\chi^2 = -0.92$, d.f. = 35, significance level = 0.363, accept H_0.

The majority of spin-off businesses were subsequently located less than ten miles away from the "host incubator". It appears from Table 4.23 that off-Park firms were more likely to spin out businesses which located less than ten miles away than is the case for the Science Park firms.

Table 4.23   Location of New Businesses Established by Former Employees of Surveyed Firms: 1992 Follow-on Survey

Location of new businesses	Science Parks		Off-Park		Total	
	No.	%	No.	%	No.	%
1. This site	2	12.5	2	11.8	4	12.1
2. Less than 10 miles away	7	43.8	12	70.6	19	57.6
3. 10–59 miles away	4	25.0	3	17.6	7	21.2
4. Elsewhere	3	18.8	0	0.0	3	9.1
Total	16	100.1	17	100.0	33	100.0

As anticipated, new firm spin-offs from Science Park firms have a greater propensity to be located subsequently on a Science Park (22.2 per cent compared with 5.6 per cent) (Table 4.24).

Table 4.24   New Businesses Established by Former Employees Located on a Science Park: 1992 Follow-on Survey

Located on a Science Park	Science Parks		Off-Park		Total	
	No.	%	No.	%	No.	%
1. Yes	4	22.2	1	5.6	5	13.9
2. No	14	77.8	17	94.4	31	86.1
Total	18	100.0	18	100.1	36	100.0

Few of the surveyed firms have any financial involvement in new businesses established by former employees (11.1 per cent for both Science Park and off-Park firms) (Table 4.25).

Table 4.25   Does the Firm Have any Financial Involvement in New Businesses Established by Former Employees: 1992 Follow-on Survey

Financial Involvement	Science Parks		Off-Park		Total	
	No.	%	No.	%	No.	%
1. Yes	2	11.1	2	11.1	4	11.1
2. No	16	88.9	16	88.9	32	88.9
Total	18	100.0	18	100.0	36	100.0

However, these new business start-ups are overwhelmingly positioned in the same industrial sector as their former employers (83.3 per cent compared with 83.3 per cent) (Table 4.26).

Table 4.26   Are the New Businesses Established by Former Employees Positioned in the Same Sector as Surveyed Firms: 1992 Follow-on Survey

Same sector	Science Parks		Off-Park		Total	
	No.	%	No.	%	No.	%
1. Yes	15	83.3	15	83.3	30	83.3
2. No	3	16.7	3	16.7	6	16.7
Total	18	100.0	18	100.0	36	100.0

Also, to a greater extent, new business spin-offs from Science Park firms established in the same industrial sector by former employees do not compete directly with surveyed firms (60.0 per cent compared with 20.0 per cent), although not in a statistically significant direction (Table 4.27).

Table 4.27 Do New Businesses Established in the Same Sector by Former Employees Compete Directly with Surveyed Firms: 1992 Follow-on Survey

Compete directly	Science Parks No.	%	Off-Park No.	%	Total No.	%
1. Yes	6	40.0	12	80.0	18	60.0
2. No	9	60.0	3	20.0	12	40.0
Total	15	100.0	15	100.0	30	100.0

$\chi^2 = 3.47$, d.f. = 1, significance level = 0.0624, accept H_0.

4.5.2 Employment, sales and profits: size and change recorded by independent single-plant firms

Analysis of the 1986 survey data (Monck et al., 1988, p 214) confirmed results from other analytical and survey work which have shown that the median surviving manufacturing firms reached a peak employment within three to four years of start-up. Storey (1985) in his study of new independent manufacturing firms in north-east England found:

> "...firms to have virtually half their 'ultimate' (year eleven) employment within the first year and to have two-thirds of their ultimate employment in the third year....These results make it clear that the main creators of gross new jobs, in the small firm sector, are new firms less than six years old. Once firms are more than six years old, as a group, they are unlikely to add significantly to gross new job creation at least for the following five years" (p 32).

Table 4.28 Employment Distribution in Surveyed Independent Single-Plant Firms: 1992 Follow-on Survey Coverage (a, b)

Employment type	Mean	Science Park Median	Total employment	No. of cases	Mean	Off-Park Median	Total employment	No. of cases	Mean	Total Median	Total employment	No. of cases
Male full-time	16.3	8	439	27	13.4	7	402	30	14.8	8	841	57
Male part-time	0.7	0	18	27	0.3	0	8	30	0.5	0	26	57
Female full-time	7.2	1	194	27	5.8	3	173	30	6.4	2	367	57
Female part-time	0.7	0	19	27	1.1	1	32	30	0.9	0	51	57
Total	27.3	12	764	28	21.2	12	658	31	24.1	12	1422	59

Notes: (a) Male and female employment totals do not sum to the total employment value because three firms refused to provide a male/female employment breakdown.
(b) No statistically significant differences were recorded between the two samples mean employment sizes.

Therefore, it must be appreciated that surveyed independent single-plant firms (particularly the older cohort of off-Park firms) may have already recorded their most significant increases in employment generation (for a similar conclusion see American Electronics Association, 1978; Morse, 1976 – quoted in Oakey and Rothwell, 1986)[4]. Table 4.28 indicates there are no statistically significant differences between the two samples with regard to their present total employment profile. This is also the case when male/female and full-/part-time employment are taken into account.

A comparison of Table 4.29 with 4.30 shows that surveyed independent single-plant Science Park firms recorded larger mean total employment increases since 1986 than their more mature off-Park counterparts (for a detailed breakdown of employment change in all surveyed Science Park firms refer to Table 4.31). Twenty-two surveyed Science Park firms (88.0 per cent) recorded absolute increases in employment, compared with only ten off-Park firms: 45.4 per cent. In addition, more off-Park firms recorded contracting levels of total employment in 1992 (two Science Park firms: 8.0 per cent compared with 10 off-Park firms: 45.5 per cent). Ninety-two jobs were lost in these ten off-Park firms compared with only three jobs lost in the two contracting Science Park firms. Moreover, the 22 growing Science Park firms created an additional 313 gross new jobs compared with only 239 gross new jobs generated by the ten expanding off-Park firms. As a result the total level of net employment change is markedly higher in the Science Park sample (310 net jobs created compared to only 147 net jobs). However, total employment increases in Science Park firms are not statistically significantly larger than those recorded by off-Park firms ("t"= 0.62, d.f.= 45, accept H_0 at the 0.05 level of significance, one-tailed test) (mean absolute changes of 12.4 and 6.7 employees in surveyed Science Park and off-Park firm, respectively).[5]

Table 4.29 Total Employment Change Since 1986 in Independent Single-Plant Firms Located on a Science Park: 1992 Follow-on Survey

| Total employment size in 1986 | Total employment size in 1992 | | | | | | | | Total | |
| | 1–5 | | 6–10 | | 11–20 | | > 21 | | | |
	No.	%	No.	%	No.	%	No.	%	No.	%
1–5	5	50.0	4	40.0	1	10.0	0	0.0	10	100.0
6–10	1	10.0	2	20.0	4	40.0	3	30.0	10	100.0
11–20	0	0.0	0	0.0	1	25.0	3	75.0	4	100.0
≥ 21	0	0.0	0	0.0	0	0.0	1	100.0	1	100.0
Total	6	24.0	6	24.0	6	24.0	7	28.0	25	100.0

Mean	12.4
Median	6
Total gross employment increase	310

Table 4.30 Total Employment Change Since 1986 in Off-Park Independent Single-Plant Firms: 1992 Follow-on Survey

| Total employment size in 1986 | Total employment size in 1992 | | | | | | | | Total | |
| | 1–5 | | 6–10 | | 11–20 | | > 21 | | | |
	No	%	No	%	No	%	No	%	No	%
1–5	4	57.1	2	28.6	1	14.3	0	0.0	7	100.0
6–10	1	16.7	4	66.7	0	0.0	1	16.7	6	100.1
11–20	0	0.0	2	28.6	3	42.9	2	28.6	7	100.1
≥ 21	4	0.0	0	0.0	2	100.0	0	0.0	2	100.0
Total	5	22.7	8	36.4	6	27.3	3	33.3	22	100.0

Mean	6.7
Median	0
Total gross employment increase	147

Closer examination of Tables 4.29 and 4.30 indicates that a small number of firms provide the bulk of employment increases, a result which is consistent with previous studies which have shown that most employment growth from small firm activity is concentrated in a small number of "high-flying" firms (for a similar conclusion see Oakey and Rothwell, 1986, p 276; Storey et al., 1987b, p 152; Garnsey and Cannon-Brookes, 1992, p 28). In fact, five firms in both subsamples contributed most of the gross employment creation, with the five fastest growing Science Park firms generating 216 gross new jobs (69.0 per cent of total gross new jobs), whilst the five fastest growing off-

Park firms generated 222 gross new jobs (92.9 per cent of total gross new jobs). These results confirm the earlier conclusion made by Storey and Strange (1992a) of:

"...the overwhelming importance of relatively few firms in determining employment change amongst UK Science Park firms" (pp 18–19).

Table 4.31 Number of Employees in Surveyed Science Park Firms: 1992 Follow-on Survey Coverage

Firm	Male F/T	Male P/T	Male Total	Female F/T	Female P/T	Female Total	Grand Total	Grand total Change since 1986 No.	%	
1. (ISP)	8	0	8	3	1	4	12	8	200	
2. (Sub)	12	0	12	2	0	2	14	-2	-13	
3. (Sub)	16	0	16	5	0	2	21	12	133	(m)
4. (Sub)	23	0	23	22	0	22	45	–	–	(m)
5. (I)	2	0	2	4	0	4	6	3	50	
6. (Sub)	12	0	12	2	0	2	14	-5	-26	
7. (ISP)	8	0	12	1	0	1	9	4	80	
8. (Sub)	16	1	17	2	1	3	20	10	100	
9. (Sub)	19	0	19	7	0	7	26	16	160	
10. (ISP)	60	0	60	35	0	35	95	78	459	
11. (ISP)	100	0	100	22	1	23	123	10	9	(m)
12. (I)	130	0	130	70	0	70	200	184	1150	
13. (Sub)	4	0	4	5	1	6	10	5	100	
14. (Sub)	59	0	59	21	0	21	80	-66	-45	
15. (ISP)	0	0	0	3	1	4	4	-2	-33	
16. (Sub)	23	0	23	14	0	14	37	–	–	(m)
17. (I)	7	0	7	1	0	1	8	3	38	
18. (I)	4	0	4	0	0	0	4	1	33	
19. (I)	30	0	30	15	0	15	45	30	200	
20. (I)	2	0	2	5	3	8	10	3	43	
21. (Sub)	22	1	23	4	0	4	27	22	440	(m)
22. (ISP)	1	0	1	1	0	1	2	0	0	
23. (ISP)	2	0	2	1	0	1	3	-1	-25	
24. (ISP)	2	2	4	1	0	1	5	4	400	
25. (I)	5	0	5	12	3	15	20	17	568	(m)
26. (ISP)	14	0	14	4	0	4	19	8	73	
27. (Sub)	–	–	–	–	–	–	–	–	–	(m)
28. (I)	20	0	20	6	1	7	27	19	238	(m)
29. (I)	4	2	6	5	1	6	12	–	–	
30. (Sub)	23	1	24	8	2	10	34	16	89	
31. (ISP)	18	0	18	2	0	2	20	12	150	(m)
32. (I)	4	0	4	9	1	10	14	11	367	
33. (ISP)	1	4	5	0	0	0	5	2	67	
34. (ISP)	33	2	35	26	5	31	66	–	–	
35. (ISP)	55	0	55	39	6	45	100	–	–	
36. (Sub)	15	5	20	12	1	13	33	-23	-41	
37. (ISP)	19	0	19	1	1	2	21	12	133	
38. (ISP)	5	2	7	2	1	3	10	7	233	
39. (Sub)	–	–	–	–	–	–	80	75	1500	
40. (I)	25	0	25	17	0	17	42	37	740	
41. (I)	28	2	30	20	0	20	50	–	–	
42. (Sub)	43	0	43	5	2	7	50	37	285	
43. (Sub)	22	0	22	54	17	71	93	77	481	
44. (ISP)	4	1	5	1	0	1	6	2	50	
45. (ISP)	20	0	20	4	1	5	25	19	317	
46. (ISP)	23	0	23	9	0	9	32	22	220	
47. (Sub)	1	2	3	0	0	0	3	-3	-50	(m)
48. (ISP)	6	2	8	0	0	0	8	6	300	
49. (ISP)	10	0	10	5	0	5	15	5	50	
50. (ISP)	7	0	7	1	0	1	8	2	33	
51. (ISP)	1	0	1	0	1	1	2	1	100	
52. (ISP)	7	0	7	30	1	31	38	22	138	(m)
53. (ISP)	13	0	13	1	0	1	14	8	133	
54. (Sub)	139	0	139	46	0	46	185	176	1956	(m)
55. (I)	4	0	4	4	0	4	8	5	167	
56. (ISP)	8	0	8	1	0	1	9	–	–	
57. (ISP)	–	–	–	–	–	–	93	75	417	
58. (ISP)	7	5	12	0	0	0	12	5	72	
59. (ISP)	7	0	7	1	0	1	8	1	14	

Notes:
(I)   = Independent firm
(ISP) = Independent single-plant firm
(Sub) = Subsidiary
(m)   = Firm engaged in a merger/take-over since 1986

Table 4.32 indicates that independent single-plant firms in the Science Park sample currently have larger mean values of sales turnover for the financial year 1990–91 (£1,572,846 compared with £760,962) than their off-Park counterparts, although not in a statistically significant direction ("t"= 1.44, d.f.= 51, accept H_0 at the 0.05 level of significance, one-tailed test).

Table 4.32   Level of Sales (£s) of Independent Single-plant Businesses During the Financial Year 1990–91: 1992 Follow-on Survey

Level of sales (£s), 1990–91	Science Park		Off-Park		Total	
	No.	%	No.	%	No.	%
≤250,000	6	23.1	9	33.3	15	28.3
250,001–500,000	7	26.9	6	22.2	13	24.5
500,001–1,000,000	5	19.2	6	22.2	11	20.8
1,000,001–5,000,000	6	23.1	6	22.2	12	22.6
≥5,000,001	2	7.7	0	0.0	2	3.8
Total	26	100.0	27	99.9	53	100.0
Mean	1,572,846		760,962		1,159,245	
Median	500,000		450,000		500,000	
Standard deviation	2,754,578		818,765		2,037,405	

Similarly, Tables 4.33 and 4.34 show that Science Park firms have recorded larger absolute increases in sales turnover than off-Park firms (£800,522 compared with £461,239 – mean values) but again it is not a statistically significant difference between the two groups ("t" = 1.28, d.f. = 46, accept H_0 at the 0.05 level of significance, one-tailed test). Even so, there is no statistically significant difference between the two samples with regard to sales turnover (£s) in 1990–91 per employee (£46,530 compared with £55,040 – mean values).

Table 4.33   Sales Turnover (£s) Change Since 1986 in Independent Single-plant Firms Located on a Science Park: 1992 Follow-on Survey

| Sales turnover size in 1986 | Sales turnover (£s), 1990–91 | | | | | | | | Total | |
| | <250,000 | | 250,001 –500,000 | | 500,001– 1,000,000 | | >1,000,001 | | | |
	No.	%	No.	%	No.	%	No.	%	No.	%
≤ 250,000	5	31.3	6	37.5	2	12.5	3	18.8	16	100.1
250,001–500,000	0	0.0	0	0.0	0	0.0	1	100.0	1	100.0
500,001–1,000,000	0	0.0	0	0.0	3	75.0	1	25.0	4	100.0
≥ 1,000,001	0·	0.0	0	0.0	0	0.0	2	100.0	2	100.0
Total	5	21.7	6	26.1	5	21.7	7	30.4	23	99.9
Mean	800,522									
Median	300,000									

Table 4.34 Sales Turnover (£s) Change Since 1986 in Off-Park Independent Single-plant Firms: 1992 Follow-on Survey

Sales turnover size in 1986	Sales turnover (£s), 1990/91								Total	
	<250,000		250,001 –500,000		500,001 –1,000,000		>1,000,001			
	No.	%	No.	%	No.	%	No.	%	No.	%
≤ 250,000	5	31.3	6	37.5	2	12.5	3	18.8	16	100.1
250,001–500,000	0	0.0	2	40.0	3	60.0	0	0.0	5	100.0
500,001–1,000,000	0	0.0	0	0.0	0	0.0	2	100.0	2	100.0
≥ 1,000,001	0	0.0	0	0.0	0	0.0	2	100.0	2	100.0
Total	8	32.0	6	24.0	5	20.0	6	24.0	25	100.0
Mean	461,239									
Median	280,000									

The profitability measure of performance follows the same pattern. The majority of respondents of independent single-plant surveyed firms, on as well as off Science Parks, indicated their businesses had made a net profit before tax in the financial year 1990–91 (70.4 per cent and 73.3 per cent of firms on Science Park and off-Park locations, respectively) (Table 4.35). During a recessionary study period it is reassuring to note that less than 30 per cent of surveyed firms in both samples indicated that they broke even or made a loss during 1990–91.

Table 4.35 Did the Independent Single-plant Business make a Net Profit Before Tax During the Financial Year 1990–91?: 1992 Follow-on Survey

Profit during 1990–91	Science Park		Off-Park		Total	
	No.	%	No.	%	No.	%
1. Yes	19	70.4	22	73.3	41	71.9
2. No	8	29.6	8	26.7	16	28.1
Total	27	100.0	30	100.0	57	100.0

$X^2 = 0.00$, d.f. = 1, significance level = 1.0000, accept H_0.

4.5.3 Current ambitions for the independent single-plant businesses and anticipated future growth

Results from the 1986 survey indicated that firms had:

"...ambitious growth expectations for the future. Almost three-quarters of firms want to diversify and expect to more than quadruple employment in five years' time. In turn, almost a third have ambitions for obtaining a public listing, at least on the Unlisted SecuritiesMarket" (Monck et al., 1988, p 209).

During a recessionary period it is not surprising to note that independent single-plant firms surveyed in 1992 had more modest expectations for the future (Table 4.36). It is important to note here that respondents were allowed to make more than one response and therefore can have had multiple current ambitions for their businesses. Over 51 per cent of firms in both subsamples suggested they wanted to consolidate their businesses by maintaining the business ownership and structure (51.9 per cent compared with 53.3 per cent). A further 22 per cent of respondents on Science Parks and 30 per cent of off-Park firms were considering an "exit route" (Birley and Westhead, 1988, 1990b, 1990c) by selling out to another business. Also, in marked contrast to the 1986 survey, less than 4 per cent of surveyed firms on and off the park suggested they wanted to obtain a full stock exchange listing (3.7 per cent compared with 3.3 per cent). Since the off-Park firms are older it is not surprising that a larger proportion of these respondents were considering retiring from the business (0.0 per cent compared with 16.7 per cent). However, over 29 per cent of respondents in both groups indicated that they intended growing by diversifying into related areas (29.6 per cent compared with 30.0 per cent). A further 11 per cent of respondents in both groups expected to increase the survival and growth chances of their firms by involving more equity partners (11.1 per cent compared with 13.3 per cent). Table 4.36 also indicates that a slightly larger proportion of off-Park respondents were considering a drive for acquisition of other businesses (3.7 per cent and 6.7 per cent of respondents on Science Park and off-Park locations, respectively).

Table 4.36   Respondents Current Ambitions for the Independent Single-plant Business: 1992 Follow-on Survey

Profit during 1990–91	Science Park		Off-Park		Total	
	No.	%	No.	%	No.	%
1. Maintain the business ownership and structure as at present	14	51.9	16	53.3	30	52.6
2. Expand the business by involving equity partners	3	11.1	4	13.3	7	12.3
3. Take the business to the USM or obtain a full listing	1	3.7	1	3.3	2	3.5
4. Sell out to another business	6	22.2	9	30.0	15	26.3
5. Retire from the business	0	0.0	5	16.7	5	8.8
6. Drive for acquisition of other business	1	3.7	2	6.7	3	5.3
7. Diversify into other, unrelated areas	2	7.4	2	6.7	2	3.5
8. Diversify into related areas	8	29.6	9	30.0	17	29.8
9. Other	4	14.8	6	20.0	10	17.5
Valid cases	27		30		57	

Despite the recessionary conditions, Table 4.37 indicates that more than 80 per cent of respondents still expected their independent single-plant business would grow in employment in the future (83.3 per cent and 82.1 per cent of respondents on Science Park and off-Park locations, respectively). Table 4.38 shows that over 88 per cent of respondents on and off Science Parks indicated that their businesses would grow their sales turnover in the future (95.7 per cent compared with 88.5 per cent).

Table 4.37   Respondents Believe that the Independent Single-plant Business Would Grow in Employment Size in the Future: 1992 Follow-on Survey

Future growth in employment size	Science Park		Off-Park		Total	
	No.	%	No.	%	No.	%
1. Decrease	0	0.0	2	7.1	2	3.8
2. No change	4	16.7	3	10.7	7	13.5
3. Increase	20	83.3	23	82.1	43	82.7
Total	24	100.0	28	99.9	52	100.0

Table 4.38 Respondents Believe that the Independent Single-Plant Business Would Grow Its Sales Turnover in the Future: 1992 Follow-on Survey

Future growth in sales turnover	Science Park No.	%	Off-Park No.	%	Total No.	%
1. No change	1	4.3	3	11.5	4	8.2
2. Increase	22	95.7	23	88.5	45	91.8
Total	23	100.0	26	100.0	49	100.0

Given the severe recessionary conditions in which the 1992 survey was undertaken there appears to be considerable optimism about the future amongst respondent firms. In this respect there is little difference between on- and off-Park firms.

4.6 Summary and conclusions

This chapter described the characteristics of the 109 firms interviewed in both 1986 and 1992. The purpose was to compare the Science Park sample with the off-Park sample. It showed:

1.   The off-Park sample is older.

2.   Twenty per cent of both off-Park and Science Park firms have been merged/acquired since 1986.

3.   The acquirers of Science Park firms were more likely to see the benefits in terms of obtaining managerial expertise, whilst those acquiring off-Park firms placed greater emphasis on acquiring technical expertise.

4.   Independent single-plant Science Park establishments have recorded faster rates of employment growth than comparable off-Park establishments. Eighty-eight per cent of Science Park establishments report increased employment between 1986 and 1992, compared with only 46 per cent of off-Park establishments.

5.   The five fastest growing Science Park firms created 69 per cent of total gross new jobs on Parks, whilst the fastest growing off-Park firms generated 93 per cent of total gross new jobs off-Park.

6.   Over 80 per cent of firms, both on- and off-Park, expect their businesses to grow in terms of employment in the future.

Part II

A New Sample of High Technology Firms in 1992

Chapter 5

Sample Derivation

The post-1986 population of all 448 organisations located on Science Parks in the United Kingdom in 1992 were identified by UKSPA. From this list 110 organisations were randomly selected covering Science Parks in the government-designated "assisted" and "non-assisted" areas. This list of 110 organisations formed the sampling frame for the "new sample" survey. As in the 1986 survey:

> "...we have chosen to regard all businesses currently located on a Science Park in the UK as being high-tech firms" (Monck et al., 1988, p 104).

The questionnaires were administered by staff from the various regional offices of KPMG Peat Marwick as they were in 1986. Seventy-one interviews were conducted with randomly selected Science Park organisations throughout the United Kingdom (65 per cent response rate).

Surveyed Science Park organisations were then "matched" with a similar group of off-Park organisations based on the same selection criterion adopted during the 1986 study: industry, ownership type, age of the organisation and the location of the business. A variety of data bases were searched for appropriate "matched" businesses (for example, the ICC on-line database, Yellow Pages and the FAME database). As is normally the case, the matching of "young high tech" firms proved to be a time-consuming exercise. Existing databases, whilst containing detailed information on more mature businesses were found to be deficient with regard to "young high tech firms". Off-Park sample selection problems were compounded due to the high level of business closures recorded during the recent recession. Nevertheless, 71 off-Park organisations were identified, and interviews were successfully completed by KPMG Peat Marwick. The field-work interviews were undertaken during the period September 1992 to March 1993. During that time, interviews were conducted both with Science Park tenants and with "comparable" organisations not located on a Science Park. As found in Part I with regard to the follow-on survey, it was not possible to obtain complete information from all organisations, and this explains why some tables do not display responses from all firms surveyed.

Chapter 6

Comparing the 1986 and 1992 Samples

6.1 Geographical coverage

Begg and Cameron (1988) in their study of the regional distribution of high technology employment in Great Britain found that:

> "High technology manufacturing and services are not evenly spread throughout Great Britain. The rest of South East and London dominate, with almost one out of every two British employers in high technology located in this area. But only the rest of the South East and, to a markedly lesser extent, the South West and East Anglia show above national average relative concentrations of this type of employment" (p 375).

Their detailed study also revealed that:

> "As a whole, high technology activity exhibits a clear preference for cities in the South of the country, which has some 50 per cent more high technology jobs (relative to total employment) than the North. The strong showing of New Towns in high technology manufacturing ensures that new towns, of which more are in the South-East, North-West and Scotland, are also preferred locations. Urban areas in regions which were designated as intermediate or development areas for regional policy assistance in 1981, many of which have since seen the scale of incentives available to them cut back, are shown to fare worst as locations for high technology" (Begg and Cameron, 1988, p 371).

Nevertheless, Begg and Cameron (1988) concluded that:

> "The combination of new infrastructure, a 'clean' image, a vigorous labour force and flexible attitudes by development corporations to land and property requirements for growth have combined to attract a markedly above average share of high technology activity, almost regardless of region" (p 375).

This perceived need for a new infrastructure by high technology firms has been matched by a growth in the number of Science Parks in the United Kingdom. Reflecting the expansion of the Science Park movement throughout the United Kingdom, Table 6.1 indicates that 27 Science Park locations were randomly selected for "new sample" interviews in 1992. As was the case in the 1986 survey, coverage varied somewhat from one Science Park to another.

Table 6.1   Science Park Locations: 1992 New Sample

Science Park location	Number interviewed in 1992	%
1. Aberdeen	3	4.2
2. Aberystwyth	2	2.8
3. Antrim	3	4.2
4. Aston	4	5.6
5. Billingham	1	1.4
6. Birmingham	4	5.6
7. Brunel	1	1.4
8. Cambridge	4	5.6
9. Cambridge Saint John's	4	5.6
10. Cardiff	2	2.8
11. Durham	2	2.8
12. Glasgow	5	7.1
13. Hull	2	2.8
14. Liverpool	1	1.4
15. Loughborough	1	1.4
16. Manchester	2	2.8
17. Nottingham	2	2.8
18. Oxford	2	2.8
19. Reading	3	4.2
20. Sheffield	2	2.8
21. Southampton	2	2.8
22. South Bank	3	4.2
23. Stirling	5	7.1
24. Surrey	4	5.6
25. Swansea	2	2.8
26. Warwick	4	5.6
27. Wrexham	1	1.4
Total	71	99.6

Further, Table 6.2 indicates that the "matching" of surveyed Science Park firms was not successful according to "location". Relatively more Science Park interviewed firms were in Scotland and the West Midlands, whilst markedly more off-Park interviews were conducted with firms in south-east England.

Table 6.2   Location of Firms by Standard Region: 1992 New Sample

Standard Region	Science Park		Off-Park		Total	
	No.	%	No.	%	No.	%
1. East Anglia	8	11.3	9	12.7	17	12.0
2. East Midlands	3	4.2	3	4.2	6	4.2
3. North	3	4.2	4	5.6	7	4.9
4. North-west	3	4.2	2	2.8	5	3.5
5. South-east	15	21.1	38	53.5	53	37.3
6. South-west	0	0.0	1	1.4	1	0.7
7. Yorkshire and Humberside	4	5.6	3	4.2	7	4.9
8. West Midlands	12	16.9	3	4.2	15	10.6
9. Northern Ireland	3	4.2	1	1.4	4	2.8
10. Scotland	13	18.3	7	9.9	20	14.1
11. Wales	7	9.9	0	0.0	7	4.9
Total	71	99.9	71	99.9	142	99.9

Overall, a significantly larger proportion of surveyed Science Park firms were located in the "north" (67.6 per cent compared with 32.4 per cent) (Table 6.3) and government-designated "assisted" areas (47.1 per cent compared with 15.7 per cent) (Table 6.4).

Table 6.3   North/South Location of Firms: 1992 New Sample

Location	Science Park		Off-Park		Total	
	No.	%	No.	%	No.	%
1. North	48	67.6	23	32.4	71	50.0
2. South	23	32.4	48	67.6	71	50.0
Total	71	100.0	71	100.0	142	100.0

χ^2 = 16.23, d.f. = 1, significance level = 0.0001, reject H_0.

Table 6.4   Government Designated "Assisted" Area Location of Firms:

Location	Science Park		Off-Park		Total	
	No.	%	No.	%	No.	%
1. Non-assisted	36	52.9	59	84.3	95	68.8
2. Assisted	32	47.1	11	15.7	43	31.2
Total	68	100.0	70	100.0	138	100.0

X^2 = 14.37 d.f. = 1, significance level = 0.0002, reject H_0.

In the 1986 survey there were fewer differences with respect to geography between the on- and off-Park firms. The difficulties of matching on four criteria (ownership, age, sector and geography) meant that one of the criteria was relaxed. Geography was identified as the least important of the criteria and therefore the most likely to be relaxed, provided the other three were fully satisfied. Nevertheless, a geographic dimension was still incorporated because during the 1986 survey several differences were identified between firms located in the "north" as opposed to the "south".

6.2   Ownership characteristics

The two samples were, however, successfully matched with regard to ownership characteristics. Like the follow-on samples, approximately two-thirds of the "new sample" comprised independent firms (66.2 per cent compared with 67.6 per cent) (Table 6.5).

Table 6.5   Ownership Characteristics of Firms: 1992 New Sample

Ownership characteristics	Science Park		Off-Park		Total	
	No.	%	No.	%	No.	%
1. Independent	47	66.2	48	67.6	95	66.9
2. Subsidiary	24	33.8	23	32.4	47	33.1
Total	71	100.0	71	100.0	142	100.0

X^2 = 0.00, d.f. = 1, significance level = 1.0000, accept H_0.

6.3   Age of surveyed businesses

Data on the age of all surveyed firms was obtained and no statistically significant difference was recorded between the two samples (Table 6.6). However, the mean average age of surveyed off-Park firms was slightly higher than their Science Park counterparts (10.2 compared with 13.5 years).

Table 6.6   Age of Firms: 1992 New Sample

Age of surveyed firms (years)	Science Park		Off-Park		Total	
	No.	%	No.	%	No.	%
1. < 4	13	18.3	9	12.7	22	15.5
2. 4–9	36	50.7	30	42.3	66	46.5
3. 10–25	20	28.2	25	35.2	45	31.7
4. 26–50	0	0.0	4	5.6	4	2.8
5. > 50	2	2.8	3	4.2	5	3.5
Total	71	100.0	71	100.0	142	100.0
Mean	10.2		13.5		11.8	
Median	6.0		9.0		8.0	

"t" = –1.35, d.f = 140, significance level = 0.180, accept H_0.

It will be recalled that the average age of the off-Park firms in the 1986 survey was markedly higher than that of the Science Park firms. In this respect the "matching" in the 1992 survey is better than that in the 1986 survey.

6.4 Sectoral coverage and functions

Samples of surveyed Science Park and off-Park firms were successfully matched with regard to sectoral composition. Table 6.7 shows the most frequently cited industrial activities in both samples are technical and consulting services (18.8 per cent compared with 17.6 per cent), computer software (13.3 per cent compared with 14.1 per cent), design and development services (6.7 per cent compared with 7.0 per cent), computer services including repair (6.1 per cent compared with 4.5 per cent), computer hardware (5.5 per cent compared with 7.0 per cent) and finance and business services (4.8 per cent compared with 8.5 per cent).

Table 6.7 Surveyed Firms Engaged in the Following Industrial Activities: 1992 New Sample (Number of Mentions)

Industrial activities	Science Park No.	Science Park %	Off-Park No.	Off-Park %	Total No.	Total %
1. Computer hardware	9	5.5	14	7.0	23	6.3
2. Computer-aided design products and services	2	1.2	10	5.0	12	3.3
3. Computer peripherals	5	3.0	6	3.0	11	3.0
4. Computer services including repair	10	6.1	9	4.5	19	5.2
5. Computer software	22	13.3	28	14.1	50	13.7
6. Electronic components incl. semi-conductors	2	1.2	2	1.0	4	1.1
7. Microprocessor application projects	3	1.8	3	1.5	6	1.7
8. Lasers	2	1.2	2	1.0	4	1.1
9. Fibre optics	1	0.6	1	0.5	2	0.6
10. Analytical and scientific instruments	7	4.2	4	2.0	11	3.0
11. Other electronic and communications related equipment	7	4.2	7	3.5	14	3.8
12. Genetic/monoclonal products	0	0.0	0	0.0	0	0.0
13. Pharmaceutical and fine chemicals	6	3.6	5	2.5	11	3.0
14. Medical equipment and instrumentation	5	3.0	5	2.5	10	2.8
15. Other health products	5	3.0	2	1.0	7	1.9
16. Biotechnology products and services (non-medical)	4	2.4	3	1.5	7	1.9
17. Coal, gas and oil equipment and machinery	3	1.8	2	1.0	5	1.4
18. Geological, marine and other environmental products and services	8	4.8	8	4.0	16	4.4
19. Energy conservation equipment	0	0.0	0	0.0	0	0.0
20. Chemicals and allied products	1	0.6	3	1.5	4	1.1
21. Process controls, automation and robotics	2	1.2	6	3.0	8	2.2
22. Mechanical equipment and machinery	1	0.6	3	1.5	4	1.1
23. Electrical equipment and machinery	2	1.2	1	0.5	3	0.8
24. Other products for retail and consumer markets	3	1.8	3	1.5	6	1.7
25. Finance and business services	8	4.8	17	8.5	25	6.9
26. Technical and consulting services	31	18.8	35	17.6	66	18.1
27. Design and development services	11	6.7	14	7.0	25	6.9
28 Other	5	3.0	6	3.0	11	3.0
Total	165	99.6	199	99.7	364	100.0

Compared with the 1986 sample, fewer "new sample" Science Park firms in 1992 were engaged in hardware and systems (down from 26 per cent to 16 per cent), software (down from 15 per cent to 13 per cent) and microelectronics (down from 10 per cent to 7 per cent). The only difference to be borne in mind is that in 1986 each surveyed firm was assigned to its principal industrial sector, whilst in 1992 firms were asked to indicate the industrial activities of their current output (Table 6.8). This suggests that the Science Park "new sample" is more evenly spread across a range of industrial activity groups than was the case for the 1986 Science Park sample.

Table 6.8   Industrial Activities of Firms: 1992 New Sample (Number of Mentions)

Industrial activities	Science Park		Off-Park		Total	
	No.	%	No.	%	No.	%
1. Hardware and systems	26	15.8	39	19.6	65	17.9
2. Software	22	13.3	28	14.1	50	13.7
3. Microelectronics	12	7.3	12	6.0	24	6.6
4. Instrumentation	8	4.8	5	2.5	13	3.6
5. Automation	4	2.4	8	4.0	12	3.3
6. Electrical equipment	2	1.2	1	0.5	3	0.8
7. Medical	10	6.1	7	3.5	17	4.7
8. Pharmaceutical	6	3.6	5	2.5	11	3.0
9. Fine Chemicals	1	0.6	3	1.5	4	1.1
10. Biotechnology	4	2.4	3	1.5	7	1.9
11. Mechanical	4	2.4	5	2.5	9	2.5
12. Environmental	8	4.8	8	4.0	16	4.4
13. Other manufacturing	3	1.8	3	1.5	6	1.6
14. Design and development	11	6.7	14	7.0	25	6.9
15. Analysis and testing/ other technical services	31	18.8	35	17.6	66	18.1
16. Financial and business service	8	4.8	17	8.5	25	6.9
17. Other	5	3.0	6	3.0	11	3.0
Total	165	99.8	199	99.8	364	100.0

Table 6.9 shows the sectors in which surveyed firms currently earned income. With regard to industrial activities, less than 12 per cent of surveyed firms in both samples indicated income was earned from manufactured products. A higher proportion of Science Park firms suggested they earned income from "soft" activities such as consultancy work (22.7 per cent compared with 18.7 per cent) and training (15.5 per cent compared with 13.6 per cent). Conversely, a larger proportion of off-Park firms gained more income from manufactured products (9.7 per cent compared with 11.5 per cent), licences (5.3 per cent compared with 9.4 per cent) and contract design work (5.8 per cent compared with 8.5 per cent).

Table 6.9   Industrial Activities from which Firms Currently Earn Income: 1992 New Sample (Number of Mentions)

Industrial activities from which income is earned	Science Park		Off-Park		Total	
	No.	%	No.	%	No.	%
1. Manufactured products	20	9.7	27	11.5	47	10.6
2. Software (software packages)	16	7.7	19	8.1	35	7.9
3. Bespoke software	22	10.6	26	11.1	48	10.9
4. Consultancy work	47	22.7	44	18.7	91	20.6
5. Contract research	18	8.7	16	6.8	34	7.7
6. Contract design work	12	5.8	20	8.5	32	7.2
7. Sub-contract production work	5	2.4	8	3.4	13	2.9
8. Testing / analysis	14	6.8	11	4.7	25	5.7
9. Licence income	11	5.3	22	9.4	33	7.5
10. Training	32	15.5	32	13.6	64	14.5
11. Other	10	4.8	10	4.3	20	4.5
Total	207	100.0	235	100.1	442	100.0

Even sharper contrasts between the two samples are apparent in relation to the single most important activity as a source of income (Table 6.10). Off-Park firms had a greater propensity to earn income from consultancy work (21.1 per cent compared with 25.4 per cent), manufactured products (16.9 per cent compared with 23.9 per cent) and bespoke software (9.9 per cent compared with 12.7 per cent). Conversely, Science Park firms were more likely to stress the importance of income generated from training (14.1 per cent compared with 7.0 per cent) and contract research (9.9 per cent compared with 2.8 per cent).

Table 6.10   Single Most Important Activity as a Current Source of Income: 1992 New Sample

Age of surveyed firms (years)	Science Park		Off-Park		Total	
	No.	%	No.	%	No.	%
1. Manufactured products	12	16.9	17	23.9	29	20.4
2. Software (software packages)	7	9.9	8	11.3	15	10.6
3. Bespoke software	7	9.9	9	12.7	16	11.3
4. Consultancy work	15	21.1	18	25.4	33	23.2
5. Contract research	7	9.9	2	2.8	9	6.3
6. Contract design work	5	7.0	4	5.6	9	6.3
7. Sub-contract production work	2	2.8	4	5.6	6	4.2
8. Testing / analysis	3	4.2	2	2.8	5	3.5
9. Licence income	3	4.2	2	2.8	5	3.5
10. Training	10	14.1	5	7.0	15	10.6
Total	71	100.0	71	99.9	142	99.9

6.5 Summary and conclusions   This chapter examined the characteristics in 1992 of 142 firms, 71 of which became established on a Science Park after 1986. These organisations were compared with 71 off-Park firms "matched" on the grounds of having similar ownership, being of similar age, being located in a similar region and operating in similar sectors.

This chapter found that:

1.   The matching is imperfect in terms of geography with more Science Park firms being surveyed in Scotland and the West Midlands, and more off-Park firms being located in south-east England.

2.   The matching is perfect in terms of ownership.

3.   There is no statistically significant difference in the ages of the two groups of firms.

4.   Sectoral comparison is good, except that the off-Park sample was more likely to earn income from manufacturing.

Part III

Themes and Issues

Chapter 7

The "Route Map"

Part I described the derivation and characteristics of a sample of high technology firms, located on and off United Kingdom Science Parks, which survived between 1986 and 1992. Part II described the derivation and characteristics of a sample of firms located on United Kingdom Science Parks, which established their businesses after 1986, and a sample of "matched" firms, operating in similar sectors, of a similar age, in similar locations, but which were not located on Science Parks.

Table 7.1 summarises the current position, showing that in total 251 firms were interviewed in 1992. Of these 109 were firms which survived between 1986 and 1992, and 142 were those in the "new" 1992 sample. The table also shows that 130 of the firms in the aggregate sample were located on a Science Park, and 121 were off-Park firms.

Table 7.1   The Distribution of Firms

Sample type	Science Park	Off-Park	Total
1986 Survivors sample	59	50	109
1992 "New" sample	71	71	142
Total	130	121	251

The purpose of Part III is to examine a set of key themes and issues which relate to making an assessment of the impact of United Kingdom Science Parks. Each of these key issues will constitute a chapter in this Part. Our purpose here is to provide the reader with a "route map" through these issues. The route map is shown in Table 7.2. Further, the table shows that the key issues can be categorised most simply into three: the people, the firm and the environment.

Table 7.2   Themes

	The people	The firm			The environment		
		Technological Sophistication	Financing/ Performance	Management/ Markets	Technology Diffusion	Science Park Location	HEI Links
Chapter Number	8	9/10	13	14	12	15	11
1. Science Park/ off-Park	✓	✓	✓	✓	✓	✓	✓
2. Assisted/ non-assisted	✓	✓	✓	✓	✓	✓	✓
3. Fast growth/ others		✓	✓	✓	✓	✓	✓
4. NTBF/ other indep.	✓	✓	✓	✓	✓	✓	✓
5. < 10 years/ > 10 years	✓	✓	✓	✓	✓	✓	✓
6. Managed/ non-man. Parks		✓	✓	✓	✓	✓	✓

We have chosen to subdivide the latter two issues into three parts. Our interest in the high technology firm was related to three specific issues: its technological sophistication, its financing and performance and its management and markets.

Environmental issues are also subdivided into technology diffusion, the impact of a Science Park location and links with higher educational institutions (HEIs).

In total, the seven headings constitute the columns of the table and broadly correspond to the subjects discussed in Part III of the report. The particular chapters to which they refer are shown at the head of the columns.

Thus far, discussion has focused exclusively upon a distinction between firms located on Science Parks and firms located elsewhere (off-Park). Yet this was not the only categorisation of the 251 firms interviewed in 1992. Table 7.2 shows in row 1 the familiar distinction between Science Park and off-Park firms, but the subsequent five rows show that other categories may yield useful insights.

For example, row 2 shows that Science Park firms may be classified according to whether they are located in the "non-assisted" or the "assisted" areas of the United Kingdom. Analyses along this division may yield insights into the role which high technology firms play in regional economic development and whether these differ from one part of the country to another.

The third row of the table shows that a distinction can be made between those firms which have grown rapidly (with regard to employment change), and those which have grown either modestly, not at all, or contracted in size. The purpose of making such a distinction would be so that the respects in which these types of firm differed could be examined with a view perhaps to targeting policy more effectively.

The fourth row of the table shows that a distinction may usefully be made between new technology-based firms (NTBFs) and other independent firms located on and off Science Parks. In principle, firms located on Science Parks would normally be high technology enterprises. In practice, a small proportion are not in these categories: they include advisory and support services, non-profit-making organisations associated with universities, and sellers and distributors of scientific equipment who do not have in-house advanced technological expertise. Since Park firms are matched in terms of sector by off-Park firms it may be useful to examine NTBFs only.

The fifth row of the table seeks to analyse the firm and its environment according to the age of the firm. Younger firms tend both to grow more rapidly and to have a higher risk of closure. It also seems plausible that they will, in their early years of life, be more active in networking, patenting and the development of new products. Categorising firms according to age would enable these issues to be tested.

Finally, some Science Parks are "managed" more intensively than others. In some, a wide range of support services are available. A full-time manager may exist, together with assistants, his/her job being in part to improve networking between the firms themselves and with the local HEI. It might, therefore, be expected that, on the more intensively managed Science Parks, firms would be more aware of the role of the manager and more appreciative of his or her efforts. Also, it might be expected that such firms would perform better in terms of growth and survival.

The analysis for each of these cross-cutting themes has been conducted, but space constrains it being presented in full. Therefore, we have had to be selective in the material which is presented in the subsequent chapters. Our strategy has been to identify, for each key issue (one per chapter), a set of alternative hypotheses to be tested. In some cases these hypotheses relate to only one of the cross-cutting themes, whereas in others a number of the themes are included.

Chapter 8

The Founders of High Technology Firms

8.1 Introduction

Recognition of the role which fast-growing small and medium enterprises play in creating employment in the United Kingdom has generated an upsurge of interest in those characteristics of an entrepreneur which are associated with business success. This interest has focused on whether it is possible to identify some form of "identikit" of the successful entrepreneur.

The research conducted to date suggests that there are three key groups of influences upon the ultimate success of a new business:

- the background characteristics of the entrepreneur
- the characteristics of the business itself
- the strategy employed by the business.

In essence, these groups of characteristics can be seen as separate in time. The background characteristics of the entrepreneur are identified prior to the business starting whereas the firm characteristics are identified when the business starts, e.g. the sector in which it operates, its legal form, etc. Strategy characteristics are decisions which are taken by the business owners once the firm is in operation.

In principle it would be desirable, particularly for financial institutions, to be able to identify the characteristics of successful businesses as a way of more closely targeting their lending policies. Ideally this identification would take place before, or at the same time, as the business starts. The background characteristics of the entrepreneur are then a topic which is of interest to several organisations engaged in the support of small enterprises.

Unfortunately, research to date does not enable the identikit picture of the successful entrepreneur to be drawn. In part, this is because the ingredients for success will differ according to the sector in which the firm operates, macro-economic circumstances and the nature of competition which the firm faces, as well as in differences in the criteria used to judge success. Nevertheless, in his review of research in this area, one of the current authors, Storey (1994), concluded that some elements within the entrepreneur's background do seem to be associated broadly with business success. Of particular importance here are the educational attainment of the entrepreneur, age and motivation.

This chapter will examine these and other elements of the entrepreneur's background to determine the extent to which those founding high technology businesses differ from the more typical small business owner. Second, it will assess whether there are any clear differences between the backgrounds of entrepreneurs who establish businesses on Science Parks, compared with those establishing high technology businesses elsewhere. Finally, it will examine whether there is evidence that the background profile of the high technology entrepreneur changed during the mid- to late 1980s.

The focus for this discussion has to be on independent businesses only. Subsidiary operations are excluded from the analysis on the grounds that it is the background of the business owner–founder which is of prime interest, rather than manager of the establishment.

8.2 The derivation of hypotheses

In this section four hypotheses are derived and presented, with the remainder of the chapter focusing upon their testing.

Hypothesis 1: The profile of the high technology business founder differs from that of the "typical" small business owner.

There are a number of reasons why the high tech founder might be expected to differ from his or her conventional counterpart. The most obvious of these is that those establishing high technology businesses would be expected to have more levels of formal education, since the technology employed is more sophisticated.

If the high tech business founder has more years of formal education, then it might be expected that the average age at which the individual started the business will be higher for the high tech founder. A further factor which could emphasise this age difference is that the capital costs of establishing high technology businesses will, on balance, be likely to be higher than those for establishing businesses in the more conventional sectors. Since financing often requires an input of personal capital and this personal capital is likely to increase with age, the influence of education on age of start up is reinforced.

Given the likelihood that the high tech founder will have higher educational qualifications than business founders generally, it is to be expected that they are less likely to be unemployed. Unemployment, or the threat of unemployment of the founder, is known to be a major stimulus to the formation of new businesses. It seems unlikely that high technology business owners would be as motivated by the threat of unemployment in starting new firms as is the case for those in the conventional sectors.

Hypothesis 2: The background profile of the high technology entrepreneur is closer to that of the "successful" entrepreneur than is the case for business owners in conventional sectors.

Research to date broadly suggests that the more successful entrepreneurs are those with higher educational qualifications, who are more mature when they establish their business, are less motivated by the threat of unemployment and who often establish their business in partnership with another individual.

If Hypothesis 1 is correct, then it suggests that the personal characteristics of high technology entrepreneurs more closely resemble those of successful entrepreneurs, than those of business founders more generally.

Hypothesis 3: The background profile of the Science Park entrepreneur is different from that of the high technology business founder located elsewhere.

A priori, a case either for supporting or rejecting Hypothesis 3 could be presented. The case for rejecting it is that Science Parks merely constitute a location for high technology businesses and that, providing the business itself qualifies as high technology, then it is unlikely that the founders of the businesses will differ. The "added value" which the Park provides would be expected to influence the business once established, rather than the background of the individuals who establish it.

The converse argument is that Science Parks are normally associated with HEIs and provide a particularly suitable location for individuals with academic links with that institution – especially for those who have formerly worked there and who have an essentially academic rather than a business background.

Hypothesis 4: The profile of the high technology entrepreneur has changed over the last five or six years.

Here again an a priori case can be made for either rejecting or accepting the hypothesis. The case for accepting the hypothesis is that during the 1980s the government saw a key objective of economic policy as being the creation of an "enterprise culture". In essence this involved the encouragement to a much wider range of individuals than had hitherto been the case to consider the option of becoming a business owner. The negative side of this was that certain groups whose employment had previously been secure felt more threatened and hence more likely to consider the option of entrepreneurship. Illustrations of these include government scientists and university academics. For all these reasons it might be expected that the background of high tech entrepreneurs would have changed.

The converse argument is that the technological skills required to establish a "high tech" business did not change during the 1980s. Since these skills could be considered to be a prerequisite for business formation in the high tech sector, it is likely that there will have been little change.

8.3 The samples of firms

To test these alternative hypotheses, results from four surveys will be discussed:

1. the original 1986 UKSPA survey

2. the 1992 survey, discussed in Part II, which replicated the 1986 UKSPA survey (referred to as the "new sample" survey)

3. a study of new businesses in all the sectors established in the county of Cleveland during the 1970s (Storey, 1982)

4. the study of new businesses in all sectors established in the county of Cleveland during the 1980s (Storey and Strange, 1992b).

The two UKSPA surveys have been discussed earlier in Parts I and II of this document. However, if we are to compare high technology businesses on the one hand with a wider and more representative range of independent businesses on the other, it is necessary to have a survey which also asks similar questions to those put to the owners of high technology businesses. For these reasons a comparison is made with new businesses established in Cleveland. The first study examines businesses established during the 1970s in that county, and the second covers businesses established during the 1980s. These constituted random samples of new firms, covering all sectors with the exception of retailing, where the questions asked were in many cases identical to those asked of firms in the UKSPA surveys. The Cleveland surveys contain face-to-face interviews with 159 new firm founders in the 1979 study and 209 interviews (of whom 176 were founders of the business) in the 1990 survey.

The Cleveland responses provide a sharp contrast to those obtained from the UKSPA and "new sample" survey. Although Cleveland is located in an area of very high unemployment, the sectoral composition of the new businesses formed in that area was close to that of a representative sample of new business starts in the United Kingdom. In this sense it provides a valuable contrast to the high technology businesses which are the focus of this work. Its limitation is that it reflects trends in an area of high unemployment, rather than in a more prosperous part of the United Kingdom. Where this is likely to influence the validity of the comparison reference is made in the text to take this into account.

8.4   The results

This section presents the results of an examination of the background of entrepreneurs establishing high technology businesses, compared with those establishing businesses in the Cleveland surveys. Six main elements of this background will be compared: gender, education, age, prior unemployment, prior business experience, prior part-time business ownership and other current business interests.

8.4.1.   Gender

Table 8.1 shows the gender of business owners in the surveys. It indicates that in the 1992 "new sample" survey, 95 per cent of individuals defined as key business owners were male. This pattern was the case both for businesses located on and off Science Parks. The figure in parenthesis in the fourth column shows that in the 1986 UKSPA survey 98 per cent of key business founders were males.

Table 8.1   Gender of Key Business Founder: 1992 New Sample

Gender of key founder	Science Park 1992 %	Off-Park 1992 %	All 1992 %	1986 %	Cleveland 1990 %	1979 %
1. Male	98	93	95	(98)	75	(89)
2. Female	2	7	5	(2)	25	(11)

There is a striking contrast with the results from the Cleveland survey conducted in 1990 where females constituted 25 per cent of key business founders. It is also interesting to note that the proportion of female-owned businesses rose sharply from 11 per cent in the 1979 survey to 25 per cent in the survey 11 years later.

8.4.2.   Educational qualifications

Table 8.2 shows the educational qualifications of business founders in the surveys. In the 1992 "new sample" survey 100 per cent of business founders on Science Parks claimed to have formal educational qualifications, with this being slightly higher than the 84 per cent of off-Park founders. Overall, 92 per cent of business founders in the 1992 "new sample" UKSPA survey have some formal educational qualifications.

Table 8.2   Educational Qualifications of Founders: 1992 New Sample

Paper qualifications of key founder	Science Park 1992 %	1986 %	Off-Park 1992 %	1986 %	All 1992 %	1986 %	Cleveland 1990 %	1979 %
1. With qualifications	100	(75)	84	(79)	92	(76)	65	(71)
2. Without qualifications	0	(25)	16	(21)	8	(24)	35	(29)
1. With degree	87	(64)	82	(52)	85	(60)	5	(7)
2. With higher degree	62	(52)	32	(16)	48	(45)	n.a.	(n.a.)

n.a = not available

This percentage is markedly higher than those found either in the 1986 UKSPA survey or in the two Cleveland surveys. In the 1986 UKSPA survey only 76 per cent of the founders claimed to have formal educational qualifications, whilst in the most recent Cleveland survey only

65 per cent of business founders were formally qualified. This suggested that individuals who established high technology businesses both on and off Science Parks in more recent years were more likely to have educational qualifications than was the case in the past. This is the opposite trend to that observed amongst founders of new businesses in Cleveland, where educational levels of business founders appeared to be falling generally.

The table also examines the nature of these educational qualifications. It shows that in the 1992 "new sample" survey 85 per cent of business owners with educational qualifications had a degree. This was the case both for on- and off-Science Park businesses – except that more off-Park owners did not have any formal qualifications. The contrast with the Cleveland study is stark. Here, only 5 per cent of individuals with qualifications had a degree.

The final row of the table shows the proportion of key business founders with a higher degree. Here there are marked differences between founders of businesses on Science Parks, compared with off-Park founders. Thus, 62 per cent of Science Park business founders had a higher degree, compared with only 32 per cent of off-Park founders. It is interesting to note that a similar difference in likelihood of having a higher degree was also apparent in the 1986 UKSPA survey, where only 16 per cent of off-Park founders had such a qualification, compared with 52 per cent of Science Park founders. Less than 1 per cent of founders of businesses in either of the Cleveland studies had a higher degree.

Overall, these results demonstrate that founders of high technology businesses are much more likely to have high educational qualifications than founders of businesses in more conventional sectors. They also demonstrate that, whilst having a degree is virtually a prerequisite for establishing a high technology business, founders of businesses on Science Parks continue to be more likely to have higher degrees than founders of off-Park businesses. Crudely, it suggests the Science Park founder has a more "academic" background, than his or her off-Park counterpart.

8.4.3 *Age of business founder*

Table 8.3 shows that in the 1992 "new sample" survey 64 per cent of business founders were between 31 and 50 years of age when they established their business; 18 per cent were under 30 years of age and 18 per cent were more than 50 years of age. There was no difference in this respect between Science Park and off-Park owners. A difference emerges when the comparison is made with the 1990 Cleveland survey results. Here 31 per cent of business owners were less than 30 years of age when they established the business and only 5 per cent were more than 50 years of age. This suggests that the founder of a high technology business is likely to be significantly older than the founder of a business in other sectors.

Table 8.3   Age of Key Founder at Time of Business Start-Up: 1992 New Sample

Age of key founder at start-up business	Science Park 1992 %	Off-Park 1992 %	All 1992 %	1986 %	Cleveland 1990 %	1979 %
< 30 years	17	19	18	(21)	31	(43)
30–50 years	66	63	64	(69)	64	(52)
50+ years	17	18	18	(10)	5	(5)

When compared with the prior surveys Table 8.3 shows that the age profile of the entrepreneur in the 1986 UKSPA survey is broadly similar to that in the "new sample" survey. However, the Cleveland survey suggests that new business owners in that county in the 1980s were older than those establishing new businesses in the 1970s.

8.4.4. The role of unemployment

Table 8.4 shows that 23 per cent of business founders in the 1992 "new sample" survey claimed to have been unemployed or to be likely to become unemployed immediately prior to starting their business. This compares with 19 per cent of founders in the 1986 UKSPA survey. In both surveys there is little difference in this respect between Science Park and off-Park founders.

Table 8.4   Whether Key Business Founder was Unemployed or Likely to be Unemployed Prior to Establishing the Surveyed Business: 1992 New Sample

Key founder unemployed	Science Park		Off-Park		All		Cleveland	
	1992 %	1986 %	1992 %	1986 %	1992 %	1986 %	1990 %	1979 %
1. Yes	26	(18)	20	(20)	23	(19)	44	(28)

However, the table does make it clear that the founders of high technology new businesses were much less likely to be motivated by unemployment, or the threat of it, than is the case for founders of businesses in the more conventional sectors. Thus, the 1990 Cleveland survey reports that 44 per cent of new business founders in that county were unemployed or likely to become unemployed immediately prior to starting their business. Even in a decade of relatively low levels of unemployment – the 1970s – the 1979 Cleveland survey found that 28 per cent of founders were unemployed. The 23 per cent in the 1992 "new sample" survey therefore suggests that comparatively few high tech founders are "pushed" into starting a business.

8.4.5   Prior business experience

It is sometimes argued that individuals who have been in business before as an owner are more likely to be successful than individuals with no prior ownership experience (for a discussion see Birley and Westhead, 1993a). This appears to be based on the principle that such individuals will have learned from their prior experience, and any mistakes which they made.

Table 8.5 shows that 31 per cent of business founders in the 1992 "new sample" survey claimed to have prior business ownership experience. This constituted a rise from 22 per cent in the 1986 survey and was particularly marked amongst those founders of off-Park businesses where the proportion with prior business experience rose from 22 per cent to 37 per cent between the 1986 and 1992 surveys.

Table 8.5   Prior Business Experience of Key Founder: 1992 New Sample

Key founder been in business before	Science Park		Off-Park		All		Cleveland	
	1992 %	1986 %	1992 %	1986 %	1992 %	1986 %	1990 %	1979 %
1. Yes	26	(22)	37	(22)	31	(22)	16	(34)

The reverse pattern appears to be the case in the two Cleveland surveys, where during the 1970s, 34 per cent of business founders claimed to have prior business experience, compared with only 16 per cent of those founding a business in the 1980s.

8.4.6 Part-time experience

One important way in which the entrepreneur can "test the water" is to begin a business on a part-time basis. This enables the individual to assess the market place for a product or service, to determine whether he/she and/or their family are suited to business ownership, without having to take the risk of losing a full-time source of income. In this sense the business begun on a part-time basis may be based upon more accurate assessments of the market place and be a less risky option for the entrepreneur.

Table 8.6 shows that 28 per cent of businesses in the "new sample" survey were started on a part-time basis. This is identical to the proportion of businesses in the 1986 UKSPA survey which were begun on a part-time basis.

Table 8.6   Part-time Business Experience of Key Founder: 1992 New Sample

Business started on a part-time basis	Science Park		Off-Park		All		Cleveland	
	1992	1986	1992	1986	1992	1986	1990	1979
	%	%	%	%	%	%	%	%
1. Yes	31	(31)	25	(21)	28	(28)	9	(22)

Although they are not statistically significantly different, it is interesting to note that in both the surveys a higher proportion of Science Park owners began their business on a part-time basis than is the case for off-Park owners. We attributed this to the stronger presence on Parks of academics who commercialised ideas emanating from their own research, and began their business on the Science Park on a part-time basis, only moving in on a full-time basis once the market-place was more certain.

8.4.7 Other business interests

Respondents were also asked whether they had an ownership interest in businesses other than the one which was being surveyed. The purpose of this question was to identify whether the entrepreneur who established the high technology business was a "portfolio owner" defined as an individual who has an ownership in, and derives income from, more than one business.

The "new sample" survey shows that 30 per cent of high technology business owners have an interest in other businesses. This is virtually identical to the 28 per cent found in the 1986 UKSPA survey. In both the 1986 and 1992 surveys there was a slightly higher likelihood for the off-Park owner to have other business interests than the Science Park business owner, but these differences were marginal.

The general pattern is that where other businesses are owned, the number is small – with just over half the respondents having ownership interest in only one other business. Usually these businesses were established after the surveyed business.

8.5   Conclusions

This chapter identified four alternative hypotheses which were to be tested.

Hypothesis 1: The profile of the high technology business founder differs from that of the "typical" small business owner.

It is undoubtedly the case that the background of the high technology business founder is very different from that of the typical small business owner. The high technology business founder is much more likely to be male, and very much more likely to have higher educational qualifications. For example, 85 per cent of high technology business founders in the late 1980s had a degree, compared with 5 per cent of business founders in all the sectors (excluding retail) in Cleveland.

The high technology business founder is generally older than the founder of the business in the more conventional sectors, and is very much less likely to be "pushed" into entrepreneurship by the threat, or experience, of unemployment.

Thirty-one per cent of high technology business founders in the "new sample" claimed to have had prior experience as a business owner; this is virtually double that for individuals in all sectors starting their business in Cleveland.

Again, almost 30 per cent of high technology business founders claimed to have started their business on a part-time basis. This figure is three times as high as that reported by founders of businesses in Cleveland.

There can be no doubt that the profile of the high technology business founder in the respects identified above is fundamentally different from that of the more typical small business owner.

Hypothesis 2: The background profile of the high technology entrepreneur is closer to that of the "successful" entrepreneur than is the case for business owners in conventional sectors.

It would be misleading to suggest that there is uniformity amongst researchers on the background characteristics of the entrepreneur which are associated with business success. However, the general pattern which emerges from research on this topic indicates that in a number of key respects the founders of high technology businesses have a background profile which is closer to that of successful business founders than is the case for new business founders generally.

Where success is defined to be either business survival and/or business growth, the pattern of research results suggests that individuals with high levels of education, those who start their business in middle age and who are less motivated by the threat of unemployment are more likely to establish successful businesses. In these respects the high technology business founder "fits the bill" much more closely than his or her conventional sector counterpart.

The key reservation to this statement, however, is that the background of the entrepreneur is only one of three major components which influence the success of the business. The other main influences, relating to the firm itself and to the strategies which the firm adopts, are not examined here.

Hypothesis 3: The background profile of the Science Park entrepreneur is different from that of the high technology business founder located elsewhere.

Differences between these two groupings do appear. The first is that the Science Park entrepreneur is very much more likely to hold a higher degree than is the case for off-Park business founders. This finding emerges not only from the 1992 "new sample" survey, but also from the 1986 UKSPA survey.

The second major difference is that in the 1992 "new sample" survey the Science Park founder was very much less likely to have had prior business experience, than his off-Park counterpart. The Science Park founder was also (slightly) less likely to have other business interests.

The general pattern then appears to be that Science Parks, not surprisingly, contain a higher proportion of individuals whose career has been devoted to academic, rather than business matters. The (slightly) higher proportion of Science Park business founders who began on a part-time basis is also compatible with this explanation, and it is interesting that in both the 1986 and 1992 surveys a higher proportion of Science Park owners began their business on a part-time basis.

Hypothesis 4: The profile of the high technology entrepreneur has changed over the last five or six years.

The evidence presented in this chapter does not support this hypothesis. The most striking findings are those of the comparative continuity and consistency in the background profile of high technology entrepreneurs between the 1986 and 1992 surveys.

High technology entrepreneurs continue to be dominated by males (98 per cent in 1986 compared with 95 per cent in 1992). The proportion of individuals beginning their business on a part-time basis is precisely the same (28 per cent), the age profile of entrepreneurs has hardly altered at all, nor has the proportion of founders "pushed" into business ownership by the threat of unemployment. The only marked difference between the two surveys is the increase from 60 per cent to 85 per cent in the proportion of high technology business founders with a degree and the increase in the proportion of founders with prior business experience. Nevertheless, the general pattern which emerges is that the characteristics of the high technology business founder have remained essentially unchanged over the six-year period.

This is in marked contrast to findings from the Cleveland study, which investigates groups of new firm founders in the 1970s and the 1980s. Its message is that the new business founder in the 1980s is much more likely to be motivated by the threat of unemployment, likely to be substantially older, very much more likely to be female and less likely to have been a business owner. It suggested that the "Enterprise Culture" of the 1980s brought into business ownership very different types of individuals from those who started businesses in the 1970s. None of these findings, however, seem to apply to the high technology business founder.

Chapter 9

Technological Sophistication

9.1 Introduction

The problems of defining "high" technology were discussed in detail in the Monck et al. (1988) study. In 1986 the majority of surveyed firms were:

> "...classified as "high tech" ...[and they were] very different from run-of-the-mill firms of a similar age" (Monck et al., 1988, p 140).

In the 1986 study it was also made clear that Science Parks select firms on the basis that they are engaged in:

> "...high technology, R & D intensive, knowledge-based or leading-edge businesses" (Monck et al., 1988, p 140).

Nevertheless, a distinction was made between those at the technological frontiers and those in a less advanced position. Firms were asked to rate (self-rate) the technological content and the relative novelty of their products, and/or the knowledge input to their services, in terms of being "leading-edge", "advanced" or "established" technology/knowledge. Firms were asked three questions and they could make one or more responses to each of these questions. Monck et al. (1988) subsequently suggested that:

> "Those firms stating that their product contains leading-edge or advanced technology, or is entirely novel; or firms stating that the service they supply is based on leading-edge knowledge, were all classified as being leading-edge firms. Firms stating that their product contains established technology or has little technological content, or their product is not particularly novel or firms that provide a service which is not unique, were classified as being high-tech firms. Following these criteria, 84 firms (30 per cent) out of the total sample of 284 were rated leading-edge and 183 (64 per cent) high-tech. The remaining 17 firms (6 per cent) are omitted from the following analyses, since they occupied an 'intermediate' status" (p 140).

For the current study an even narrower definition of leading-edge, as opposed to merely high tech, was adopted based on self-rated responses. Manufacturing firms which stated that their product(s) contained leading-edge technology or the product(s) were entirely novel; or firms stating that the service(s) they supplied were based on leading-edge knowledge, were all classified as leading-edge firms. It is also important to note here that firms were asked to make only one response to each of the three stated questions, and:

> "The answers to such questions are fraught with familiar problems of precise interpretation. For example, where the firm has more than a single product, or where attempts are made to compare across market places, different standards of novelty may apply" (Storey and Strange, 1992a, p 25).

Although there are reservations about questions of this type, some reassurance can be derived from the fact that in more than half the cases for both subsamples the same individuals (or founders) were questioned.

In this section six alternative hypotheses are presented. The remainder of this chapter tests each hypothesis in turn.

Hypothesis 1: Manufacturing firms located on Science Parks will be more likely to produce manufactured products using more sophisticated technology than their off-Park counterparts.

Hypothesis 2: Manufacturing firms located on Science Parks will be more likely to manufacture "entirely novel products" compared with off-Park firms.

Hypothesis 3: Service firms located on Science Parks are less likely to be engaged in the provision of a "standard" service than off-Park firms.

Hypothesis 4: More mature Science Park firms are less likely to produce manufactured products based on the "application of advanced technology".

Hypothesis 5: More mature Science Park firms are less likely to manufacture "entirely novel products".

Hypothesis 6: More mature Science Park firms are more likely to be engaged in activities with a standard service.

These hypotheses were initially tested on the follow-on sample (Section 9.3), then on the "new sample" (Section 9.4). The two samples were then combined and the hypotheses tested (Section 9.5).

9.3 The technological level of firms in the follow-on sample

Table 9.1 indicates there are no statistically significant differences in the current technological content of manufactured products produced by Science Park and off-Park firms. In both subsamples over 69 per cent of firms asserted the technological content of their manufactured products was at least "application of advanced technology" (72.2 per cent and 69.7 per cent of firms on Science Park and off-Park locations, respectively).

Table 9.1 Technological Content of Any Manufactured Products Produced by Firms: 1992 Follow-on Survey

Technological Content	Science Park No.	%	Off-Park No.	%	Total No.	%
1. Application of advanced technology	13	72.2	23	69.7	36	70.6
2. Application of established technology	5	27.8	10	30.3	15	29.4
3. Little technological content	0	0.0	0	0.0	0	0.0
Total	18	100.0	33	100.0	51	100.0

$\chi^2 = 0.00$, d.f. = 1, significance level = 1.0000, accept H_o.

Virtually the same proportion of manufacturing firms on Science Parks thought they produced "entirely novel products" as was the case for off-Park firms (27.8 per cent compared with 24.2 per cent) (Table 9.2). With regard to the uniqueness of any service, over 45 per cent of surveyed firms in both samples suggested their service(s) were "based on leading-edge knowledge".

Table 9.2 Degree of Novelty of Manufactured Products Produced by Firms: 1992 Follow-on Survey

Degree of novelty	Science Park		Off-Park		Total	
	No.	%	No.	%	No.	%
1. Entirely novel products	5	27.8	8	24.2	13	25.5
2. Significant novel enhancements	6	33.3	18	54.5	24	47.1
3. Similar to, but better than, products already in existence	7	38.9	7	21.2	14	27.5
Total	18	100.0	33	99.9	51	100.1

Table 9.3, however, shows that a somewhat larger proportion of Science Park firms perceived they supplied a standard service (33.9 per cent and 19.0 per cent of firms on Science Park and off-Park locations, respectively).

Table 9.3 Uniqueness of Any Service Which Firms Provide: 1992 Follow-on Survey

Uniqueness of service	Science Park		Off-Park		Total	
	No.	%	No.	%	No.	%
1. Based on "leading-edge" knowledge	26	46.4	19	45.2	45	45.9
2. Knowledge new to UK	2	3.6	5	11.9	7	7.1
3. Not available elsewhere in region	9	16.1	10	23.8	19	19.4
4. Standard service	19	33.9	8	19.0	27	27.6
Total	56	100.0	42	99.9	98	100.0

Over the last six years the evidence suggests that surveyed firms generally perceive themselves as providing products and/or services which have high technology characteristics. Even so, there were a significant number of firms, particularly on Science Parks, who suggested their services were "standard". (For a similar conclusion see Massey et al., 1992, p 46.)

Table 9.4a   Novelty of Products and Services of Science Park Firms, 1986 and 1992

(a) Technological content of product

	Leading-edge technology, based on latest research	Application of advanced technology	Application of established technology	Little technological content	Not applicable
1.		#	+		
2.			+		#
3.		#	+		
4.			+		#
5.				#	+
6.				#	+
7.		+		#	
8.				#	+
9.	#	+			
10.	#	+			
11.		+		#	
12.		+	#		
13.				#	+
14.		+		#	
15.				#	+
16.				#	+
17.	#	+			
18.			#		+
19.		#	+		
20.				#	+
21.				#	+
22.				#	+
23.				#	+
24.				#	+
25.				#	+
26.		+		#	
27.		#	+		
28.		+		#	
29.				#	+
30.				#	+
31.		#			
32.				#	+
33.		#	+		
34.			+	#	
35.	#	+			
36.		+		#	
37.				#	+
38.			+	#	
39.	#	+			
40.				#	+
41.	#				+
42.				#	+
43.				#	+
44.		#	+		
45.	#	+			
46.		+		#	
47.		+		#	
48.				#	+
49.		+		#	
50.			+	#	
51.				#	+
52.				#	+
53.				#	+
54.		+		#	
55.				#	+
56.		+	#		
57.		+	#		
58.				#	+
59.				#	+

(b) Novelty of Product

	Entirely novel products	Significant novel enhancements to an existing product	Similar to, but better than, products already in existence	Not applicable
1.		+	#	
2.			+	#
3.		# +		
4.			+	#
5.				# +
6.				# +
7.	+			#
8.				# +
9.	#		+	
10.	# +			
11.	+			#
12.			# +	
13.				# +
14.	+			#
15.				# +
16.				# +
17.		+	#	
18.			#	+
19.	#	+		
20.				# +
21.				# +
22.				# +
23.				# +
24.				# +
25.				# +
26.	+			#
27.	+		#	
28.			+	#
29.				# +
30.				# +
31.		#		
32.			+	# +
33.			# +	
34.			+	#
35.	# +			
36.	+			#
37.				# +
38.	+			#
39.	#	+		
40.				# +
41.		#		+
42.				# +
43.				# +
44.		#	+	
45.		# +		
46.		+		#
47.	+			#
48.				# +
49.		+		#
50.	+			#
51.				# +
52.				# +
53.				# +
54.		+		#
55.				# +
56.		+	#	
57.	+	#		
58.				# +
59.				# +

(c) Uniqueness of service

	A service based on leading-edge knowledge	A service based on knowledge new to UK	A service not elsewhere in the region	A standard service	Not applicable
1.			# +		
2.				# +	
3.			# +		
4.		+		#	
5.			+	#	
6.	#		+		
7.	#	+			
8.	#	+			
9.				#	+
10.		+		#	
11.	#	+			
12.				#	+
13.	#	+			
14.	#	+			
15.	#			+	
16.	#	+			
17.	#				
18.				# +	
19.			#		
20.				# +	
21.	#	+			
22.	#	+			
23.				# +	
24.			+	#	
25.	#		+		
26.		+	#		
27.			+	#	
28.	#		+		
29.		+	#		
30.	#	+			
31.					#
32.			+	#	
33.				#	+
34.	#	+			
35.		+			#
36.		+ #			
37.	#	+			
38.	#		+		
39.	#			+	
40.		+		#	
41.		+ #			
42.	#	+			
43.	#		+		
44.					# +
45.	#	+			
46.		+		#	
47.		+		#	
48.			# +		
49.		+	#		
50.			# +		
51.				# +	
52.	#			+	
53.	#			+	
54.	#	+			
55.		+	#		
56.		+		#	
57.	#	+			
58.	#	+			
59.		+		#	

Notes: # = 1992   + = 1986

9   TECHNOLOGICAL SOPHISTICATION

To examine changes over time the responses to the three questions from Science Park firms are shown in Table 9.4. This table is presented in three sections. The first section shows firm responses to assessing the technological content of the product(s); the second section shows self-assessments of the novelty of the product(s) itself; and the third section shows assessments of the uniqueness of the service(s). To reiterate, firms during the 1986 survey which had more than a single product or service were allowed to list more than one category per question, but in the 1992 survey they were allowed to list only a single category per question.

At a finer level of analysis this table confirms the broad empirical evidence presented in Tables 9.1 to 9.3 that there has been little overall change in the firms' own perceptions of the novelty of products or services over the six-year period. We were unable to find evidence suggesting that surviving Science Park firms were becoming either more or less innovative over a six-year period. On Science Parks there appears to be a greater variability amongst manufacturing businesses than service firms. The latter generally stayed in the same technological sophistication category over the six-year period.

9.4 The technological level of firms in the "new sample"

No statistically significant differences between Science Park and off-Park firms were observed between the technological level of businesses in the "new sample" (based on one self-rated response). Over 73 per cent of surveyed manufacturing firms perceived that the technological content of their manufactured product was based on, at least, the "application of advanced technology" (80 per cent compared with 74 per cent) (Table 9.5). Further, over a third of surveyed firm respondents in both groups said they produced "entirely novel products" (40.0 per cent compared with 37.0 per cent) (Table 9.6).

Table 9.5 Technological Content of Any Manufactured Products Produced by Firms: 1992 New Sample

Technological Content	Science Park No.	%	Off-Park No.	%	Total No.	%
1. Leading edge technology	8	40.0	10	37.0	18	38.3
2. Application of advanced technology	8	40.0	10	37.0	18	38.3
3. Application of established technology	4	20.0	3	11.1	7	14.9
4. Little technological content	0	0.0	4	14.8	4	8.5
Total	20	100.0	27	99.9	47	100.0

Table 9.6 Degree of Novelty of Manufactured Products Produced by Firms: 1992 New Sample

Degree of novelty	Science Park No.	%	Off-Park No.	%	Total No.	%
1. Entirely novel products	8	40.0	10	37.0	18	38.3
2. Significant novel enhancements	6	30.0	9	33.3	15	31.9
3. Similar to, but better than, products already in existence	6	30.0	8	29.6	14	29.8
Total	20	100.0	27	99.9	47	100.0

$\chi^2 = 0.07$, d.f. = 2, significance level = 0.9671, accept H_o.

It is also interesting to note that over 57 per cent of respondents on and off Science Parks suggested their service(s) was based on "leading-edge" knowledge (57.6 per cent and 69.2 per cent, respectively) (Table 9.7).

Table 9.7   Uniqueness of Any Service Which Firms Provide: 1992 New Sample

Uniqueness of service	Science Park		Off-Park		Total	
	No.	%	No.	%	No.	%
1. Based on "leading-edge" knowledge	38	57.6	45	69.2	83	63.4
2. Knowledge new to UK	8	12.1	3	4.6	11	8.4
3. Not available elsewhere in region	13	19.7	8	12.3	21	16.0
4. Standard service	7	10.6	9	13.8	16	12.2
Total	66	100.0	65	99.9	131	100.0

χ^2 = 4.30, d.f. = 3, significance level = 0.2312, accept H_0.

9.5 The technological level of firms in the total sample, 1992

No statistically significant differences were recorded between the technological level of Science Park and off-Park firms in the total sample (the follow-on and the "new sample" combined). The majority of respondents perceived the technological content of their manufactured products was based on at least "advanced technology" (76.3 per cent compared with 71.7 per cent) and at least 30 per cent of respondents on and off Science Parks indicated they had "entirely novel products" (34.2 per cent compared with 30.0 per cent). Further, over 52 per cent of respondents on and off Science Parks indicated their service was based on "leading-edge" knowledge (52.5 per cent compared with 59.8 per cent).

It is also suggested that the technological content of the surviving firms in the follow-on sample have lower technological sophistication than those in the 1992 "new sample". A comparison of, for example, Table 9.2 with Table 9.6 shows that 26 per cent of the follow-on group have entirely new products, compared with 38 per cent of the "new sample". Similarly, a comparison of Table 9.3 with Table 9.7 shows that only 46 per cent of the follow-on survey firms classified their services as "leading-edge" compared with 63 per cent of "new sample" firms.

The total Science Park sample was further explored with regard to the age of the surveyed business. Surveyed firms less than ten years old, like their more mature counterparts, generally manufactured products based on the "application of advanced technology" (84.2 per cent compared with 75.0 per cent). Contrary to expectation, a larger proportion of respondents based in firms which were ten or more years of age indicated that they had "entirely novel products" (26.3 per cent compared with 41.7 per cent). However, as hypothesised, a significantly larger proportion of mature (ten or more years of age) rather than young Science Park firms provided a "standard service" activity (14.3 per cent compared with 23.3 per cent) (Table 9.8).

Table 9.8   Uniqueness of Any Service Which the Firms Provide: Total Science Park Sample by Age of the Business

Uniqueness of service	1–9 years		> 10 years		Total	
	No.	%	No.	%	No.	%
1. Based on "leading-edge" knowledge	35	55.6	23	53.5	58	54.7
2. Knowledge new to UK	10	15.9	0	0.0	10	9.4
3. Not available elsewhere in region	9	14.3	10	23.3	19	17.9
4. Standard service	9	14.3	10	23.3	19	17.9
Total	63	100.1	43	100.1	106	99.9

χ^2 = 9.14, d.f. = 3, significance level = 0.0275, reject H_o.

9.6 Conclusions

Six hypotheses have been tested in this chapter. We conclude that:

1. The evidence from the follow-on sample does not support Hypotheses 1, 2 or 3. It finds no difference in the technological sophistication of the outputs between Science Park and off-Park firms.

2. For surviving Science Park firms there does not appear to be evidence of this group, as a whole, becoming either more or less innovative. Amongst Science Park firms there appears to be a greater variability amongst manufacturing than service firms. The latter generally stayed in the same technological sophistication category over the six-year period.

3. The evidence from the "new sample" survey also does not confirm Hypotheses 1, 2 or 3. The technological sophistication of off-Park firms is therefore very similar to that of Science Park firms.

4. For the above reasons, no support for Hypotheses 1, 2 or 3 was found in the combined sample.

5. The technological sophistication of Science Park firms varies with their age. Hypothesis 4, that mature Science Park firms are less likely to produce manufactured products based on the "application of advanced technology" was not confirmed. Contrary to expectation, it appears that mature Science Park firms (ten or more years of age) are more likely to manufacture "entirely novel products". Hypothesis 5 is, therefore, rejected. However, supporting Hypothesis 6 to a statistically significant extent, more mature Science Park firms were found to be engaged in service activities based on a standard technology.

Chapter 10

Inputs to Research and Development: R & D Expenditures and QSEs

10.1 Introduction

From the outset it is appreciated that "...innovation is inherently a multidimensional concept that cannot be measured by a one dimensional instrument" and consequently we must gather a range of "indicators of innovation" (Hansen, 1992, pp 38 and 43).

Analysis of the 1986 survey results revealed statistically significant differences in R & D intensity between on- and off-Science Park firms but Monck et al. (1988) did add the important provisos:

> "...these should not be exaggerated, and many partly reflect differences in the age of the two samples" (p 157).

Nevertheless, it was suggested by Monck et al. (1988) that:

> "The proportion of qualified scientists and engineers (QSEs) employed in a firm (as a percentage of total employment) is one indication of R & D effort and intensity. Technological capability and innovativeness has been linked to the percentage of QSEs employed, in many studies, with one recent study even defining "high technology" sectors in terms of the percentage of QSEs employed (Markusen et al., 1986). Hence the proportion of QSEs to other employees in a firm can be used as an indicator of "R & D intensity": the higher the percentage of QSEs, the greater the R & D effort"[6] (p 154).

During the 1986 survey it was found that Science Park firms had significantly higher R & D intensity in terms of QSEs employed than off-Park firms.

A second indication of the technological capability of firms is the financial resources invested in R & D (see Angelmar, 1984). The most conventional measures of R & D intensity are financial indicators. For example, Nelson et al. (1967) found that up to the 1,000-employee level there was a disproportionate increase in R & D spending with increases in firm size.

The 1986 survey also took financial levels of R & D investment and expressed them as percentage of turnover. This measure has been used by Cohen and Klepper (1990) who found that the overall R & D intensity of the firm was independent of its prior period sales. Monck et al. (1988) noted,

> "...for those off-park firms with some R & D expenditure, expenditure tends to be a lower percentage of turnover than for park firms. Thus, for example, 28 per cent of park firms recorded very high percentages of R & D expenditure (over 40 per cent of turnover) compared with only 15 per cent of off-park firms" (p 156).

A similar proxy measure is also constructed in the present study.

It has been suggested that a further indicator of the technical capability of firms is given by the respondents' view of the thrust of their R & D activity: to what aims is it directed?

10.2 Derivation of hypotheses

In this section five alternative hypotheses are presented. The remainder of this chapter tests each in turn.

Hypothesis 1: Science Park firms will record higher levels of R & D intensity than off-Park firms with regard to QSEs engaged in R & D.

Hypothesis 2: Science Park firms will record higher levels of R & D spending (£s) than off-Park firms.

Hypothesis 3: Science Park firms will record higher R & D spending (£s) as a proportion of turnover than off-Park firms.

Hypothesis 4: Science Park firms will be more likely to indicate that they have ambitious research thrusts and that their primary research thrust or direction of R & D is "radical new research".

Hypothesis 5: Mature Science Park firms with larger financial reserves will invest more heavily than off-Park firms in R & D inputs.

These hypotheses are tested in Section 10.3 in the follow-on sample, and in Section 10.4 in the "new sample". Finally, in Section 10.5 when the two samples are combined. Section 10.6 presents the conclusion.

10.3 Inputs to R & D in the follow-on sample

The evidence from the follow-on survey confirms the earlier findings presented in the 1986 survey. Supporting Hypothesis 1, the mean percentage of total employees that have QSEs engaged in R & D was higher in Science Park firms (means of 31.5 per cent and 22.2 per cent recorded by Science Park and off-Park firms, respectively), although only at 10 per cent significance level here (two-tailed test) (Table 10.1). It is also interesting to note from this table that a larger proportion of off-Park firms (18.4 per cent), rather than Science Park firms (12.8 per cent), indicated that they had no QSEs engaged in R & D. We tentatively infer from this evidence that Science Park firms on this input measure are slightly more QSE-intensive.

Table 10.1 Percentage of Qualified Scientists and Engineers (QSEs) Engaged in R & D Employed by Firms: 1992 Follow-on Survey

Percentage QSEs	Science Park		Off-Park		Total	
	No.	%	No.	%	No.	%
0	5	12.8	7	18.4	12	15.6
1–20	10	25.6	16	42.1	26	33.8
21–40	15	38.5	10	26.3	25	32.5
41–60	5	12.8	1	2.6	6	7.8
61–80	1	2.6	3	7.9	4	5.2
81–100	3	7.7	1	2.6	4	5.2
Total	39	00.0	38	99.9	77	100.1

"t"= 1.67, d.f. = 75, significance level = 0.098, reject H_o (1-tailed test).

Table 10.2 shows that Hypothesis 2 is not supported. There is no statistically significant difference in the mean absolute level of total R & D expenditure per year (£s) between the two groups (those refusing to supply information or answering "not applicable" are not included in these figures). The majority of firms in both samples indicated that their R & D expenditure was either nil or £50,000 or less.

Table 10.2   Total R & D Expenditure Per Year (£s): 1992 Follow-on Survey

Total R & D	Science Park		Off-Park		Total	
(£s)	No.	%	No.	%	No.	%
0	5	18.5	6	25.0	11	21.6
1–50,000	8	29.6	8	33.3	16	31.4
50,001–100,000	1	3.7	4	16.7	5	9.8
100,001–150,000	2	7.4	3	12.5	5	9.8
150,001–500,000	9	33.3	1	4.2	10	19.6
≥ 500,001	2	7.4	2	8.3	4	7.8
Total	27	99.9	24	100.0	51	100.0

"t"= -0.74, d.f. = 49, significance level = 0.468, accept H_0.

In Table 10.3 total R & D expenditure is expressed as a proportion of total turnover. (For this variable more valid responses were available for analysis.) No statistically significant differences were observed between the two samples, with the majority of firms indicating proportions of 20 per cent or less. The mean percentage figure reported by Science Park firms was 19.5 per cent compared with 16.6 per cent recorded by off-Park firms. Hence, we conclude there is no significant difference between the R & D expenditure intensity of Science Park and off-Park firms, and that Hypothesis 3 cannot be accepted.

Table 10.3   R & D Expenditure as a Percentage of Total Turnover: 1992 Follow-on Survey

Total R & D	Science Park		Off-Park		Total	
No.	%	No.	%	No.	%	No.
0	5	11.9	6	15.8	11	13.8
1–20	25	59.5	25	65.8	50	62.5
21–40	8	19.0	1	2.6	9	11.3
41–60	1	2.4	4	10.5	5	6.3
61–80	1	2.4	2	5.3	3	3.8
81–100	2	4.8	0	0.0	2	2.5
Total	42	100.0	38	100.0	80	100.2

"t"= 0.56, d.f. = 78, significance level = 0.575, accept H_0.

Table 10.4 also shows that Hypothesis 4 cannot be accepted. This table indicates the respondents' view(s) of the thrust of their R & D activity and the technical capability of surveyed firms. It is important to note here that respondents were allowed to make more than one response and therefore can have multiple R & D thrusts. Further, the percentage figures in the table relate to the total number of valid responses per subsample.

Table 10.4   Thrust or Direction of R & D in Firms: 1992 Follow-on Survey

Total R & D	Science Park		Off-Park		Total	
	No.	%	No.	%	No.	%
1. No significant research	14	23.7	4	8.2	18	16.7
2. Product improvements	14	23.7	15	30.6	29	26.9
3. Extension of existing range of products	18	30.5	24	49.0	42	38.9
4. Development of complementary products	20	33.9	17	34.7	37	34.3
5. Radical new research	12	20.3	16	32.7	28	25.9
Valid cases	59		49		108	

The main differences between firms in the two samples relate to the "no significant research" and "extension of existing range of products". Contrary to expectation, a larger proportion of Science Park, than off-Park firms suggested "no significant research" (23.7 per cent compared with 8.2 per cent). The over-riding R & D thrust of off-Park firms was an "extension of existing range of products" (30.5 per cent compared with 49.0 per cent). Interestingly, nearly a quarter of firms in both groups claimed "radical new research". However, with regard to the latter statements it was earlier appreciated by Monck et al. (1988):

> "...these responses are themselves unverifiable, and doubts must be raised over the claims around "radical new research" in small firms which are close to the market" (p 144).

10.4 Inputs to R & D in the "new sample"

In the "new sample", there were no statistically significant differences in the percentage of QSEs engaged in R & D (means of 27.6 per cent and 19.0 per cent recorded by Science Park and off-Park firms, respectively) (Table 10.5). There are, however, striking differences between Table 10.5 and Table 10.1. The latter shows that only 16 per cent of firms in the follow-on survey had no QSEs, compared with 47 per cent of firms in the "new sample" survey.

Table 10.5   Percentage of Qualified Scientists and Engineers (QSEs) Engaged in R & D Employed by Firms: 1992 New Sample

Percentage QSEs	Science Park		Off-Park		Total	
	No.	%	No.	%	No.	%
0	22	44.9	20	50.0	42	47.2
1–20	9	18.4	7	17.5	16	18.0
21–40	2	4.1	6	15.0	8	9.0
41–60	4	8.2	2	5.0	6	6.7
61–80	8	16.3	3	7.5	11	12.4
81–100	4	8.2	2	5.0	6	6.7
Total	49	100.1	40	100.0	89	100.0

"t" = 1.30, d.f. = 87, significance level = 0.198, accept H_0.

As found in the follow-on survey Hypothesis 2 cannot be accepted. On this measure firms on and off Science Parks recorded broadly similar levels of total R & D expenditure per year (£s) (means of £362,425 and £431,196 recorded by Science Park and off-Park firms, respectively) (Table 10.6). Given the above findings it is not surprising that a higher proportion of "new sample" firms report no R & D expenditure (50 per cent), compared with those in the follow-on survey (22 per cent).

Table 10.6   Total R & D Expenditure Per Year (£s): 1992 New Sample

Total R & D (£s)	Science Park		Off-Park		Total	
	No.	%	No.	%	No.	%
0	22	55.0	21	45.7	43	50.0
1–50,000	6	15.0	6	13.0	12	14.0
50,001–100,000	5	12.5	3	6.5	8	9.3
100,001–150,000	1	2.5	2	4.3	3	3.5
150,001–500,000	3	7.5	5	10.9	8	9.3
≥ 500,001	3	7.5	9	19.6	12	14.0
Total	40	100.0	46	100.0	86	100.1

"t" = -0.28, d.f. = 84, significance level = 0.782, accept H_0.

Table 10.7 shows Hypothesis 3 cannot be accepted because, on average, firms in both samples recorded similar levels of R & D expenditure as a percentage of total turnover (means of 18.2 per cent and 13.5 per cent recorded by Science Park and off-Park firms, respectively).

Table 10.7   R & D Expenditure as a Percentage of Total Turnover: 1992 New Sample

Total R & D	Science Park		Off-Park		Total	
	No.	%	No.	%	No.	%
0	22	40.0	21	32.3	43	35.8
1–20	20	36.4	34	52.3	54	45.0
21–40	3	5.5	6	9.2	9	7.5
41–60	4	7.3	0	0.0	4	3.3
61–80	1	1.8	2	3.1	3	2.5
81–100	5	9.1	2	3.1	7	5.8
Total	55	100.1	65	100.0	120	99.9

"t" = 0.96, d.f. = 118, significance level = 0.337, accept H_0.

Finally, with regard to the fourth indicator of technical capability, no clear differences emerge between the two samples with regarded to stated R & D thrusts (Table 10.8). Hence, Hypothesis 4 cannot be accepted. Approximately, one-third of respondents in both samples indicated there was going to be "no significant research". Nearly one-third of respondents in both groups suggested an "extension of existing range of products". However, a slightly larger proportion of Science Park respondents anticipated "radical new research" (26.1 per cent compared with 15.7 per cent).

Table 10.8   Thrust or Direction of R & D in Firms: 1992 New Sample

Thrust of R & D	Science Park		Off-Park		Total	
	No.	%	No.	%	No.	%
1. No significant research	21	30.4	23	32.9	44	31.7
2. Product improvements	10	14.5	23	32.9	33	23.7
3. Extension of existing range of products	21	30.4	23	32.9	44	31.7
4. Development of complementary products	21	30.4	23	32.9	44	31.7
5. Radical new research	18	26.1	11	15.7	29	20.9
Valid cases	69		70		139	

10.5   Inputs to R & D in the total sample, 1992

Only one statistically significant difference was recorded between the total 1992 Science Park and off-Park samples (the follow-on and the "new sample" combined). As hypothesised, the mean percentage of QSEs engaged in R & D was significantly higher in Science Park firms (means of 29.3 per cent and 20.5 per cent respectively) (Table 10.9). However, no statistically significant contrasts were recorded with respect to the other measures of inputs to R & D.

Table 10.9   Percentage of Qualified Scientists and Engineers (QSEs) Engaged in R & D Employed by Firms: Total Sample 1992

Percentage QSEs %	Science Park		Off-Park		Total	
	No.	%	No.	%	No.	%
0	27	30.7	27	34.6	54	32.5
1–20	19	21.6	23	29.5	42	25.3
21–40	17	19.3	16	20.5	33	19.9
41–60	9	10.2	3	3.8	12	7.2
61–80	9	10.2	6	7.7	15	9.0
81–100	7	8.0	3	3.8	10	6.0
Total	88	100.0	78	99.9	166	99.9

"t" = 2.00, d.f. = 164, significance level = 0.047, reject H_0.

To test Hypothesis 5 the total Science Park sample was analysed with respect to firm age. Only one R & D input measure yielded a statistically significant difference between young and more mature firms. As hypothesised, more mature Science Park firms (ten or more years of age) on average recorded significantly higher levels of total R & D expenditure per year (£s) than younger firms (means of £78,946 and £651,434) (Table 10.10).

Table 10.10   Total R & D Expenditure Per Year (£s): Total Science Park Sample by Age of the Business

Total R & D (£s)	1–9 years		≥ 10 years		Total	
	No.	%	No.	%	No.	%
0	16	44.4	10	43.5	26	44.1
1–50,000	9	25.0	3	13.0	12	20.3
50,001–100,000	4	11.1	1	4.3	5	8.5
100,001–150,000	1	2.8	1	4.3	2	3.4
150,001–500,000	6	16.7	4	17.4	10	16.9
≥ 500,001	0	0.0	4	17.4	4	6.8
Total	36	100.0	23	99.9	59	100.0

"t" = -1.74, d.f. = 57, significance level = 0.095, reject H_0 (1-tailed test).

10.6 Conclusions

This chapter identified five hypotheses each of which were tested. We conclude that:

1. Based on empirical evidence from the follow-on and the total 1992 samples we find that Science Park firms are slightly more QSE-intensive than their off-Park counterparts. Hypothesis 1 is therefore supported.

2. Whilst QSEs engaged in R & D are a relatively high proportion of the labour force of Science Park firms other dimensions of "innovativeness" suggest few differences between Science Park and off-Park firms. Using R & D expenditure-related measures and R & D thrusts or directions, the off-Park firms are equally likely in 1992 to be deemed to be innovative. Hypotheses 2, 3 and 4 cannot therefore be supported.

3. Only for one R & D measure – total R & D expenditure per year (£s) – did the data confirm Hypothesis 5: more mature Science Park firms invest more heavily in R & D.

4. The firms in the "new sample" are much more likely to have no QSEs and no R & D expenditure than those in the follow-on survey. This is a serious finding in the light of the results from Chapter 9 which suggested that it was the follow-on survey firms which had the lower technological sophistication.

Chapter 11

Inputs to R & D: Links with Higher Education Institutions (HEIs)

11.1 Introduction

The focus on expenditure inputs to the innovation process has been criticised by some commentators. For example:

> "Firms that devote relatively larger quantities of resources to innovation may actually be less innovative if they are not as efficient at converting those resources into commercialized innovations. A second problem with the R&D input approach is that some firms may not be able to report resources devoted to innovation separately from resources devoted to other functions within the firm....This problem is most likely to occur in small firms. Thus it is suspected that small firms systematically under-report their levels of R&D" (Hansen, 1992, p 37).

Consequently, this chapter explores the importance of alternative input measures of R & D. It is assumed that:

> "...university science parks might be able to generate regional high-technology networks" (van Dierdonck et al., 1991, p 111);

and consequently:

> "Links with the local university or HEI are fundamental to the Science Park ethos ...." (Monck et al., 1988, p 145)[7].

Further:

> "This is a key principle of science parks, whereby firms on the park can build contacts with the host academic institution and benefit from the use of academic resources. In this way small firms which cannot afford to employ full-time research expertise in specific areas, or cannot justify the cost of purchasing expensive scientific equipment, can have access to them within the host academic institution" (Massey et al., 1992, p 38).

It was suggested by Monck et al. (1988, pp 167–168) that the forms of linkage between individual firms and the HEI might include:

- the transfer of people, including founder-members of firms, key personnel and staff into employment in firms

- the transfer of knowledge (often embodied in the above personnel)

- contract or sponsoring research in the university by researchers and students

- contract development, design analysis, testing, evaluation, etc.

- access to university facilities such as library materials, especially journals

- less formal interchange with academics which may lead to the important exchange of information, or provide access to a network of people and resources.

For example, Segal Quince & Partners (1985) in their study of the Cambridge Phenomenon revealed that informal contacts were of fundamental importance leading to the evolution of this cluster of high technology companies. The importance of informal contacts has, however, been questioned by MacDonald (1987). Sceptical views of university – industry relationships have also been presented by Lowe (1985), Miller and Cote (1987), Joseph (1989) and Shachar and Felsenstein (1992). However, Bishop (1988, p 161) in his study of 79 high technology establishments (defined as those engaged in aerospace, micro-electronics, medical equipment and biotechnology) in the three Travel-to-Work Areas of Bristol, Plymouth and Exeter in south-west England found that 39 establishments (49 per cent) had some links with an academic institution. Firms with over 100 workers were significantly more likely to have a link with an academic institution than firms with less than 50 employees. With regard to the types of link:

> "...32 of the 39 firms with linkages had industrial research linkages, whilst only just over half had linkages in management training" (Bishop, 1988, p 161).

A study of high technology firms located on Science Parks in Belgium and Holland by van Dierdonck et al. (1991, p 122) osberved linkages to the local Science Park environment but found them "rather sparse".

These researchers went on further to argue:

> "...that a science park is not necessarily the most effective way to become involved in industrial science and technology. A multitude of other mechanisms exist" (p 122).

Moreover, results from the 1986 Science Park survey showed only limited evidence of "tapping-in" by Science Park firms to academic resources (Massey et al., 1992, p 38) and, contrary to expectation, research links between academic institutions and surveyed firms on Science Parks were no more evident than similar links with firms located off-Park. On the basis of their analysis of the 1986 survey data, Massey et al. (1992) concluded that:

> "...significantly more park firms than off-park firms mentioned "informal contacts with academics" and the use of academic facilities such as computers, libraries or dining facilities as being important.... However, the depth of these links is unclear. Our interviews with park establishments suggest that research links with the host academic institution are usually in firms that already had such links. In many cases even these decrease over time. And firms which move on to science parks with no previous academic research links do not usually forge them." (p 138)

This clearly is a major issue which can be tested empirically. In the current study, therefore, surveyed firms were asked to identify links with the HEI.

11.2 Derivation of hypotheses

In this section six hypotheses are presented. The remainder of this chapter tests each in turn.

Hypothesis 1: More of the Science Park firms interviewed in 1986 will, by 1992, mention using the resources of local HEIs.

Hypothesis 2: Science Park firms will be more likely than off-Park firms to have contacted a HEI.

Hypothesis 3: Science Park firms will be more likely than off-Park firms to have "formal" contacts with the resource networks in the HEI.

Hypothesis 4: Science Park firms will seek closer links with the local HEI than off-Park firms.

Hypothesis 5: Science Park firms will be more likely than off-Park firms to have attended technical seminars and events at the local HEI.

Hypothesis 6: Science Park firms located in "assisted" areas will have stronger links with their local HEIs than Science Park firms located elsewhere.

11.3   Inputs to R & D in the follow-on sample: links with HEIs

Table 11.1 indicates the extent of "tapping-in" by those firms surveyed in 1986 compared to that recorded in the follow-on samples. With regard to the 1986 survey data, Monck et al. (1988) suggested:

> "Important caveats need to be inserted into any interpretation of these results. The bald tabulations provide us with no insight into the importance or value of the links, or the depth of the relationships established. There may also be bias in the sense that the off-park firms, being older and better established, have had a greater opportunity to create such links." (p 172)

Moreover, it is important to note here that the 1986 survey results relate to the percentage of firms mentioning each factor as being one of the three most important links with the HEI, whilst the 1992 "tapping-in" evidence relates to the percentage of responding surveyed firms mentioning any link with an HEI.

Table 11.1 suggests that over time there has been an increase in the proportion of Science Park firms reporting informal contacts with academics in the HEI. Both Science Park and off-Park firms have, over the six-year period, increased their contact with HEIs by employing academics on a part-time basis/consultancy basis, engaging students on projects, the employment of recent graduates and the use of HEI facilities such as the library. Science Park firms, in particular have commercialised their activities by selling their own skills and services to HEIs.

Table 11.1   Links with the Local University, Polytechnic or Institute of Higher Education (HEI): 1992 Follow-on Survey (a) (b)

Contact with HEI		Science Park		Off-Park	
		1986 Survey %	1992 Survey %	1986 Survey %	1992 Survey %
1.	Informal contact with academics	60	76	45	45
2.	Employment of academics on a part-time/consultancy basis	28	46	28	29
3.	Sponsor research trials or projects	14	31	15	12
4.	Access to specialist equipment	38	39	30	22
5.	Test/analysis in HEI	12	22	13	10
6.	Student projects	22	51	24	31
7.	Employment of recent graduates	30	44	30	39
8.	Training by HEI	4	10	7	6
9.	Assistance by business in HEI teaching programme	5	17	10	2
10.	Other formal links	1	12	0	4
Use of facilities					
11.	Computer	19	22	7	4
12.	Library	48	68	19	24
13.	Recreation	30	32	7	4
14.	Conferences	15	22	12	14
15.	Dining	22	24	6	4
16.	Audio-visual	10	14	4	2
17.	University as a customer	15	37	16	14
18.	Other	5	5	3	6
	Valid cases	183	59	101	49

Notes: (a) Percentage of surveyed firms in 1986 mentioning each factor as being one of the three most important links with the HEI.
(b) Percentage of responding surveyed firms in 1992 mentioning any link with a HEI.

Table 11.2 shows a significantly larger proportion of surveyed Science Park firms in 1992 indicated they had links with an HEI than was the case for off-Park firms (95.0 per cent and 73.5 per cent of firms on Science Park and off-Park locations, respectively) (χ^2= 8.13, d.f.= 1, reject H_0 at the 0.01 level of significance). This supports Hypothesis 2.

For those off-Park firms indicating a link with a local HEI, Table 11.2 indicates that over 61 per cent of firms giving valid responses had developed informal contacts with academics. This is even more frequently mentioned by Science Park firms (80.4 per cent). More than 40 per cent of firms on and off Science Parks indicated they had research links in the form of student projects (53.6 per cent compared with 41.7 per cent). Off-Park firms were more likely to have provided employment for recent graduates (46.4 per cent compared with 52.8 per cent). Table 11.2 also shows that a markedly larger proportion of Science Park firms had utilised HEI library facilities (71.4 per cent and 33.3 per cent of firms on Science Park and off-Park locations, respectively). Moreover, a larger proportion of Science Park firms had used the university as a customer (39.3 per cent compared with 19.4 per cent).

Respondents were then asked to indicate the importance of links with HEIs for the operation of their business. Each respondent was asked to score each link on a scale between one to five, where one was "extremely important" and five was "unimportant". Interestingly, Table 11.3 shows that both Science Park and off-Park firms stressed the importance of "formal" contacts with HEIs for the operation of their businesses. Science Park firms regarded the following as important factors in a relationship with an HEI (mean score of 2.2): the employment of recent graduates (2.2); access to specialist equipment (2.4); university as a customer (2.3); and access to computer facilities (2.4). Similarly, off-Park firms stressed the importance of "formal" contacts with access to: specialist equipment (mean score of 1.9); use of a computer (2.0); conference attendance (2.0); the sponsorship of trials or research projects in the HEI (2.2); use of the library (2.3); and the employment of recent graduates (2.4). Although no statistically significant differences were recorded between the two subsamples, it was the off-Park firms which were more likely to regard informal contacts with academics (3.0 compared with 2.4) as important.

Table 11.2   Links with the Local University, Polytechnic or Institute of Higher Education (HEI) as a Proportion of Total Valid Cases: 1992 Follow-on Survey

Contact with HEI		Science Park		Off Park		Total	
		No.	%	No.	%	No.	%
1.	Informal contact with academics	45	80.4	22	61.1	67	72.8
2.	Employment of academics on a part-time/consultancy basis	27	48.2	14	38.9	41	44.6
3.	Sponsor research trials or projects	18	32.1	6	16.7	24	26.1
4.	Access to specialist equipment	23	41.1	11	30.6	34	37.0
5.	Test/analysis in HEI	13	23.2	5	13.9	18	19.6
6.	Student projects	30	53.6	15	41.7	45	48.9
7.	Employment of recent graduates	26	46.4	19	52.8	45	48.9
8.	Training by HEI	6	10.7	3	8.3	9	9.8
9.	Assistance by business in HEI teaching programme	10	17.9	1	2.8	11	12.0
10.	Other formal links	7	12.5	2	5.6	9	9.8
Use of facilities							
11.	Computer	13	23.2	2	5.6	15	16.3
12.	Library	40	71.4	12	33.3	52	56.5
13.	Recreation	19	33.9	2	5.6	21	22.8
14.	Conferences	13	23.2	7	19.4	20	21.7
15.	Dining	14	25.0	2	5.6	16	17.4
16.	Audio-visual	8	14.3	1	2.8	9	9.8
17.	University as a customer	22	39.3	7	19.4	29	31.5
18.	Other	3	5.4	3	8.3	6	6.5
	Valid cases	56	95.0	36	73.5	92	85.2
	No contact	3	5.0	13	26.5	16	14.8
	No response	0		1		1	

Table 11.3 Importance of the HEI Link in Relation to the Operation of Firms: 1992 Follow-on Survey (scores ranged from 1 "extremely important" to 5 "unimportant") (a)

Importance of link with HEI	Science Park Mean	SD	Off-Park Mean	SD	Total Mean	SD
1. Informal contact with academics	3.0	1.5	2.4	1.4	2.8	1.5
2. Employment of academics on a part-time/consultancy basis	2.7	1.3	2.6	1.6	2.7	1.4
3. Sponsor research trials or projects	2.9	1.3	2.2	1.6	2.7	1.4
4. Access to specialist equipment	2.4	1.2	1.9	0.8	2.2	1.1
5. Test/analysis in HEI	2.2	0.9	2.8	1.5	2.4	1.1
6. Student projects	3.1	1.4	3.2	1.3	3.2	1.3
7. Employment of recent graduates	2.2	1.1	2.4	1.3	2.3	1.2
8. Training by HEI	3.0	1.8	3.0	0.0	3.0	1.4
9. Assistance by business in HEI teaching programme	4.0	0.8	3.0	–	3.9	0.8
10. Government scheme involving an HEI	3.2	1.6	3.5	0.7	3.3	1.4
Use of facilities						
11. Computer	2.4	1.5	2.0	1.4	2.4	1.4
12. Library	2.6	1.4	2.3	1.5	2.6	1.4
13. Recreation	3.0	1.4	3.0	2.8	3.0	1.5
14. Conferences	2.8	1.5	2.0	1.2	2.5	1.4
15. Dining	2.7	1.4	3.5	0.7	2.8	1.3
16. Audio-visual	3.0	1.2	3.0	–	3.0	1.1
17. University as a customer	2.3	1.6	2.6	1.5	2.4	1.6
18. Other	3.0	1.7	3.0	2.0	3.0	1.7

Note: (a) Scores are presented for only those firms indicating a link.

For both groups of firms the single most important link reported was informal contact with academics (29.8 per cent and 31.0 per cent of firms on Science Park and off-Park locations, respectively) (Table 11.4)[8]. Overall, the results suggest a perhaps surprising amount of formal and informal contact between HEIs and off-Park firms, to the extent that there are smaller differences between on- and off-Park firms in this respect than might have been expected. Nevertheless, according to most criteria, contact levels between HEIs and firms was greater amongst the Science Park group.

The second key result was that, in contrast to the Cambridge Phenomenon finding, the contacts which the firm has which were regarded as the most important for the operation of its business were the formal, rather than the informal ones. Even so, the single most important link with HEIs, for on- and off-Park firms, was informal contact with academics. For Science Park firms the three other most important links were having the university as a customer (17.0 per cent compared with 3.4 per cent), employment of recent graduates (12.8 per cent compared with 17.2 per cent) and access to library facilities (12.8 per cent compared with 6.9 per cent). To a slightly greater extent, off-Park firms stressed the importance of the sponsorship of trials or research projects in the HEI (4.3 per cent compared with 10.3 per cent).

We conclude on the basis of the above discussion that there is limited evidence from the follow-on samples to support Hypothesis 3. Also, Science Park firms do not record more frequent "formal" contacts with the HEIs than off-Park firms. Both groups, nevertheless, value the importance of "formal" contacts with HEIs.

Table 11.4 The Single Most Important Link Reported by Firms and the Local University, Polytechnic or Institute of Higher Education (HEI): 1992 Follow-on Survey

Single most important HEI Link	Science Park No.	Science Park %	Off-Park No.	Off-Park %	Total No.	Total %
1. Informal contact with academics	14	29.8	9	31.0	23	30.3
2. Employment of academics on a part-time/consultancy basis	4	8.5	3	10.3	7	9.2
3. Sponsor research trials or projects	2	4.3	3	10.3	5	6.6
4. Access to specialist equipment	2	4.3	2	6.9	4	5.3
5. Test/analysis in HEI	0	0.0	0	0.0	0	0.0
6. Student projects	0	0.0	1	3.4	1	1.3
7. Employment of recent graduates	6	12.8	5	17.2	11	14.5
8. Training by HEI	0	0.0	0	0.0	0	0.0
9. Assistance by business in HEI teaching programme	0	0.0	0	0.0	0	0.0
10. Other formal links	1	2.1	1	3.4	2	2.6
Use of facilities						
11. Computer	0	0.0	0	0.0	0	0.0
12. Library	6	12.8	2	6.9	8	10.5
13. Recreation	1	2.1	0	0.0	1	1.3
14. Conferences	0	0.0	1	3.4	1	1.3
15. Dining	1	2.1	0	0.0	1	1.3
16. Audio-visual	1	2.1	0	0.0	1	1.3
17. University as a customer	8	17.0	1	3.4	9	11.8
18. Other	1	2.1	1	3.4	2	2.6
Total	47	100.0	29	99.6	76	99.9

11.4 Development of inputs leading to R & D fostered by HEIs in the follow-on sample

To explore the need for "tapping-in", respondents in the follow-on survey were asked to indicate whether they sought closer links between their businesses and the local HEI. Table 11.5 shows over 52 per cent of respondents in both subsamples believe closer links would be desirable/beneficial (69.1 per cent and 52.5 per cent of firms on Science Park and off-Park locations, respectively). More than 57 per cent of respondents in both groups, however, felt the HEI could make its services and facilities more accessible to firms (64.6 per cent and 57.1 per cent of firms on Science Park and off-Park locations, respectively) (Table 11.6).

Table 11.5 Respondents Believe that Closer Links Between the Firm and the Local HEI are Desirable/Would Be Beneficial to the Firm: 1992 Follow-on Survey

Closer links with HEI are beneficial to firm	Science Park No.	Science Park %	Off-Park No.	Off-Park %	Total No.	Total %
1. Yes	38	69.1	21	52.5	59	62.1
2. No	17	30.9	19	47.5	36	37.9
Total	55	100.0	40	100.0	95	100.0

$\chi^2 = 2.05$, d.f. = 1, significance level = 0.1523, accept H_o.

Table 11.6 Could the HEI Make Its Services and Facilities More Accessible to Firms: 1992 Follow-on Survey

HEI make facilities more accessible	Science Park No.	Science Park %	Off-Park No.	Off-Park %	Total No.	Total %
1. Yes	31	64.6	24	57.1	55	61.1
2. No	17	35.4	18	42.9	35	38.9
Total	48	100.0	42	100.0	90	100.0

$\chi^2 = 0.26$, d.f. = 1, significance level = 0.6131, accept H_o.

It is disconcerting that a majority of respondents in both subsamples reported that no one from the local HEI had ever visited them to discuss the HEIs facilities (60.4 per cent and 67.4 per cent of firms on Science Park and off-Park locations, respectively) (Table 11.7). Even though a visit is more likely to have been made to a Science Park firm than to an off-Park firm, the fact that more than half of long-established firms have not been visited is disappointing. Perhaps even more striking is the evidence presented in Table 11.8 which indicates that 59 per cent of Science Park firms reported their firm had not been visited by anyone from a Science Park to discuss HEI facilities (58.5 per cent and 87.2 per cent of firms on Science Park and off-Park locations, respectively). The evidence here certainly suggests that this is an area needing attention.

Table 11.7   Has Anyone from the Local HEI Ever Visited to Discuss the HEI's Facilities: 1992 Follow-on Survey

Person from HEI to discuss the HEI's facilities	Science Park		Off-Park		Total	
	No.	%	No.	%	No.	%
1. Yes	21	39.6	14	32.6	35	36.5
2. No	32	60.4	29	67.4	61	63.5
Total	53	100.0	43	100.0	96	100.0

$\chi^2 = 0.25$, d.f. = 1, significance level = 0.6157, accept H_0.

Table 11.8   Has Anyone from the Local Science Park Ever Visited Firms to Discuss the HEI's Facilities: 1992 Follow-on Survey

Person from Science Park to discuss the HEI's facilities	Science Park		Off-Park		Total	
	No.	%	No.	%	No.	%
1. Yes	22	41.5	5	12.8	27	29.3
2. No	31	58.5	34	87.2	65	70.7
Total	53	100.0	39	100.0	92	100.0

$\chi^2 = 7.59$, d.f. = 1, significance level = 0.0059, reject H_0.

The importance of this is emphasised by the finding that the majority of Science Park firms report that the local HEI has been useful in either recruiting or retaining highly skilled staff, either in an active or passive way (55.6 per cent and 42.9 per cent of firms on Science Park and off-Park locations, respectively) (Table 11.9).

Table 11.9   Respondents Believe that the Presence of a Local HEI Has Been Useful in Either Recruiting or Retaining Highly Skilled Staff, Either in an Active or Passive Way: 1992 Follow-on Survey

HEI useful in recruiting skilled staff	Science Park		Off-Park		Total	
	No.	%	No.	%	No.	%
1. Yes	30	55.6	18	42.9	48	50.0
2. No	24	44.4	24	57.1	48	50.0
Total	54	100.0	42	100.0	96	100.0

$\chi^2 = 1.06$, d.f. = 1, significance level = 0.3036, accept H^0.

Even so, more than one-third of respondents in both subsamples said that they had never been invited to any technical seminars at the local HEI (42.6 per cent compared with 34.9 per cent) (Table 11.10). For those invited, 74.2 per cent of Science Park firm respondents attended compared with 66.7 per cent of off-Park respondents (Table 11.11).

Table 11.10   Respondent Ever Been Invited to any Technical Seminars at the Local HEI: 1992 Follow-on Survey

Invited to any technical seminars	Science Park No.	%	Off-Park No.	%	Total No.	%
1. Yes	31	57.4	28	65.1	59	60.8
2. No	23	42.6	15	34.9	38	39.2
Total	54	100.0	43	100.0	97	100.0

$\chi^2 = 0.32$, d.f. = 1, significance level = 0.5732, accept H_0.

Table 11.11   Did the Respondent Attend the Technical Seminars at the Local HEI: 1992 Follow-on Survey

Attend technical seminars	Science Park No.	%	Off-Park No.	%	Total No.	%
1. Yes	23	74.2	18	66.7	41	70.7
2. No	8	25.8	9	33.3	17	29.3
Total	31	100.0	27	100.0	58	100.0

$\chi^2 = 0.11$, d.f. = 1, significance level = 0.7346, accept H_0.

It is pleasing to note here that 90.9 per cent of Science Park firms and 83.3 per cent of off-Park firms viewed these technical seminars as being useful (Table 11.12).

Table 11.12   Did the Respondent View the Technical Seminars at the Local HEI as Being Useful: 1992 Follow-on Survey

Technical seminars Useful	Science Park No.	%	Off-Park No.	%	Total No.	%
1. Yes	20	90.9	15	83.3	35	87.5
2. No	2	9.1	3	16.7	5	12.5
Total	22	100.0	18	100.0	40	100.0

A similar set of questions were asked about events at the local HEI intended to inform firms about the HEIs skills and facilities. Virtually 60 per cent of respondents in both subsamples suggested that they had never been invited to any such events (63.3 per cent compared with 57.1 per cent) (Table 11.13).

Table 11.13   Respondent Ever Been Invited to any Events at the Local HEI Designed to Inform Them of the HEI's Skills and Facilities: 1992 Follow-on Survey

Invited to any events to show the HEI's skills and facilities	Science Park No.	%	Off-Park No.	%	Total No.	%
1. Yes	20	37.0	18	42.9	38	39.6
2. No	34	63.3	24	57.1	58	60.4
Total	54	100.0	42	100.0	96	100.0

$\chi^2 = 0.14$, d.f. = 1, significance level = 0.7128, accept H_0.

For those invited, two-thirds of respondents in both groups attended (80.0 per cent compared with 66.7 per cent) (Table 11.14). Whilst all those attending from a surveyed Science Park firm suggested the event was of interest, this was the case for only 66.7 per cent of off-Park respondents (Table 11.15).

Table 11.14 Did the Respondent Ever Attend Events at the Local HEI Designed to Inform Them of the HEI's Skills and Facilities: 1992 Follow-on Survey

Attended events to show the HEI's skills and facilities	Science Park		Off-Park		Total	
	No.	%	No.	%	No.	%
1. Yes	16	80.0	12	66.7	28	73.7
2. No	4	20.0	6	33.3	10	26.3
Total	20	100.0	18	100.0	38	100.0

Table 11.15 Was the Event at the Local HEI Designed to Inform Them of the HEI's Skills and Facilities of Interest to Respondents: 1992 Follow-on Survey

Event at HEI of interest	Science Park		Off-Park		Total	
	No.	%	No.	%	No.	%
1. Yes	16	100.0	8	66.7	24	85.7
2. No	0	0.0	4	33.3	4	14.3
Total	16	100.0	12	100.0	28	100.0

The low level of contact with HEIs may, in part, be because surveyed firms are not aware of HEI events and technical facilities. Table 11.16 shows over 57 per cent of respondents in both subsamples indicated their firm had not received copies of the local HEI's newsletter (57.4 per cent compared with 69.0 per cent). For those receiving a newsletter it is interesting to note that a larger proportion of off-Park respondents suggested there were no items which were of interest (15.4 per cent compared with 46.2 per cent) (Table 11.17). Whilst the majority of surveyed Science Park firm respondents were interested in general news items (60.9 per cent) and seminar/lecture programmes (47.8 per cent).

Table 11.16 Respondent Received Copies of the Local HEI's Newsletter: 1992 Follow-on Survey

Received copies of HEI's newsletter	Science Park		Off-Park		Total	
	No.	%	No.	%	No.	%
1. Yes	23	42.6	13	31.0	36	37.5
2. No	31	57.4	29	69.0	60	62.5
Total	54	100.0	42	100.0	96	100.0

χ^2 = 0.91, d.f. = 1, significance level = 0.3390, accept H_0.

Table 11.17 Items Regarded as of Interest by Respondents who had Received Copies of the Local HEI's Newsletter: 1992 Follow-on Survey

Items of interest in the HEI's newsletter	Science Park		Off-Park		Total	
	No.	%	No.	%	No.	%
1. New appointments	9	39.1	3	23.1	12	33.3
2. General news items	14	60.9	3	23.1	17	47.2
3. Seminar/lecture programmes	11	47.8	4	30.8	15	41.7
4. Details of leisure facilities/events	7	30.4	0	0.0	7	19.4
5. Other	3	13.0	0	0.0	3	8.3
6. None	2	15.4	6	46.2	8	22.2
Valid cases	23		13		36	

The above suggests Hypotheses 4 and 5 are not supported. Firms on- and off-Science Parks appreciate that closer links between their business and HEIs is desirable and beneficial. Off-Park firms are willing to attend technical seminars and events at the local HEI designed to inform them of the HEIs skills and facilities. This all suggests that HEIs could do more to improve the awareness of the business community of their skills and facilities. It is reassuring to note that, where links are established and awareness is high, this is seen to be useful.

11.5 Inputs to R & D links with HEIs: the "new sample"

This section examines links with the HEI for firms in the 1992 "new sample". As noted earlier, in the 1986 survey Monck et al. (1988, p 171) reported the percentage of surveyed firms mentioning each factor as being one of the three most important links with the HEI. In the "new sample" survey in 1992 firms (as in the follow-on sample) could mention any link with an HEI (see Table 11.18a). Comparing the 1986 results (Table 11.1) with those for the "new sample" it is not surprising we observe an apparent increase. In both surveys 60 per cent of Science Park firms indicated they had had informal contact with academics. However, a larger proportion of Science Park firms in the 1992 "new sample" had had the following links: use of library facilities (up from 48 per cent to 62 per cent); student projects (up from 22 per cent to 38 per cent); training by the HEI (up from 4 per cent to 14 per cent); assistance by business in HEI teaching programmes (up from 5 per cent to 17 per cent); and the university as a customer (up from 15 per cent to 24 per cent). Science Park firms in 1992 were, however, less likely to have used HEI specialist equipment (down from 38 per cent to 32 per cent) and computer facilities (down from 19 per cent to 9 per cent).

The 1992 "new sample" results indicated that a larger proportion of surveyed Science Park firms had a link with an HEI than off-Park firms (87.3 per cent compared with 78.9 per cent), although not in a statistically significant direction. For those firms with an HEI link the types of links were generally very similar between firms located on and off Science Parks. Over 62 per cent of valid responding firms, in both groups, indicated they had informal contact with academics (69.4 per cent compared with 62.5 per cent) (Table 11.18b). However, a larger proportion of valid responding Science Park firms had used the HEI library (71.0 per cent compared with 30.4 per cent) or recreation facilities (40.3 per cent compared with 3.6 per cent).

Table 11.18a   Links with the Local University, Polytechnic or Institute of Higher Education (HEI) as a Proportion of Responding Firms: 1992 New Sample

Contact with HEI	Science Park		Off-Park		Total	
	No.	%	No.	%	No.	%
1. Informal contact with academics	43	60.6	35	49.3	78	54.9
2. Employment of academics on a part-time/consultancy basis	21	29.6	22	31.0	43	30.3
3. Sponsor research trials or projects	15	21.1	18	25.4	33	23.2
4. Access to specialist equipment	23	32.4	16	22.5	39	27.5
5. Test/analysis in HEI	12	16.9	9	12.7	21	14.8
6. Student projects	27	38.0	22	31.0	49	34.5
7. Employment of recent graduates	24	33.8	24	33.8	48	33.8
8. Training by HEI	10	14.1	9	12.7	19	13.4
9. Assistance by business in HEI teaching programme	12	16.9	11	15.5	23	16.2
10. Other formal links	10	14.1	6	8.5	16	11.3
Use of facilities:						
11. Computer	6	8.5	7	9.9	13	9.2
12. Library	44	62.0	17	23.9	61	43.0
13. Recreation	25	35.2	2	2.8	27	19.0
14. Conferences	16	22.5	12	16.9	28	19.7
15. Dining	18	25.4	4	5.6	22	15.5
16. Audio-visual	7	9.9	4	5.6	11	7.7
17. University as a customer	17	23.9	17	23.9	34	23.9
18. Other	5	7.0	2	2.8	7	4.9
Valid cases	62	87.3	56	78.9	118	83.1
No contact	9	12.7	15	21.1	24	16.9

Table 11.18b   Links with the Local University, Polytechnic or Institute of Higher Education (HEI) as a Proportion of Total Valid Cases: 1992 New Sample

Contact with HEI	Science Park		Off-Park		Total	
	No.	%	No.	%	No.	%
1. Informal contact with academics	43	69.4	35	62.5	78	66.1
2. Employment of academics on a part-time/consultancy basis	21	33.9	22	39.3	43	36.4
3. Sponsor research trials or projects	15	24.2	18	32.1	33	28.0
4. Access to specialist equipment	23	37.1	16	28.6	39	33.1
5. Test/analysis in HEI	12	19.4	9	16.1	21	17.8
6. Student projects	27	43.5	22	39.3	49	41.5
7. Employment of recent graduates	24	38.7	24	42.9	48	40.7
8. Training by HEI	10	16.1	9	16.1	19	16.1
9. Assistance by business in HEI teaching programme	12	19.4	11	19.6	23	19.5
10. Other formal links	10	16.1	6	10.7	16	13.6
Use of facilities:						
11. Computer	6	9.7	7	12.5	13	11.0
12. Library	44	71.0	17	30.4	61	51.2
13. Recreation	25	40.3	2	3.6	27	22.9
14. Conferences	16	25.8	12	21.4	28	23.7
15. Dining	18	29.0	4	7.1	22	18.6
16. Audio-visual	7	11.3	4	7.1	11	9.3
17. University as a customer	17	27.4	17	30.4	34	28.8
18. Other	5	8.1	2	3.6	7	5.9
Valid cases	62	87.3	56	78.9	118	83.1
No contact	9	12.7	15	21.1	24	16.9

As in the follow-on survey, respondents were asked about the importance of links between HEIs and their business. Table 11.19 shows both Science Park and off-Park firms stressed the importance of "formal" contacts with HEIs. Science Park firms regarded the following as important: "other" links (mean score of 1.8); audio-visual facilities (2.3); test/analysis facilities in a HEI (2.4); library (2.4); access to conference facilities (2.4); and having the university as a customer (2.4). Similarly, off-Park firms stressed the importance of: "formal" contacts with employment of academics on a part-time basis/consultancy basis (mean score of 2.3); training by HEI (2.3); government schemes involving an HEI (2.3); having the university as a customer (2.4); and the employment of recent graduates (2.5). No statistically significant differences were recorded between the two subsamples relating to the importance of links with the HEI.

For both groups of firms the single most important link with the HEI was ascertained (Table 11.20). For Science Park firms the most important links were library facilities (17.6 per cent and the employment of academics on a part-time/consultancy basis (11.8 per cent). Off-Park firms placed more emphasis on the employment of recent graduates (20 per cent), the university as a customer (14.5 per cent) and informal contact with academics (18.2 per cent).

The evidence from the 1992 "new sample" survey suggests that Hypothesis 3 cannot be accepted. It appears that new firms on and off Science Parks have generally developed less "formal" levels of contact(s) with local HEIs. However, it is acknowledged that part of the value of a Science Park location for a new firm is the opportunity to develop "informal" contacts early and quickly and to "tap in" to a variety of resources in the HEI on an "as and when" needed basis.

Table 11.19   Importance of the HEI Link in Relation to the Operation of Firms: 1992 New Sample (scores ranged from 1 "extremely important" to 5 "unimportant") (a)

Importance of link with HEI	Science Park		Off-Park		Total	
	Mean	SD	Mean	SD	Mean	SD
1. Informal contact with academics	3.1	1.3	3.1	1.2	3.1	1.2
2. Employment of academics on a part-time/consultancy basis	2.2	1.3	2.3	1.1	2.2	1.2
3. Sponsor research trials or projects	2.9	1.4	2.6	1.1	2.8	1.2
4. Access to specialist equipment	2.7	1.1	2.8	1.4	2.7	1.2
5. Test/analysis in HEI	2.4	1.2	3.1	1.5	2.7	1.3
6. Student projects	3.3	1.3	3.3	1.3	3.3	1.3
7. Employment of recent graduates	2.6	1.3	2.5	1.3	2.6	1.3
8. Training by HEI	2.8	1.6	2.3	1.2	2.6	1.4
9. Assistance by business in HEI teaching programme	3.3	1.7	3.3	1.3	3.3	1.5
10. Government scheme involving an HEI	3.0	1.5	2.3	0.8	2.8	1.3
Use of facilities						
11. Computer	3.0	1.7	3.3	1.0	3.2	1.3
12. Library	2.4	1.1	3.4	1.2	2.7	1.2
13. Recreation	3.3	1.2	4.0	1.4	3.4	1.2
14. Conferences	2.4	1.2	3.0	1.4	2.7	1.3
15. Dining	2.9	1.1	4.3	1.0	3.2	1.2
16. Audio-visual	2.3	1.4	3.3	1.3	2.6	1.4
17. University as a customer	2.4	1.6	2.4	1.5	2.4	1.5
18. Other	1.8	0.8	4.0	1.4	2.4	1.3

Note: (a)   Scores are presented for only those firms indicating a link.

Table 11.20   The Single Most Important Link Reported by Firms and the Local University, Polytechnic or Institute of Higher Education (HEI): 1992 New Sample

Single most important HEI Link	Science Park No.	%	Off-Park No.	%	Total No.	%
1. Informal contact with academics	6	11.8	10	18.2	16	15.1
2. Employment of academics on a part-time/consultancy basis	6	11.8	5	9.1	11	10.4
3. Sponsor research trials or projects	3	5.9	5	9.1	8	7.5
4. Access to specialist equipment	5	9.8	4	7.3	9	8.5
5. Test/analysis in HEI	1	2.0	2	3.6	3	2.8
6. Student projects	3	5.9	3	5.5	6	5.7
7. Employment of recent graduates	6	11.8	11	20.0	17	16.0
8. Training by HEI	2	3.9	1	1.8	3	2.8
9. Assistance by business in HEI teaching programme	0	0.0	4	7.3	4	3.8
10. Other formal links	1	2.0	0	0.0	1	0.9
Use of facilities						
11. Computer	0	0.0	0	0.0	0	0.0
12. Library	9	17.6	1	1.8	10	9.4
13. Recreation	0	0.0	0	0.0	0	0.0
14. Conferences	3	5.9	0	0.0	3	2.8
15. Dining	1	2.0	0	0.0	1	0.9
16. Audio-visual	0	0.0	1	1.8	1	0.9
17. University as a customer	5	9.8	8	14.5	13	12.3
Total	51	100.2	55	100.0	106	99.8

11.6 Development of inputs leading to R & D fostered by HEIs: the "new sample"

The data on the "new sample" of firms presented in Table 11.21 suggests Hypothesis 4 cannot be accepted. The majority of off-Park firms like their Science Park counterparts, suggested closer links between surveyed enterprises and the local HEI were desirable/would be beneficial (62.1 per cent compared with 55.4 per cent).

Table 11.21   Respondents Believe that Closer Links Between Firms and the Local HEI are Desirable/Would Be Beneficial to the Firm: 1992 New Sample

Closer links with HEI are beneficial to firm	Science Park No.	%	Off-Park No.	%	Total No.	%
1. Yes	41	62.1	36	55.4	77	58.8
2. No	25	37.9	29	44.6	54	41.2
Total	66	100.0	65	100.0	131	100.0

χ^2 = 0.37, d.f. = 1; significance level = 0.5447, accept H_0.

Similarly, as reported in the follow-on sample, the vast majority of firms in the "new sample" felt the HEI could make its services and facilities more accessible (55.9 per cent compared with 69.4 per cent) (Table 11.22).

Table 11.22   Could the HEI Make Its Services and Facilities More Accessible to Firms: 1992 New Sample

HEI make facilities more accessible	Science Park No.	%	Off-Park No.	%	Total No.	%
1. Yes	33	55.9	43	69.4	76	62.8
2. No	26	44.1	19	30.6	45	37.2
Total	59	100.0	62	100.0	121	100.0

χ^2 = 1.79, d.f. = 1, significance level = 0.1806, accept H_0.

Again, a majority of respondents, on and off Science Parks, reported that no one from the local HEI had ever visited them to discuss the HEI's facilities (74.3 per cent compared with 82.4 per cent) (Table 11.23). Amongst the "new sample" 41.4 per cent of Science Park firms had been visited by someone from the Science Park to discuss HEI facilities compared with 7.5 per cent of off-Park firms. This statistically significant difference is shown in Table 11.24.

Table 11.23   Has Anyone from the Local HEI Ever Visited to Discuss the HEIs Facilities: 1992 New Sample

Person from HEI to discuss the HEI's facilities	Science Park		Off-Park		Total	
	No.	%	No.	%	No.	%
1. Yes	18	25.7	12	17.6	30	21.7
2. No	52	74.3	56	82.4	108	78.3
Total	70	100.0	68	100.0	138	100.0

$\chi^2 = 0.89$, d.f. = 1, significance level = 0.3461, accept H_0.

Table 11.24   Has Anyone from a Science Park Ever Visited Firms to Discuss the HEIs Facilities: 1992 New Sample

Person from Science Park to discuss the HEI's facilities	Science Park		Off-Park		Total	
	No.	%	No.	%	No.	%
1. Yes	29	41.4	5	7.5	34	24.8
2. No	41	58.6	62	92.5	103	75.2
Total	70	100.0	67	100.0	137	100.0

$\chi^2 = 19.39$, d.f. = 1, significance level = 0.0000, reject H_0.

In contrast to the follow-on sample, firms in the "new sample" were less persuaded the local HEI had been useful in either recruiting or retaining highly skilled staff, either in an active or passive way (43.8 per cent compared with 32.3 per cent) (Table 11.25).

Table 11.25   Respondents Belief that the Presence of a Local HEI Has Been Useful in Either Recruiting or Retaining Highly Skilled Staff, Either in an Active or Passive Way: 1992 New Sample

HEI useful in recruiting skilled staff	Science Park		Off-Park		Total	
	No.	%	No.	%	No.	%
1. Yes	28	43.8	21	32.3	49	38.0
2. No	36	56.3	44	67.7	80	62.0
Total	64	100.1	65	100.0	129	100.0

$\chi^2 = 1.34$, d.f. = 1, significance level = 0.2471, accept H_0.

This may be linked to the finding that a higher proportion of respondents in the "new sample", than in the follow-on sample, indicated they had never been invited to any technical seminars at the local HEI (39.2 per cent compared with 47.8 per cent) (Tables 11.10 and 11.26).

Table 11.26   Respondent Ever Been Invited to any Technical Seminars at the Local HEI: 1992 New Sample

Invited to any technical seminars	Science Park No.	%	Off-Park No.	%	Total No.	%
1. Yes	42	60.0	30	44.1	72	52.2
2. No	28	40.0	38	55.9	66	47.8
Total	70	100.0	68	100.0	138	100.0

χ^2 = 2.88 d.f. = 1, significance level = 0.0897, accept H_0.

For those invited, a slightly larger proportion of off-Park respondents attended (69.0 per cent compared with 79.3 per cent) (Table 11.27). It is pleasing to note that over 86 per cent of respondents in both groups viewed these technical seminars as being useful (88.9 per cent compared with 87.0 per cent) (Table 11.28).

Table 11.27   Did the Respondent Attend the Technical Seminars at the Local HEI: 1992 New Sample

Attend technical seminars	Science Park No.	%	Off-Park No.	%	Total No.	%
1. Yes	29	69.0	23	79.3	52	73.2
2. No	13	31.0	6	20.7	19	26.8
Total	42	100.0	29	100.0	71	100.0

χ^2 = 0.47, d.f. = 1, significance level = 0.4918, accept H_0.

Table 11.28   Did the Respondent View the Technical Seminars at the Local HEI as Being Useful: 1992 New Sample

Technical seminars Useful	Science Park No.	%	Off-Park No.	%	Total No.	%
1. Yes	24	88.9	20	87.0	44	88.0
2. No	3	11.1	3	13.0	6	12.0
Total	27	100.0	23	100.0	50	100.0

A larger proportion of Science Park firms than off-Park firms suggested they had been invited to an event at the local HEI designed to inform them of the HEI's skills and facilities, although not in a statistically significant direction (41.2 per cent compared with 23.8 per cent) (Table 11.29).

Table 11.29   Respondent Ever Been Invited to any Events at the Local HEI Designed to Inform Them of the HEI's Skills and Facilities: 1992 New Sample

Invited to any events to show the HEI's skills and facilities	Science Park No.	%	Off-Park No.	%	Total No.	%
1. Yes	28	41.2	15	23.8	43	32.8
2. No	40	58.8	48	76.2	88	67.2
Total	68	100.0	63	100.0	131	100.0

χ^2 = 3.72, d.f. = 1, significance level = 0.0538, accept H_0.

For those invited to an event at the local HEI, over 55 per cent of respondents on and off Science Parks attended (55.6 per cent compared with 73.3 per cent) (Table 11.30). All off-Park firms attending reported the event was of interest compared with 86.7 per cent of Science Park firms (Table 11.31).

Table 11.30   Did the Respondent Ever Attend Events at the Local HEI Designed to Inform Them of the HEI's Skills and Facilities: 1992 New Sample

Attended events to show the HEI's skills and facilities	Science Park		Off-Park		Total	
	No.	%	No.	%	No.	%
1. Yes	15	55.6	11	73.3	26	61.9
2. No	12	44.4	4	26.7	16	38.1
Total	27	100.0	15	100.0	42	100.0

$\chi^2 = 0.65$, d.f. = 1, significance level = 0.4207, accept H_0.

Table 11.31   Was the Event at the Local HEI Designed to Inform Them of the HEI's Skills and Facilities of Interest to Respondents: 1992 New Sample

Event at HEI of interest	Science Park		Off-Park		Total	
	No.	%	No.	%	No.	%
1. Yes	13	86.7	9	100.0	22	91.7
2. No	2	13.3	0	0.0	2	8.3
Total	15	100.0	9	100.0	24	100.0

A significantly larger proportion of Science Park respondents indicated they received copies of the local HEI's newsletter (55.7 per cent compared with 21.7 per cent) (Table 11.32). Of those receiving a newsletter it is interesting to note (as found in the follow-on sample) that firms located on and off Science Parks suggested that general news items (46.2 per cent compared with 66.7 per cent) and seminar/lecture programmes (41.0 per cent compared with 33.3 per cent) were of interest (Table 11.33).

Table 11.32   Respondent Received Copies of the Local HEI's Newsletter: 1992 New Sample

Received copies of HEI's newsletter	Science Park		Off-Park		Total	
	No.	%	No.	%	No.	%
1. Yes	39	55.7	15	21.7	54	38.8
2. No	31	44.3	54	78.3	85	61.2
Total	70	100.0	69	100.0	139	100.0

$\chi^2 = 15.48$, d.f. = 1, significance level = 0.0001, reject H_0.

Table 11.33   Items Regarded of Interest by Respondents who had Received Copies of the Local HEI's Newsletter: 1992 New Sample

Items of interest in the HEI's newsletter	Science Park		Off-Park		Total	
	No.	%	No.	%	No.	%
1. New appointments	6	15.4	1	8.3	7	13.7
2. General news items	18	46.2	8	66.7	26	51.0
3. Seminar/lecture programmes	16	41.0	4	33.3	20	39.2
4. Details of leisure facilities/events	11	28.2	0	0.0	11	21.6
5. Other	3	7.7	2	16.7	5	9.8
6. None	9	23.1	2	16.7	11	21.6
Valid cases	39		12		51	

Based on the above discussion we conclude that Hypotheses 4 and 5 are not empirically supported. Firms newly located on Science Parks, like their off-Park counterparts, appreciated that closer links with an HEI were desirable and would be beneficial. As with the follow-on study firms, those invited to technical seminars and events at the local HEI generally attended and found them useful.

11.7 Inputs to R & D and links with HEIs: total sample, 1992

When the "new sample" of firms is combined with the follow-on study only three statistically significant differences between Science Park and off-Park firms were recorded. As hypothesised, due to the generally close relationship between Science Parks and local HEIs, it was not surprising to note that significantly more Science Park firms reported some form of link with an HEI (90.8 per cent compared with 76.7 per cent). It is also not surprising to find that Science Park firms were more likely to report that a person from a Science Park had visited them to discuss the HEI's facilities (41.5 per cent compared with 9.4 per cent) (Table 11.34), and they had received copies of the local HEI's newsletter (50.0 per cent compared with 25.2 per cent) (Table 11.35).

Table 11.34 Has Anyone from a Science Park Ever Visited Firms to Discuss the HEI's Facilities: Total Sample 1992

Person from Science Park to discuss the HEI's facilities	Science Park No.	%	Off-Park No.	%	Total No.	%
1. Yes	51	41.5	10	9.4	61	26.6
2. No	72	58.5	96	90.6	168	73.4
Total	123	100.0	106	100.0	229	100.0

χ^2 = 28.27, d.f. = 1, significance level = 0.0000, reject H_0.

Table 11.35 Respondent Received Copies of the Local HEIs Newsletter: Total Sample 1992

Received copies of HEI's newsletter	Science Park No.	%	Off-Park No.	%	Total No.	%
1. Yes	62	50.0	28	25.2	90	38.8
2. No	62	50.0	54	74.8	145	61.7
Total	124	100.0	111	100.0	235	100.0

χ^2 = 14.18, d.f. = 1, significance level = 0.0002, reject H_0.

To test Hypothesis 6 the total Science Park sample was analysed according to whether or not firms were located in an "assisted" area. Only two statistically significant differences emerged from this analysis. Contrary to expectation, Science Park firms in "assisted" areas had a significantly lower propensity to attend technical seminars at the local HEI (83.3 per cent compared with 57.1 per cent) (Table 11.36).

Table 11.36 Did the Respondent Attend the Technical Seminars at the Local HEI: Total Science Park Sample by Assisted Area Status

Attend technical seminars	Non-assisted No.	%	Assisted No.	%	Total No.	%
1. Yes	30	83.3	20	57.1	50	70.4
2. No	6	16.7	15	42.9	21	29.6
Total	36	100.0	35	100.0	71	100.0

χ^2 = 4.65, d.f. = 1, significance level = 0.0310, reject H_0.

Furthermore, Table 11.37 shows significantly fewer Science Park firms in "assisted" areas had been invited to any events at the local HEI designed to inform them of the HEIs skills and facilities (50.8 per cent compared with 30.0 per cent). These results do not suggest that firms in "assisted" areas are better linked to their local HEI. If anything, the reverse is the case and so Hypothesis 6 cannot be accepted.

Table 11.37   Respondent Ever Been Invited to any Events at the Local HEI Designed to Inform Them of the HEI's Skills and Facilities: Total Science Park Sample by Assisted Area Status

Invited to any events to show the HEI's skills and facilities	Non-assisted		Assisted		Total	
	No.	%	No.	%	No.	%
1. Yes	30	50.8	18	30.0	48	40.3
2. No	29	49.2	42	70.0	71	59.7
Total	59	100.0	60	100.0	119	100.0

$\chi^2 = 4.54$, d.f. = 1, significance level = 0.0331, reject H_0.

11.8   Conclusions   This chapter identified six hypotheses, and we conclude that:

1. Based upon the follow-on survey evidence, firms do increase their links with the local HEI over time. Hypothesis 1 is supported.

2. As suggested in Hypothesis 2, Science Park firms are significantly more likely to contact a local HEI than off-Park firms. This result emerges for the longer established firms in the follow-on survey but not for the more recently established firms in the "new sample".

3. Hypothesis 3 is not confirmed. The majority of both Science Park and off-Park firms have few "formal" links with HEIs. Nevertheless, for those with such links, these are viewed as important for business development.

4. Firms located on and off Science Parks indicated they sought closer links between their business and the local HEI. Therefore, Hypothesis 4 is not supported.

5. Contrary to expectation, Hypothesis 5 is not confirmed. Both Science Park and off-Park firms valued attending those technical seminars and events at the local HEI designed to inform them of the HEI's skills and facilities

6. Hypothesis 6 cannot be accepted. There is no evidence that firms located on Science Parks in "assisted" areas have better links with their HEIs than those located elsewhere. Indeed, in some respects, their links are weaker.

Chapter 12

Technology Diffusion: R & D Outputs

12.1 Introduction This chapter compares the outputs of R & D by Science Park and off-Park firms. One measure of output is the extent of patenting. However, it is appreciated:

> "Although patent statistics are often used as proxy measures of technological performance there are problems with comparing establishments – the tendency of firms to take out patents varies between sectors and between countries (Taylor and Silbertson 1973; Pavitt 1982)" (Massey et al., 1992, p 48).

In the 1986 survey 28 per cent of firms on Science Parks had lodged a patent in the last two years, compared with only 19 per cent of off-Park firms (Monck et al., 1992, p 157). Interestingly, when firms whose principal activity was software or business services were excluded, 34 per cent of Science Park firms had taken out one or more patents during the last year compared with 22 per cent of off-Park firms (Monck et al., 1988, p 159).

For many firms, however, it is the introduction of new products rather than patenting which is the appropriate measure of innovation:

> "For the majority of Science Park firms undertaking R & D, the ultimate purpose is the launch of new products (remembering that process innovation is not likely to be significant in Science Park firms), although some firms undertake contract R & D for client companies." (Monck et al., 1988, p 161).

In 1986, 143 firms (61 per cent) had launched at least one new product in the previous two years within their existing market or in a new market. Further, Massey et al. (1992) based on their analysis of the 1986 survey data concluded:

> "On product launches the data are less clear-cut. There is considerable variation between science-park sites in the tendency for establishments to have launched new products. . . . Overall, there is no difference between park and off-park establishments" (p 48).

The present survey also collected data on a second measure of innovativeness – the number of product/service launches in the last two years. This measure of innovation "output" has recently been utilised by Hansen (1992) in a study of firms in the United States. Even so it is appreciated:

> "Defining the concept 'new product' is inherently difficult. First, there is a difference between a product that is new for the firm, new for the industry, new for the country or new for the world. There is also a question of how radical a change is required to justify the appellation 'new'. . . [and] it is recognized that this problem is probably unsolvable. . ." (Hansen, 1992, p 39).

12.2 Derivation of hypotheses

In this chapter four hypotheses are presented. The chapter tests each in turn.

Hypothesis 1: Science Park firms (excluding those whose principal activity is software) will have recorded a larger number of patents or applications in the last twelve months than off-Park firms.

Hypothesis 2: Science Park software house firms will have recorded a larger number of copyrights or applications in the last twelve months than off-Park firms.

Hypothesis 3: Science Park firms will have introduced more new products/services in the last two years to their existing customer base than off-Park firms.

Hypothesis 4: Science Park firms will have introduced more new products/services in the last two years to new markets than off-Park firms.

Each of these hypotheses are tested, first on firms in the follow-on sample in Section 12.3, and then on firms in the "new sample" in Section 12.4.

12.3 R & D outputs in the follow-on sample

Table 12.1 shows that Hypothesis 1 cannot be accepted. The off-Park firms (who were more likely to be engaged in manufacturing activities) did not have a statistically significant higher mean level of patenting activity (mean number of patents or applications being 1.0 and 2.1 for Science Park and off-Park firms, respectively). In the follow-on survey virtually three-quarters of all responding firms indicated they had not taken out a patent or made an application to do so in the last twelve months (80.6 per cent and 65.2 per cent of firms on Science Park and off-Park, respectively).

Table 12.1   Number of Patents or Applications That Have Been Taken Out in the Last Twelve Months: 1992 Follow-on Survey (a)

Number of patents	Science Park		Off-Park		Total	
	No.	%	No.	%	No.	%
0	29	80.6	15	65.2	44	74.6
1	0	0.0	2	8.7	2	3.4
2	3	8.3	0	0.0	3	5.1
3	2	5.6	1	4.3	3	5.1
≥ 4	2	5.6	5	21.7	7	11.9
Total	36	100.1	23	99.9	59	100.1

"t"= -0.87, d.f. = 57, significance level = 0.389, accept H_0.

Note: (a) Surveyed firms whose principal activity is software are excluded

Similarly, for software houses three-quarters of firms in both sub-samples indicated they had not registered a copyright or an application for one in the last twelve months (74.1 per cent compared with 78.6 per cent) (Table 12.2). As in the case of patenting, there was no statistically significant difference between the two groups in the mean number of registered copyrights or applications (mean number of copyrights or applications being 0.6 in both Science Park and off-Park firms, respectively). Consequently, Hypothesis 2 cannot be accepted.

Table 12.2   Number of Copyrights or Applications Registered in the Last Twelve Months by Software Houses: 1992 Follow-on Survey

Number of copyrights	Science Park		Off-Park		Total	
	No.	%	No.	%	No.	%
0	20	74.1	11	78.6	31	75.6
1	2	7.4	1	7.1	3	7.3
2	3	11.1	0	0.0	3	7.3
3	1	3.7	1	7.1	2	4.9
≥ 4	1	3.7	1	7.1	2	4.9
Total	27	100.0	14	99.9	41	100.0

"t"= 0.13, d.f. = 39, significance level = 0.894, accept H_0.

The follow-on survey results also show no statistically significant differences between Science Park and off-Park firms with regard to the number of new products/services launched in the last two years to either the existing customer base (Table 12.3) or to new markets (Table 12.4). More than three-quarters of firms had introduced one or more new products/services to their existing customer base (80.8 per cent compared with 87.8 per cent) as well as into new markets (81.2 per cent compared with 76.3 per cent). Based on this evidence Hypotheses 3 and 4 cannot be confirmed.

Table 12.3   Number of New Products/Services Launched in the Last Two Years to the Existing Customer Base: 1992 Follow-on Survey

Number of new products/ services to the existing customer base	Science Park		Off-Park		Total	
	No.	%	No.	%	No.	%
0	10	19.2	5	12.2	15	16.1
1	8	15.4	10	24.4	18	19.4
2	11	21.2	12	29.3	23	24.7
3	10	19.2	8	19.5	18	19.4
≥ 4	13	25.0	6	14.6	19	20.4
Total	52	100.0	41	100.0	93	100.0

"t"= 1.24, d.f. = 91, significance level = 0.221, accept H_0.

Table 12.4   Number of New Products/Services Launched in the Last Two Years to New Markets: 1992 Follow-on Survey

Number of new products/ services to new markets	Science Park		Off-Park		Total	
	No.	%	No.	%	No.	%
0	9	18.8	9	23.7	18	20.9
1	15	31.3	9	23.7	24	27.9
2	11	22.9	8	21.1	19	22.1
3	5	10.4	6	15.8	11	12.8
≥ 4	8	16.7	6	15.8	14	16.3
Total	48	100.1	38	100.1	86	100.0

"t"= 0.39, d.f. = 84, significance level = 0.701, accept H_0.

12.4   R & D outputs in the "new sample"

No statistically significant differences between firms on and off Science Parks in the "new sample" were recorded with regard to the number of patents or applications. Table 12.5 shows the majority of firms indicated they had not taken out a patent or made an application in the last twelve months (86.4 per cent compared with 74.5 per cent). Therefore, Hypothesis 1 cannot be confirmed.

Table 12.5 Number of Patents or Applications That Have Been Taken Out in the Last Twelve Months: 1992 New Sample (a)

Number of patents	Science Park		Off-Park		Total	
	No.	%	No.	%	No.	%
0	51	86.4	38	74.5	89	80.9
1	1	1.7	3	5.9	4	3.6
2	1	1.7	0	0.0	1	0.9
3	0	0.0	3	5.9	3	2.7
≥ 4	6	10.2	7	13.7	13	11.8
Total	59	100.0	51	100.0	110	99.9

"t"= -0.09, d.f. = 108, significance level = 0.925, accept H_0.
Note: (a) Surveyed firms whose principal activity is software are excluded

Similarly, the vast majority of software houses in the "new sample" had not registered a copyright or an application for one in the last twelve months (84.2 per cent and 76.9 per cent of firms on Science Parks and off-Parks, respectively) (Table 12.6). Hypothesis 2, therefore, cannot be supported (mean number of copyrights or applications being 0.6 and 0.3 in Science Park and off-Park firms, respectively).

Table 12.6 Number of Copyrights or Applications Registered in the Last Twelve Months by Software Houses: 1992 New Sample

Number of copyrights	Science Park		Off-Park		Total	
	No.	%	No.	%	No.	%
0	16	84.2	20	76.9	36	80.0
1	2	10.5	3	11.5	5	11.1
2	0	0.0	3	11.5	3	6.7
≥ 3	1	5.3	0	0.0	1	2.2
Total	19	100.0	26	99.9	45	100.0

"t"= 0.53, d.f. = 43, significance level = 0.605, accept H_0.

Finally, no statistically significant differences between Science Park and off-Park firms were recorded in the "new sample" with regard to the number of new products/services launched in the last two years to either the existing customer base (Table 12.7) or to new markets (Table 12.8). More than 60 per cent of firms on and off Science Parks in the "new sample" had introduced one or more new products/services to the existing customer base (68.3 per cent compared with 74.1 per cent) and 60 per cent of firms in both groups had introduced new products/services to new markets. So, Hypotheses 3 and 4 cannot be supported.

Table 12.7 Number of New Products/Services Launched in the Last Two Years to the Existing Customer Base: 1992 New Sample

Number of new products/ services to the existing customer base	Science Park		Off-Park		Total	
	No.	%	No.	%	No.	%
0	19	31.7	15	25.9	34	28.8
1	13	21.7	9	15.5	22	18.6
2	8	13.3	13	22.4	21	17.8
3	7	11.7	4	6.9	11	9.3
≥ 4	13	21.7	17	29.3	30	25.4
Total	60	100.1	58	100.0	118	99.9

"t"= -0.98, d.f. = 116, significance level = 0.329, accept H_0.

Table 12.8   Number of New Products/Services Launched in the Last Two
             Years to New Markets: 1992 New Sample

Number of new products /services to new markets	Science Park No.	%	Off-Park No.	%	Total No.	%
0	23	39.7	23	39.7	46	39.7
1	13	22.4	11	19.0	24	20.7
2	6	10.3	11	19.0	17	14.7
3	2	3.4	1	1.7	3	2.6
≥ 4	14	24.1	12	20.7	26	22.4
Total	58	99.9	58	100.1	116	100.1

"t"= −1.00, d.f. = 114, significance level = 0.319, accept H_0.

12.5 Conclusions   This chapter identified four hypotheses each of which have been
tested. We conclude that:

1. Science Park firms perform similarly to off-Park firms in terms of
   the number of recorded patents or copyrights.

2. Firms on and off Science Parks continue to introduce similar
   numbers of new products/services to existing and new markets.

Chapter 13

Financing the High Technology-based Firm

13.1 Introduction

The high technology firm is often considered to present problems to a financier. The first problem is that, if it is using a sophisticated technology, the banker may be unaware of the market place for that technology. Indeed the more sophisticated the technology, the less confident the banker is likely to be in making an assessment. In this sense a high technology firm proposition may be considered to be a high risk option, even though it may also be thought to have the potential to yield high returns.

The second problem is that those individuals who have the scientific capacity and interest to develop the technology, do not necessarily have the managerial expertise to develop the business. Indeed the two sets of skills may even be mutually exclusive.

For both these reasons the provision of financing for new technology-based firms by the clearing banks may be problematic. In their analysis of bank funding to small firms Keasey and Watson (1993) argue that the short-term loan or overdraft facility, which is provided by the bulk of clearing banks in the United Kingdom, is inappropriate to high risk/high return businesses. This is because, under such financing arrangements, the bank only profits from those businesses which repay in full the loan plus the interest. The bank does not gain if the project is extremely successful. Only the owners profit from a major capital gain. In economists' jargon, the bank has a full down-side risk, but no up-side gain. For these reasons, given an uncertain market-place, it is rational for banks to prefer making loans to a low risk/low return project, than to a high risk/high return project.

Keasey and Watson argue that one way to overcome these problems is to increase the use of venture capital. The central difference between venture capital and loan/overdraft sources of finance is that, in the event of the project being successful and a high return paid to equity participants, then the venture capitalist benefits in the sense of being an equity partner. Hence, the venture capitalist is more willing to participate in the financing of high technology businesses which are deemed to be high risk yet high return, than in the financing of low risk/low return businesses.

Given the theoretical attractions of this type of investment to venture capitalists, it may be surprising to find that, at least in the United Kingdom, venture capital plays only a very modest role in high technology businesses. The ACOST (1990) study argued:

> "There is a lack of institutional venture capital to fund high risk, high growth companies, particularly those with a competitive basis in technology. In comparison with the USA, it seems that the British venture capital industry has not been as active in financing 'big ticket' start ups and of creating international businesses from the outset."

The remainder of this chapter will examine three themes. The first is the extent to which there are differences in the financing of independent technology-based firms, compared with other independent firms in the United Kingdom. The second is the extent to which there are differences amongst independent technology-based firms according to whether or not they are located on a Science Park. Third, any change in the financing of small high technology firms since 1986 will be observed.

Discussion will be limited to independent businesses only. These are defined as enterprises which are not subsidiaries of larger corporations, where the financing arrangements are likely to depend upon decisions made by the parent company.

13.2 Derivation of hypotheses

In this section six hypotheses are derived and presented, with the remainder of the chapter focusing upon the testing of each of these hypotheses.

Hypothesis 1: New independent technology-based firms will use different sources of finance to start the business, compared with independent businesses in other sectors.

There are a number of reasons why this hypothesis might be expected to be confirmed. The first is that, as we have noted in the introduction, independent technology businesses are likely to be deemed high risk and high return. For these reasons they are more likely to be attractive to providers of venture capital and external investors, than is the case for small independent businesses more generally. The second reason is that high tech firms are more likely to be owned and managed by an educated individual than is the case for independent businesses more generally. Research on the characteristics of bank lending suggests that educated entrepreneurs are more likely to be in receipt of bank lending at start-up than less educated individuals (Storey, 1994). Third, owners of independent businesses in the high technology sector are more likely to have access to personal assets which can be used as collateral for the business – most notably house ownership (Cressy, 1993).

Hypothesis 2: Independent technology-based businesses will use a greater range of sources of finance as the business develops.

Independent technology-based businesses, run by individuals with high educational attainment, are likely, in general, to be better networked into a range of sources of finance. There is a considerable prestige in owning and managing a sophisticated technological business which, whilst it may present assessment problems to bankers, has considerably greater prestige than the hairdressing, car repairing or clothing manufacture proposals which much more frequently pass across bank managers' desks.

Furthermore, particularly in "assisted" areas, the high technology business is likely to be a focus of attention amongst those concerned with promoting local economic development. It, therefore, is more likely to be in receipt of public funding than the independent business in the more conventional sectors.

Hypothesis 3: Independent technology-based businesses are more likely to be constrained by a shortage of finance than is the case for independent businesses in other sectors.

Although there are advantages for a business in the high technology sectors, there may also be disadvantages. If the business grows, and growth rates may be higher in high technology businesses than elsewhere, then the business could still consider itself constrained by a "shortage" of finance, perhaps even more so than other independent businesses. This argument is presented by Oakey (1984) who argues that high technology businesses experience particular difficulties because of their R & D expenditure in the development of new products, many of which have a long lead time before they yield sales income. Further, he claims that new products in the high technology sector have relatively short lives, and so it is necessary to be continually developing new products to replace those which become obsolete. Oakey also argues that ensuring the appropriate phasing of expenditure on new product development is a particularly serious problem facing high technology businesses. Hence high technology firms, even though they have greater access to finance, may be more likely than small firms in other sectors to be constrained in their growth.

Hypotheses 4: Being located on a Science Park reduces the financing problems facing independent high technology businesses.

There are a number of reasons why location on a Science Park may ease the financing problems of independent high technology businesses. The first is that there is likely to be a greater pool of knowledge about appropriate sources of finance for high technology businesses, amongst both clients on the Park and in the contact network of the Science Park manager. Indeed a key function of the manager is to ensure that tenants are aware of financing alternatives and ensure that providers of finance are aware of a group of businesses on a Science Park with particular financing needs and requirements. The second is that the Park may constitute a magnet attracting providers or finance looking for suitable clients. Finally, in "assisted" areas, the Science Park is likely to be a focus for public sector financing sources.

Hypothesis 5: Loans to high technology businesses are more likely to be secured.

We have already observed that the high technology business is likely to be perceived of as being high risk and high return. From the point of view of the bank the only way in which it can provide any loan/overdraft facility and minimise its down-side risk is to ensure the loan is secured. This security may take the form either of the assets within the business and/or personal guarantees given by the owner of the business. It may also be the case that the amount borrowed by a high technology small firm may be higher, on average, than the amount borrowed by other conventional businesses. Cressy (1993) shows that the likelihood of the loan being secured increases with the sum borrowed.

Hypothesis 6: High technology independent businesses will be served by different bankers from independent businesses more generally.

Provision of finance for independent high technology businesses may be considered to be a specialism. In making their assessments bankers need to be aware of the particular market-place into which the product is being sold. In some extreme cases there will only be possibly a few people in the world who are able to make an accurate assessment of the scale of the market for a genuinely innovative product. Hence it seems plausible to argue that bankers for independent high technology businesses will differ from those independent businesses more generally.

13.3 The sample of firms   To test these hypotheses the results of four surveys will be discussed:

1. the 1986 UKSPA survey

2. the 1992 follow-up of the 1986 UKSPA survey (referred to as the follow-on survey)

3. the 1992 survey which replicates the 1986 UKSPA survey (referred to as the "new sample" survey)

4. a study of new businesses in all sectors established in the County of Cleveland during the 1980s (referred to as the Cleveland survey) (Storey and Strange, 1992b).

All four surveys have been discussed earlier with the Cleveland study being described in Chapter 8.

The Cleveland responses provide a sharp contrast to those in the high technology surveys. It will be recalled from Chapter 8 that individuals establishing businesses in Cleveland have a very different educational and work history background, compared with those included in the high technology surveys. For example, only 5 per cent of Cleveland respondents have a degree compared with 85 per cent of founders in the UKSPA "new sample" survey. Similarly, 44 per cent of founders of businesses in Cleveland were unemployed or likely to become unemployed immediately prior to starting their business, compared with 23 per cent in the UKSPA "new sample" survey.

Whilst the backgrounds of new firm founders in Cleveland were very different from founders of high technology businesses, the Cleveland founders were, in fact, more representative of small business owners in general, than those included in the UKSPA surveys. Finally, in comparing the surveys, it is important to recognise that Cleveland is an "assisted" area. In this sense there is likely to be a greater involvement of public funding in the start-up of businesses, than would be the case in a "non-assisted" area.

13.4 Finance at start-up   Table 13.1 shows the sources of finance used to establish a business in the UKSPA "new sample" survey and in the Cleveland survey. A total of nine sources of finance are identified. The first column reports the results of respondents located on a Science Park in 1992 and the second reports the results of respondents located off-Park. The third column combines the data to provide a picture for independent high technology businesses in aggregate. The fourth column reports comparable responses of new business founders in Cleveland.

The table shows the frequency with which each source of finance was mentioned by respondents, so that each respondent may mention more than a single source. Hence the total number of mentions exceeds the total number of valid cases. The column marked "%" expresses the proportion of mentions as a percentage.

Sources of finance		Science Park		Off-Park		Total		Cleveland All Sectors	
		No.	%	No.	%	No.	%	No.	%
1.	Personal savings	33	78.6	27	62.8	60	70.6	144	81.8
2.	House Mortgage	3	7.1	4	9.3	7	8.2	10	5.6
3.	Loans from friends/relations	0	0.0	1	2.3	1	1.2	11	6.3
4.	Loan/overdraft from clearing bank	13	31.0	16	37.2	29	34.1	57	32.3
5.	Venture capital from clearing bank	1	2.4	0	0.0	1	1.2	–	–
6.	Venture capital from other sources	9	21.4	6	14.0	15	17.6	–	–
7.	Loan from finance company	1	2.4	0	0.0	1	1.2	2	1.1
8.	Finance from public agency/local authority/ government department	6	14.3	5	11.6	11	12.9	15	8.5
9.	Other	6	14.3	8	18.6	14	16.5	13	7.4
	Valid Cases	42		43		85		176	

The table makes a number of important points. First, there are no significant differences between the sources of finances mentioned by founders of high technology firms on Science Parks, compared with their off-Park counterparts. Second, there are strong similarities with sources of finance used by the founders of new businesses in Cleveland. Thus, apparently about one-third of business start-ups in both the Cleveland and the "new sample" surveys used loans or overdrafts from a clearing bank initially.

Differences between the two surveys do occur in one major and one minor respect. The major difference is the total absence from the Cleveland survey of any form of venture capital either from a clearing bank or from other sources in the start-up of new businesses. This contrasts with the "new sample" survey where 17.6 per cent of firms claimed to use venture capital from other sources at start-up. Although it is not statistically significant, it is interesting to note that this was more characteristic of firms on the Science Park, than amongst the off-Park sample. The minor respect in which the Cleveland and the "new sample" surveys differ is that the use of personal savings in the former appears to be slightly more frequent.

Finally, respondents to the "new sample" survey mentioned an average of 1.63 sources of finance to start their business, compared with the 1.43 sources mentioned by respondents to the Cleveland survey. This suggests that founders of high technology firms are more likely to use a wider range of sources of finance at start-up. There is no difference in this respect between on- and off-Science Park firms.

13.5   Most important sources of finance at start-up

Table 13.1 in the previous section examined the sources of finance mentioned by respondents in the "new sample" and the Cleveland surveys. An alternative perspective is to identify the single most important source of finance at start-up.

Table 13.2 shows the sources of finance defined to be most important in establishing the business. The first three sets of columns present the results from the "new sample" survey with a distinction being made between firms located on and off Science Parks. In column three the aggregate results for the "new sample" survey are presented. Finally, in column four a comparison is made with the 1986 UKSPA sample, with the figures being given in percentage terms.

In the "new sample", for approximately half of the firms, the personal savings of the individual were the single most important source of funding for the business. This was true for both Science Park and off-Park firms. The only slight difference to emerge is that amongst the nine Science Park firms which used external venture capital other than from a clearing bank, six identified it as the single most important source to establish a business, compared with only one of the six off-Park firms which used venture capital. This suggests that venture capital may be more prevalent as a major source of finance to firms currently located on Science Parks.

Table 13.2   Most Important Source of Finance Used to Establish the Business – All Independent Firms

Most important source of finance	Science Park		Off-Park		Total		1986 UKSPA Sample
	No.	%	No.	%	No.	%	%
1. Personal savings	21	53.8	20	54.1	41	53.9	61
2. House mortgage	1	2.6	1	2.7	2	2.6	2
3. Loans from friends/relations	0	0.0	1	2.7	1	1.3	–
4. Loan/overdraft from clearing bank	4	10.3	8	21.6	12	15.8	17
5. Venture capital from clearing bank	1	2.6	0	0.0	1	1.3	–
6. Venture capital from other sources	6	15.4	1	2.7	7	9.2	15
7. Finance from public agency/local authority government department	2	5.1	0	0.0	2	2.6	7
8. Other	4	10.3	6	16.2	10	13.2	8
Valid cases	39	100.0	37	100.0	76	100.0	

Comparing the 1992 "new sample" survey with the 1986 UKSPA sample is slightly problematic because of differences in the categories used. For example, in the 1986 UKSPA survey, personal savings were separated from finance derived from ownership in an existing business. In the 1992 survey, however, the latter category was not separately included, so we have been forced to combine categories. The 1986 survey also separately identified private sources of venture capital, but in the 1992 survey these have been added into "venture capital from other sources". Given these problems there appear to be few changes in the most important sources of finance to start businesses over this six-year period. Personal savings continue to dominate, with loans and overdrafts being mentioned by a similar proportion of respondents (approximately 16 per cent). There was a slight fall in the proportion of firms mentioning finance from public agencies but we attributed this to the higher proportion of firms in the "new sample" survey being located outside the "assisted" areas. There is, however, a suggestion that venture capital was a more important source of start-up finance in the recent survey, than was the case in 1986.

13.6   Current sources of finance

Respondents were also asked about current sources of finance used in the last twelve months. The responses given in the "new sample" survey, the follow-on survey and the Cleveland survey are reported in Table 13.3. The general pattern which emerges appears to be fairly consistent across all three surveys. Only in the Cleveland survey were fewer respondents referring to the use of loan or overdraft facilities at the clearing banks.

Table 13.3   Sources of Finance Used in the Last Twelve Months:
             Independent Firms

Sources of finance	"New Sample" Survey		Follow-On Survey		Cleveland Survey	
	No.	%	No.	%	No.	%
1. Personal savings	17	19.1	16	20.3	39	21.8
2. Profits from business	56	62.9	59	74.7	121	67.6
3. Loan/overdraft from clearing bank	44	49.4	40	50.6	59	33.0
4. Venture capital from clearing bank	2	2.2	1	1.3		
5. Other venture capital	7	7.9	4	5.1	35	19.6
6. Loan from financial companies	4	4.5	11	13.9		
7. Finance from public agency	9	10.1	9	11.4		
8. Sale of share capital	8	9.0	5	6.3		
9. Other	14	15.7	3	3.8		
Valid Cases	89		79		179	
Mentions per case	1.81		1.87		1.42	

The dominant element in the financing of existing independent businesses is the re-investment of profit which was referred to by between two-thirds and three-quarters of respondents. Personal savings continued to be used by about one-fifth of respondents. Loan or overdraft facilities were used by approximately half of the high technology businesses, but only by about one-third of the Cleveland survey respondents.

Whilst the distribution of sources of finance are broadly similar, it is apparent that the Cleveland survey firms were less likely to utilise the range of sources of finance which were used by the high technology businesses. This is reflected in the fact that in the Cleveland survey the number of sources of finance mentioned by each firm as being used in the last twelve months was 1.42. This is virtually identical to the average number of sources of finance used by firms at start-up. It differs sharply from the high technology firms where the number of sources of finance used in the last twelve months was 1.81 in the "new sample" survey and 1.87 in the follow-on survey. Both of these are a marked increase over the average number of sources of finance mentioned at start-up. It suggests that, as the high technology firm matures, it is more likely to draw upon a wider range of sources of finance than is the case for independent firms more generally.

In both the "new sample" survey and the follow-on survey an analysis was conducted to see whether sources of current finance differed between firms on and off Science Parks. No statistically significant difference was observed in either of the two surveys.

13.7   Finance as a constraint upon growth

It was argued above that the high technology businesses may be more constrained by a "shortage" of finance than other types of independent businesses. This is because, although the high technology firm may have greater access to sources of finance because of its more rapid rates of growth, these may be more quickly exhausted. We are not able to explicitly test this matter since the questions asked in the high technology surveys are not replicated elsewhere. Nevertheless, Table 13.4 aggregates replies from firms in both the "new sample" and follow-on surveys to a question about the extent to which access to finance has restricted the growth of their firm (as distinct from merely aggravating existing cash-flow difficulties) at any stage. It distinguishes the replies according to whether or not the firm was located on a Science Park.

Table 13.4 Did Problems over Access to Finance Restrict the Growth of the Firm (as Distinct from Merely Aggravating Existing Cash-Flow Difficulties) at Any Stage? – All Independent Firms: Total Sample 1992

Growth restricted by problems with access to finance	Science Park No.	%	Off-Park No.	%	Total No.	%
1. Yes – in the first year	6	7.1	2	2.3	8	4.7
2. Yes – currently	13	15.3	5	5.8	18	10.5
3. Yes – at other time	2	2.4	7	8.1	9	5.3
4. Yes – continually	21	24.7	22	25.6	4	25.1
5. No	43	50.6	50	58.1	93	54.4
Total	85	100.1	86	99.9	171	100.0

Overall, approximately half the firms indicated they had not at any stage been constrained, but the remaining half indicated there had been constraints upon their growth at some point in their history. Indeed, virtually a quarter of the firms indicated that access to finance was a continual constraint and had been so since the business began.

We find some difficulty interpreting this finding since the nature of the constraint is likely to vary from one firm to another. Nevertheless, the fact that cash-flow difficulties were specifically excluded suggests that, at least in the minds of the business owners, their growth was constrained by access to finance.

When we examine the Science Park sample in total – i.e. combine the "new sample" and the follow-on survey firms – we find Science Park firms in "assisted" areas were much more likely to report restrictions upon their growth attributable to problems of obtaining access to finance (as distinct from merely aggravating existing cash-flow difficulties) (Table 13.5). Thus, approximately 58 per cent of Science Park firms located in "assisted" areas reported their growth being restricted, compared with only 40 per cent of Science Park businesses located in "non-assisted" areas.

Table 13.5 Did Problems over Access to Finance Restrict the Growth of the Firm (as Distinct from Merely Aggravating Existing Cash-Flow Difficulties) at Any Stage? – All Independent Firms: Total Science Park Sample by Assisted Area Status

Growth restricted by problems with access to finance	Non-assisted No.	%	Assisted No.	%	Total No.	%
1. Yes – in the first year	1	2.4	5	11.6	6	7.1
2. Yes – currently	6	14.3	7	16.3	13	15.3
3. Yes – at other time	0	0.0	2	4.7	2	2.4
4. Yes – continually	10	23.8	11	25.6	21	24.7
5. No	25	59.5	18	41.9	43	50.6
Total	42	100.0	43	100.1	85	100.1

The frequency with which firms reported their growth being restricted by access to finance contrasts with the Aston Business School (1991) survey which indicated that very few businesses were unable to obtain appropriate packages of finance. Although it is unclear to what extent firms were seeking alternative sources of finance but were being turned down, it suggests this is an area which is worthy of further investigation.

| 13.8 | The role of guarantees | In Section 13.1. we observed that high technology businesses were likely to be perceived by financiers as high risk/high reward projects. We hypothesised in Section 13.2 that bankers would be expected to respond to this type of proposal by attempting to minimise their down-side risk and ensuring that loans are secured on either the assets of the business or on the personal property of the business owners or on both. |

The extent to which this is the case is shown in Table 13.6a and Table 13.6b. Table 13.6a takes the independent firms in both the "new sample" and follow-on surveys and distinguishes between those located on and off Science Parks. It reports the responses of firms as to whether or not security against the assets of the firm are taken in respect of any loans or overdrafts provided by the bank. Overall, 64 per cent of firms reported their loans to be secured against the assets of the business, and in this respect there was no difference according to whether or not the firm is located on a Science Park. Similarly, Table 13.6b takes the same set of firms and asks about the extent to which personal guarantees are required to cover loans or bank overdrafts. Here, 55 per cent of firms replied that some form of personal guarantees were required which again was similar for both firms located on and off Science Parks.

Table 13.6a   Does the Bank Require from the Firm or its Directors any Security Against the Assets of the Firm – All Independent Firms: Total Sample 1992

Security against assets of the firm	Science Park		Off-Park		Total	
	No.	%	No.	%	No.	%
1. Yes	29	63.0	41	65.1	70	64.2
2. No	17	37.0	22	34.9	39	35.8
Total	46	100.0	63	100.0	109	100.0

$\chi^2 = 0.00$, d.f. = 1, significance level = 0.9867, accept H_0.

Table 13.6b   Does the Bank Require Personal Guarantees – All Independent Firms: Total Sample 1992

Personal guarantees required	Science Park		Off-Park		Total	
	No.	%	No.	%	No.	%
1. Yes	27	56.3	36	54.5	63	55.3
2. No	21	43.8	30	45.5	51	44.7
Total	48	100.1	66	100.0	114	100.0

$\chi^2 = 0.00$, d.f. = 1, significance level = 1.0000, accept H_0.

We have also examined the extent to which provision of guarantees varied according to the age of the business or the geographical area in which the firm is located. We found no evidence that the proportion of firms required to give guarantees varied either according to whether or not the business was more than ten years old, or whether or not it was located in an "assisted" area.

These results support the hypotheses that high technology firms are more likely to have their loans and overdrafts secured either by business or personal guarantees. A study by Binks et al. (1993) of over 6,100 small firms reported that only 34 per cent of firms were required to give personal collateral for overdrafts.

13.9 The high technology banker It was hypothesised in Section 13.2 earlier that the provision of banking expertise to high technology businesses was a specialism. The extent to which this is the case is shown in Table 13.7, which shows the clearing bank which holds the main business account of the high technology independent businesses included in both the "new sample" survey and the follow-on survey. A distinction is made between businesses located on and off Science Parks.

It does not provide any support for the view that the distribution of market share amongst the bankers is significantly different for the high technology sector from that in the small business sector as a whole.

Table 13.7 shows that National Westminster Bank was the bank referred to most frequently by respondents in the survey, having a 26 per cent market share. This was closely followed by Barclays at 24 per cent. The only slight surprise is that the market share of the Midland Bank was as high as 17 per cent, and higher than Lloyds at 15 per cent.

Table 13.7   Clearing Bank where Main Business Account is Held: Total Sample 1992

Clearing bank	Science Park		Off-Park		Total	
	No.	%	No.	%	No.	%
National Westminster	15	21.8	24	30.3	39	26.4
Barclays	18	26.1	18	22.8	36	24.3
Midland	12	17.4	13	16.5	25	16.9
Lloyds	14	20.2	8	10.1	22	14.9
Royal Bank of Scotland	5	7.2	8	10.1	13	8.8
Clydesdale	2	2.9	2	2.5	4	2.7
TSB	2	2.9	1	1.3	3	2.0
Yorkshire	0	0.0	3	3.8	3	2.0
Others	1	1.4	2	2.5	3	2.0
Total	69	100.0	79	100.0	148	100.0

These figures are broadly in keeping with those presented by Binks et al. (1993) in their study of the relationships between small businesses and banks, except that the share of the Midland Bank appears to be rather higher in this survey than elsewhere. The Binks et al. (1993) figures are 27 per cent for National Westminster, 26 per cent for Barclays, 17 per cent for Lloyds and 12 per cent for Midland.

13.10 Conclusions This chapter identified six hypotheses which were tested. We conclude that:

1. Founders of high technology businesses are likely to use a wider range of sources of finance, than founders of new businesses in the more conventional sectors. In particular, we find evidence to suggest the use of venture capital is more prevalent in high technology businesses. Although it is not statistically significant, there is weak evidence to suggest high technology firms located on Science Parks may be more likely to use venture capital than those located off-Park.

2. As the business develops the high technology firm is more likely to use a wider variety of sources of finance, than the business of comparable age, in the more conventional sectors.

3. Although we do not have strictly comparable data, we were surprised to find that approximately half of firms surveyed in 1992 claimed that restrictions over access to finance had restricted the

growth of their business at some stage. This is a substantially higher figure than that implied by the authoritative study by Aston Business School (1991) on the financing of United Kingdom small businesses.

4. The constraint upon the growth of high technology businesses appears not to be influenced by whether the firm is located on a Science Park. As noted above, the only impact which we can isolate is that Science Park firms seem to be more likely to utilise venture capital than off-Park firms.

5. There does appear to be quite strong evidence to suggest that loans to high technology businesses are more likely to be secured on both the personal guarantees of the owner and the assets of the business than loans to small businesses more generally. We attribute this to the high risk/high return problems associated with financing high technology businesses. In addition, the older and more highly qualified business founders in the high technology sector may have greater personal assets to offer as well. Banks are likely to recognise this and may consequently require secured loans.

6. There does not seem to be very much difference between the bankers which are used by independent high technology businesses, compared with those of small businesses more generally. The dominant banks are National Westminster and Barclays; the only slight difference is that Midland Bank appears to have a rather higher share in the high technology sector than it has in the small business sector more generally.

Chapter 14

Management and Markets

14.1 Introduction

Making the transition from an entrepreneur-managed to a professionally managed firm (Flamhotz, 1966; Covin and Slevin, 1990; Covin et al., 1990) is not easy. Results from the 1986 survey suggested the problems of high tech businesses were essentially similar to those of all new businesses: time constraints on management time; obtaining finance; shortages of skilled labour; and obtaining payment from large debtors (Monck et al., 1988, p 203).

The ability to manage and finance technical developments and business growth in highly competitive markets is crucial. Following the spirit of the "ecological" model (Hannan and Freeman, 1977; Pennings, 1982; Aldrich, 1990; Birley and Westhead, 1993b) we appreciate that a new and small business in new technology-based sectors can survive and grow only if it learns to adapt and consequently change rapidly in order that an appropriate organisation – environment relationship is developed. Based on the assumptions of the "ecological" model we accept that "environments" (as perceived by owner managers) for new technology-based firm formation and growth may contain contrasting available levels of resources (such as financial resources and customers). It also must be acknowledged that each market niche entered is associated with a variety of "hostile" competitors who will compete for available resources. Moreover, it is appreciated here that:

> "Munificence captures the structure and nature of the market being entered: hostility captures the structure and nature of the firms competing for that market. Thus, some new venture opportunities have much more potential than others; and, holding the quality potential of the opportunity constant, some markets are more hotly contested than others. Obviously, the most favourable circumstance for a new venture is to pursue an opportunity with high munificence under conditions of limited hostility" (Tsai et al., 1991, p 12).

For a new technology-based firm to be successful it must identify the right market(s), and then manage and finance its development. As a result, the first part of this chapter will explore in detail the evolution of an appropriate management structure in surveyed "new sample" firms to determine what managerial functions are essential for firm survival and growth.

New technology-based firms face a variety of technical, managerial, financial and regulatory problems which may impede firm development. However:

> "the ready availability of external advice and support can be of crucial importance to the small technology business in its formative years" (Monck et al., 1988, p 201).

Firms in both follow-on and the "new sample" were, therefore, asked to identify the external organisations and individuals contacted for advice during the last year, and the reasons for contacting these advisers. As in the 1986 survey:

"...the nature of management development issues with which the firms will have to contend if they are to achieve their long-term growth objectives are reviewed" (Monck et al., 1988, p 193).

The second part of this chapter explores the characteristics of the market(s) in which surveyed firms currently operate. It is widely appreciated that:

"...the ability to grow is partially dependent upon access to a suitable market..." (O'Farrell and Hitchens, 1988, p 402).

Also, it has been argued by Monck et al. (1988) that:

"A major difficulty facing new and young firms as they seek to grow is that of identifying and developing markets for their products" (p 194).

Consequently, the customer base of surveyed firms will be explored to determine the level of dependency on manufactured and/or standard software products as well as the dependency on a limited number of customers in relation to total output (by value).

14.2 Derivation of hypotheses

In this section six hypotheses are presented and tested.

Hypothesis 1: Firms located on and off Science Parks will diversify their management teams over time in order to survive and grow in selected market niches.

Hypothesis 2: Science Park firms will have more diverse management teams, with individuals coming from a variety of backgrounds/expertise.

Hypothesis 3: The support infrastructure provided by a Science Park, means its firms will be more likely to utilise formal assistance and advice from external organisations to secure its survival and growth.

Hypothesis 4: To survive and grow, firms located on and off Science Parks will, over time, increase their use of formal assistance and advice from external organisations.

Hypothesis 5: Science Park managers will emphasise the dangers of excessive income dependency upon manufactured and/or standard software products. Consequently, fewer Science Park firms will exhibit this dependency.

Hypothesis 6: Science Park managers will emphasise the danger of dependency on a small number of customers. Consequently, fewer Science Park firms will exhibit customer dependency.

14.3 Management functions in the "new sample"

Table 14.1 shows that the management teams of firms, when they began, were limited with regard to management backgrounds/expertise. Less than 51 per cent of firms on and off Science Parks had production, finance, marketing and personnel backgrounds when the business began. Very few surveyed firms had balanced management teams. Firms in both groups from the outset comprised primarily individuals with general management background (70.4 per cent compared with 77.0 per cent) and/or R & D backgrounds/expertise (55.7 per cent compared with 57.4 per cent).

Table 14.1 Backgrounds/Expertise of the Management Team When the Business Began: 1992 New Sample (a)

Management team backgrounds/expertise when business began	Science Park No.	%	Off-Park No.	%	Total No.	%
1. General management	50	70.4	47	77.0	97	73.5
2. R & D	39	55.7	35	57.4	74	56.5
3. Marketing	32	45.1	31	50.8	63	47.7
4. Finance	24	33.8	22	36.1	46	34.8
5. Personnel	14	19.7	18	29.5	32	24.2
6. Production	15	21.1	16	26.2	31	23.5

Note: (a) No statistically significant differences were recorded between firms on and off Science Parks.

As anticipated, we find supportive evidence for Hypothesis 1. Over time firms on and off Science Parks have adapted, changed and diversified their management teams (Table 14.2). These changes were overwhelmingly achieved through the recruitment of new specialists from outside the surveyed businesses. Overall, most firms at the time of this survey had management teams which included individuals from a general management background/expertise (88.7 per cent compared with 95.8 per cent). Interestingly, the vast majority of Science Park firms had expanded and diversified their management teams to a greater extent than their off-Park counterparts, although this difference is not statistically significant. The increased professional management of almost all firms is reflected in the finding that more than 66 per cent of firms on and off Science Parks employed individuals with marketing (66.2 per cent compared with 81.7 per cent) and finance (67.6 per cent compared with 78.9 per cent) backgrounds/expertise. Also, it is not surprising to note that over 67 per cent of respondents in both groups indicated they had individuals with R & D backgrounds/expertise (67.1 per cent compared with 71.8 per cent). Hypothesis 2, therefore, cannot be confirmed.

Table 14.2 Backgrounds/Expertise of the Current Management Team: 1992 New Sample (a)

Management team backgrounds/expertise when business began	Science Park No.	%	Off-Park No.	%	Total No.	%
1. General management	63	88.7	68	95.8	131	92.3
2. R & D	47	67.1	51	71.8	98	56.5
3. Marketing	47	66.2	58	81.7	105	73.9
4. Finance	48	67.6	56	78.9	104	73.2
5. Personnel	31	43.7	37	52.1	68	47.9
6. Production	26	36.6	37	52.1	63	44.4

Note: (a) No statistically significant differences were recorded between firms on and off Science Parks.

14.4 Sources of current advice and assistance: the follow-on sample

This section tests Hypothesis 3. Table 14.3 shows over 82 per cent of firms contacted external organisations and individuals for information, advice, assistance or expertise during the last year. There was no difference between firms on and off Science Parks. The two groups of firms also mentioned similar types of external organisations and individuals. The most frequently cited were central government/ government departments (e.g. the DTI) mentioned by 27 per cent overall. This group of contacts were followed by accountants (13 per cent) and HEIs (13 per cent). Science Park firms were slightly more likely to contact banks/financial institutions (10.3 per cent compared with 7.7 per cent) whilst off-Park firms were slightly more likely to use consultants (7.6 per cent compared with 13.2 per cent).

Table 14.3 External Organisations and Individuals Formally Contacted During the Last Year: 1992 Follow-on Survey (Number of Mentions)

Organisation	Science Park		Off-Park		Total	
	No.	%	No.	%	No.	%
1. Central government/government departments	37	25.5	27	29.7	64	27.1
2. Local government/local authorities	4	2.8	4	4.4	8	3.4
3. TECs	9	6.2	4	4.4	13	5.5
4. Enterprise agencies	1	0.7	3	3.3	4	1.7
5. Other public sector	1	0.7	1	1.1	2	0.8
6. Other training organisations	1	0.7	0	0.0	1	0.4
7. Universities (HEIs)	19	13.1	11	12.1	30	12.7
8. Banks/financial institutions	15	10.3	7	7.7	22	9.3
9. Accountants	19	13.1	12	13.2	31	13.1
10. Solicitors	12	8.3	5	5.5	17	7.2
11. Consultants	11	7.6	12	13.2	23	9.7
12. Other private sector	10	6.9	2	2.2	12	5.1
13. Other sources	6	4.1	3	3.3	9	3.8
Total	145	100.0	91	100.1	236	99.8
Valid cases	50	86.2	39	83.0	89	84.8
Number of cases recording no contacts	8	13.8	8	17.0	16	15.2
Don't know	1		3		4	

The reasons for contacting external organisations and individuals were also similar between the two groups. Table 14.4 shows the three most frequently mentioned reasons were professional advice (26.2 per cent compared with 20.7 per cent), finance and grant applications (22.8 per cent compared with 31.0 per cent) and information (i.e. technical, technology, overseas trade, etc.) (22.8 per cent compared with 24.1 per cent). From this we infer that a similar proportion of firms, irrespective of location, have used professional advisers (such as accountants and solicitors), academic and technical advice from HEIs and financial and technical assistance from central government departments. Hypothesis 3, which suggested that differences might exist in this respect, therefore cannot be supported.

Table 14.4 Reason for Contacting External Organisation and Individuals During the Last Year: 1992 Follow-on Survey (Number of Mentions)

Reason for contact	Science Park		Off-Park (a)		Total	
	No.	%	No.	%	No.	%
1. Professional advice	38	26.2	18	20.7	56	24.1
2. Advice – unspecified	7	4.8	6	6.9	13	5.6
3. Information – technical, technology, overseas trade, etc	33	22.8	21	24.1	54	23.3
4. Training	11	7.6	2	2.3	13	5.6
5. Finance and grant application	33	22.8	27	31.0	60	25.9
6. Running a business/business and management development	4	2.8	6	6.9	10	4.3
7. Premises	3	2.1	0	0.0	3	1.3
8. Product design/development	7	4.8	6	6.9	13	5.6
9. Other	9	6.2	1	1.1	10	4.3
Total	145	100.1	87	99.9	232	100.0

Note: (a) Four off-Park organisations were contacted but respondents could not remember the exact reason for the contact.

14.5 Sources of initial and current advice and assistance: the "new sample"

Approximately 60 per cent of all firms in the "new sample" (Table 14.5) indicated they contacted external organisations and individuals before the business was started. No difference was observed in this respect between Science Park and off-Park firms (60.0 per cent compared with 58.8 per cent). Again, the most frequently contacted external organisations and individuals were central government/government departments (e.g. the DTI) (19.2 per cent and 25.0 per cent of mentions in Science Park and off-Park firms, respectively), accountants (17.2 per cent compared with 18.8 per cent) and banks/financial institutions (13.1 per cent compared with 12.5 per cent).

Table 14.5   External Organisations and Individuals Formally Contacted Before the Business was Started: 1992 New Sample (Number of Mentions)

Organisation	Science Park No.	Science Park %	Off-Park No.	Off-Park %	Total No.	Total %
1. Central government/government departments	19	19.2	16	25.0	35	21.5
2. Local government/local authorities	5	5.1	1	1.6	6	3.7
3. TECs	6	6.1	2	3.1	8	4.9
4. Enterprise agencies	7	7.1	5	7.8	12	7.4
5. Other public sector	1	1.0	0	0.0	1	0.6
6. Universities (HEIs)	6	6.1	2	3.1	8	4.9
7. Banks/financial institutions	13	13.1	8	12.5	21	12.9
8. Accountants	17	17.2	12	18.8	29	17.8
9. Solicitors	8	8.1	9	14.1	17	10.4
10. Consultants	9	9.1	2	3.1	11	6.7
11. Other private sector	4	4.0	4	6.3	8	4.9
12. Other sources	4	4.0	3	4.7	7	4.3
Total	99	100.1	64	100.1	163	100.0
Valid cases	39	60.0	30	58.8	69	59.5
Number of cases recording no contacts	26	40.0	21	41.2	47	40.5
Don't know	6		20		26	

Table 14.6 shows the most frequently mentioned reason for contacting external organisations or individuals was to obtain professional advice (29 per cent of all firms). Other frequently cited reasons related to finance and grant applications and getting advice on technical information. No difference between firms located on and off-Park were observed in this respect.

Table 14.6   Reason for Contacting External Organisation and Individuals Before the Business was Started: 1992 New Sample (Number of Mentions)

Reason for contact	Science Park No.	Science Park %	Off-Park(a) No.	Off-Park(a) %	Total No.	Total %
1. Professional advice	29	29.3	22	34.9	51	31.5
2. Advice – unspecified	0	0.0	1	1.6	1	0.6
3. Information – technical, technology, overseas trade, etc	23	23.2	7	11.1	30	18.5
4. Training	1	1.0	1	1.6	2	1.2
5. Finance and grant application	28	28.3	13	20.6	41	25.3
6. Running a business/business and management development	4	4.0	14	22.2	18	11.1
7. Premises	6	6.1	0	0.0	6	3.7
8. Product design/development	8	8.1	5	7.9	13	8.0
Total	99	100.0	63	99.9	162	99.9

Note: (a) One off-Park respondent mentioned an organisation contacted butcould not remember the exact reason for contact.

Hypothesis 4 suggests that over time, firms would increase their contact with these external organisations and individuals. This is supported by comparing Table 14.7 and Table 14.5. The former shows that more firms made contact with external organisations in the last year, than prior to starting their business. It is also the case that the number of contacts per firm rose. However, we do not observe any differences in these respects between firms located on and off Science Parks.

Table 14.7   External Organisations and Individuals Formally Contacted During the Last Year: 1992 New Sample (Number of Mentions)

Organisation	Science Park		Off-Park		Total	
	No.	%	No.	%	No.	%
1. Central government/government departments	34	24.6	20	17.7	54	21.5
2. Local government/local authorities	4	2.9	3	2.7	7	2.8
3. TECs	5	3.6	11	9.7	16	6.4
4. Enterprise agencies	6	4.3	6	5.3	12	4.8
5. Other public sector	1	0.7	0	0.0	1	0.4
6. Universities (HEIs)	7	5.1	1	0.9	8	3.2
7. Banks/financial institutions	15	10.9	8	7.1	23	9.2
8. Accountants	29	21.0	18	15.9	47	18.7
9. Solicitors	12	8.7	10	8.8	22	8.8
10. Consultants	11	8.0	20	17.7	31	12.4
11. Other private sector	8	5.8	11	9.7	19	7.6
12. Other sources	6	4.3	5	4.4	11	4.4
Total	138	99.9	113	99.9	251	100.2
Valid cases	53	75.7	46	67.6	99	71.7
Number of cases recording no contacts	17	24.3	22	32.4	39	28.3
Don't know	1		3		4	

For established businesses, Table 14.8 shows the main reason for contacting external organisations and individuals was need of professional advice (34.8 per cent and 39.5 per cent of mentions amongst Science Park and off-Park firms, respectively) and technical information (23.9 per cent compared with 11.4 per cent). Perhaps reflecting the increased need to finance growth, a slightly larger proportion of Science Park firms mentioned they had recently contacted external organisations and individuals for finance and grant applications (23.9 per cent compared with 15.8 per cent).

Table 14.8   Reason for Contacting External Organisation and Individuals During the Last Year: 1992 New Sample (Number of Mentions)

Reason for contact	Science Park		Off Park (a)		Total	
	No.	%	No.	%	No.	%
1. Professional advice	48	34.8	45	39.5	93	36.9
2. Information – technical, technology, overseas trade, etc.	33	23.9	13	11.4	46	18.3
3. Training	7	5.1	11	9.6	18	7.1
4. Finance and grant application	33	23.9	18	15.8	51	20.2
5. Running a business/business and management development	8	5.8	11	9.6	19	7.5
6. Premises	2	1.4	1	0.9	3	1.2
7. Product design/development	6	4.3	12	10.5	18	7.1
8. Other	1	0.7	3	2.6	4	1.6
Total	138	99.9	114	99.9	252	99.9

Note: (a) One respondent mentioned a reason for contact but could not recall the organisation contacted.

14.6 Dependency in the product/service and customer bases: follow-on sample

Table 14.9 shows that firms which earned income from manufactured products and/or software (standard packages) in the follow-on samples were heavily dependent upon these activities for the majority of their total income. In fact, over 65 per cent of firms in both subsamples indicated these activities accounted for more than 60 per cent of their total income. Consequently, Hypothesis 5 cannot be confirmed.

Table 14.9   Percentage of Total Income that Comes from Manufactured and/or Standard Software Products: 1992 Follow-on Survey

Per cent of income from manufactured and standard software products	Science Park		Off-Park		Total	
	No.	%	No.	%	No.	%
1–20	5	15.2	2	5.7	7	10.3
21–40	3	9.1	2	5.7	5	7.4
41–60	3	9.1	8	22.9	11	16.2
61–80	9	27.3	9	25.7	18	26.5
81–100	13	39.4	14	40.0	27	39.7
Total	33	100.1	35	100.0	68	100.1

"t" = -0.92, d.f. = 66, significance level = 0.361, accept H_0.

However, it was reassuring to note the majority of firms in both follow-on samples (across all industrial activities) suggested they were not dependent on their three largest customers for a high proportion of their total output (by value) (Table 14.10). Over 57 per cent of firms on and off Science Parks indicated that two-fifths or less of their output went to their three largest customers. As a result, Hypothesis 6 is not empirically supported. These results confirm those presented in previous studies of new as well as small firms that only a small proportion of firms were dependent on the needs of dominant customers (see Keeble and Gould, 1984, p 8; Hitchens and O'Farrell, 1987, p 546; Birley and Westhead, 1992, p 321).

Table 14.10   Percentage of Total Output (by Value) that Goes to the Three Largest Customers: 1992 Follow-on Survey

Per cent of output that goes to the three largest customers	Science Park		Off-Park		Total	
	No.	%	No.	%	No.	%
1–20	18	38.3	17	37.8	35	38.0
21–40	12	25.5	9	20.0	21	22.8
41–60	7	14.9	6	13.3	13	14.1
61–80	3	6.4	10	22.2	13	14.1
81–100	7	14.9	3	6.7	10	10.9
Total	47	100.0	45	100.0	92	99.9

"t" = -0.41, d.f. = 90, significance level = 0.680, accept H_0.

14.7 Dependency in the product/service and customer bases: "new sample"

The evidence from the "new sample" survey shown in Table 14.11 suggests Hypothesis 5 is not supported. "New sample" firms currently earning income from manufactured products and/or software (standard packages) were heavily dependent upon these activities for the majority of their total income. Fifty-nine per cent of all firms reported these activities accounted for more than 60 per cent of their total income.

Table 14.11 Percentage of Total Income that Comes from Manufactured and/or Standard Software Products: 1992 New Sample

Per cent of income from manufactured and standard software products	Science Park No.	%	Off-Park No.	%	Total No.	%
1–20	3	14.3	7	20.0	10	17.9
21–40	5	23.8	5	14.3	10	17.9
41–60	0	0.0	3	8.6	3	5.4
61–80	4	19.0	5	14.3	9	16.1
81–100	9	42.9	15	42.9	24	42.9
Total	21	100.0	35	100.1	56	100.2

"t" = 0.00, d.f. = 54, significance level = 0.998, accept H_0.

Table 14.12 shows Science Park firms are significantly more dependent on their three largest customers for income (total output by value) (means of 54.3 per cent and 43.3 per cent for Science Park and off-Park firms, respectively). This is the opposite to that proposed in Hypothesis 6.

Table 14.12 Percentage of Total Output (by Value) that Goes to the Three Largest Customers: 1992 New Sample

Per cent of output that goes to the three largest customers	Science Park No.	%	Off-Park No.	%	Total No.	%
1–20	7	13.5	17	28.3	24	21.4
21–40	13	25.0	14	23.3	27	24.1
41–60	14	26.9	18	30.0	32	28.6
61–80	9	17.3	4	6.7	13	11.6
81–100	9	17.3	7	11.7	16	14.3
Total	52	100.0	60	100.0	112	100.0

"t" = 2.18, d.f. = 110, significance level = 0.031, reject H_0.

14.8 Management and markets: the combined sample, 1992

The combined sample supports the earlier evidence from the follow-on as well as the "new sample" that Hypothesis 3 cannot be sustained. Seventy-three per cent of firms, on and off Science Parks, reported that during the last year they had formally contacted external organisations and individuals, but no difference existed between on- and off-Park firms.

Evidence from the combined sample also rejects Hypotheses 5 and 6. It is, however, interesting to note there was no statistically significant difference between firms on and off Science Parks with regard to output dependency on their three largest customers. Over 50 per cent of firms on and off Science Parks indicated that two-fifths or less of their output went to their three largest customers.

14.9 Conclusions

This chapter identified six hypotheses which were tested. We conclude that:

1. Evidence from the "new sample" confirms Hypothesis 1. Firms on and off Science Parks have, over time, clearly diversified their management teams.

2. Hypothesis 2 is not supported in the "new sample" analysis. Firms, whether or not they were located on a Science Park, had similarly diverse management teams with individuals coming from a variety of backgrounds/expertise.

3. Based on evidence from the follow-on, "new" and total combined samples we conclude that Hypothesis 3 cannot be accepted. We see no evidence that being located on a Science Park influences the type of advice and assistance obtained by surveyed firms.

4. Hypothesis 5 is not supported. Irrespective of location, firms throughout the samples showed a heavy income dependency upon manufactured and/or standard software products.

5. Evidence from all three samples indicates that Hypothesis 6 cannot be supported. Reassuringly, the follow-on and total samples suggested that on- and off-Science Park firms did not appear to be dependent on their three largest customers for the majority of their sales (output by value). However, contrary to expectation, the evidence from the "new sample" showed that it was off-Park firms, rather than those on Science Parks, which were the least likely to be customer dependent.

Chapter 15

Science Park Location

15.1 Introduction

This chapter explores the property needs of high technology firms in the "new sample" with regard to size of premises, terms of occupation and the key location factors. The future property needs of firms are also explored in relation to the follow-on, "new sample" and the total combined sample. The value of the management support function on Science Parks is discussed in Chapter 16.

The 1986 survey showed Science Park firms occupied smaller premises than off-Park firms. Over 60 per cent of Science Park firms, compared with only 34 per cent of off-Park firms, occupied premises with less than 2,000 square feet (Monck et al., 1988, p 179). It also found that 39 per cent of tenants on Science Parks were new firms on arrival, compared with 46 per cent of off-Park firms. Finally, it revealed that a markedly larger proportion of off-Park firms owned their premises (1 per cent compared with 25 per cent) (Monck et al., 1988, p 181).

Firms in 1986 were asked about the factors which had influenced them in selecting their current premises (Monck et al., 1988, pp 182–3). For Science Park tenants the most important factors were "prestige and image of the site" (59 per cent of mentions), "access to university facilities" (33 per cent) and "previous location in the area" (32 per cent). For off-Park firms, the most significant factors were the "key founder lived locally" (62 per cent) and "cost of premises" (49 per cent). Interestingly, for the latter group, "prestige and image of the site" was given only 18 per cent of mentions and "access to universities facilities" and "scope for attracting graduates" were not mentioned at all.

With regard to future property requirements, in 1986, about one-half of respondents (51 per cent on Science Parks and 52 per cent off Science Parks) indicated their intention to move to a new site or to take additional premises within the next two years. Monck et al. (1988) concluded:

> "...the majority of current firms look to the Science Park as the prime provider of additional space. In contrast, the majority of off-park firms do not expect their additional premises needs to be met by their present location" (p 184).

Further, they went on to state:

> "...despite the higher rental levels, Science Park-based firms are more satisfied with their location and property decisions than off-park firms. It helps to explain why a higher proportion of firms on Science Parks expect to expand by remaining on site, whereas off-park firms expect to relocate elsewhere" (Monck et al., 1988, pp 185–6).

15.2 Derivation of hypotheses

In this section nine hypotheses are presented and tested.

Hypothesis 1: Firms located on Science Park "seed beds" will be more likely to have been new firms on arrival.

Hypothesis 2: Due to the Science Park estate management policy, Park firms are more likely to be tenants than off-Park firms.

Hypothesis 3: Science Park managers have particularly encouraged the start-up of new small ventures and, as a result, more Park firms will occupy small units.

Hypothesis 4a: Science Park firms are more likely to stress that their current premises were selected due to the "prestige and image of the site" than off-Park firms.

Hypothesis 4b: Science Park firms are more likely to stress that their current premises were selected due to the increased potential "access to university facilities" than off-Park firms.

Hypothesis 5: Science Park respondents will be more likely to suggest they were paying the full market rent for premises than off-Park firms.

Hypothesis 6: Science Park firms will be more likely to require additional floorspace in new or additional premises in the next two years.

Hypothesis 7: Science Park firms requiring new or additional premises will expect to expand by remaining on site, whereas their off-Park counterparts will relocate elsewhere.

Hypothesis 8: Science Park firms in "assisted" areas, due to the availability of grants, will be more likely to seek new or additional premises close to their current site than Park firms located elsewhere.

15.3 Property needs of "new sample" respondents

As indicated above, 39 per cent of Science Park tenants during the 1986 survey were new firms on arrival. The equivalent proportion in the 1992 "new sample" is only 31 per cent (34 per cent for off-Park firms). This suggests that Hypothesis 1 cannot be accepted.

Table 15.1 shows that the 1992 "new sample" results are similar to those of the 1986 survey. Supporting Hypothesis 2, a larger proportion of Science Park firms were located in leased premises (87.3 per cent compared with 64.3 per cent), whilst more off-Park firms were owner-occupiers (1.4 per cent compared with 31.4 per cent).

Table 15.1   Type of Tenure: 1992 New Sample

Type of tenure	Science Park		Off-Park		Total	
	No.	%	No.	%	No.	%
1. Own	1	1.4	22	31.4	23	16.3
2. Lease	62	87.3	45	64.3	107	75.9
3. Licence	8	11.3	1	1.4	9	6.4
4. Other	0	0.0	2	2.8	2	1.4
Total	71	100.0	70	99.9	141	100.0

Table 15.2 shows that Hypothesis 3 cannot be supported. However, it suggests Science Park firms occupy units with less than 501 square feet (20.0 per cent compared with 4.5 per cent).

Table 15.2   Size of Unit Occupied by Firms (sq. ft.): 1992 New Sample

Size of unit (sq. ft.)	Science Park		Off-Park		Total	
	No.	%	No.	%	No.	%
≤ 500	14	20.0	3	4.5	17	12.5
501–1,000	19	27.1	10	15.2	29	21.3
1,001–2,000	18	25.7	9	13.6	27	19.9
2,001–5,000	8	11.4	13	19.7	21	15.4
5,001–9,000	5	7.1	6	9.1	11	8.1
9,001–50,000	5	7.1	22	33.3	27	19.9
> 50,000	1	1.4	3	4.5	4	2.9
Total	70	99.8	66	99.9	136	100.0

"t"= −1.45, d.f. = 134, significance level = 0.151, accept H_0.

Over 63 per cent of respondents in both groups suggested other sites were seriously considered before the surveyed premises was chosen (Table 15.3).

Table 15.3   Were Any Other Sites Seriously Considered Before this Site was Chosen?: 1992 New Sample

Other sites seriously considered	Science Park		Off-Park		Total	
	No.	%	No.	%	No.	%
1. Yes	43	65.2	39	63.9	82	64.6
2. No	23	34.8	22	36.1	45	35.4
Total	66	100.0	61	100.0	127	100.0

χ^2 = 0.00, d.f. = 1, significance level = 1.0000, accept H_0.

Table 15.4 shows the three most important factors identified by respondents in influencing their choice of location. As suggested in Hypothesis 4a, Science Park firms were much more likely to emphasise the "prestige and overall image of the site" (50.7 per cent compared with 25.0 per cent) than off-Park firms. Also, supporting Hypothesis 4b, Science Park firms had a greater propensity to mention "access to facilities of HEI/centre of research" (17.4 per cent compared with 3.3 per cent) and "prestige of being linked to the HEI/centre of research" (11.6 per cent compared with 0.0 per cent).

Table 15.4   Three Most Important Factors in Influencing the Firm to Locate in Surveyed Location: 1992 New Sample (a)

Three most important location factors	Science Park No.	Science Park %	Off-Park No.	Off-Park %	Total No.	Total %
1. Key founder lived locally	16	23.2	22	36.7	38	29.5
2. Key founder worked previously in locality	3	4.3	5	8.3	8	6.2
3. Key founder worked at local HEI/centre of research	6	8.7	1	1.7	7	5.4
4. Firm was already based in the area	18	26.1	23	38.3	41	31.8
5. Cost of premises	26	37.7	28	46.7	54	41.9
6. Access to facilities of HEI/centre of research	12	17.4	2	3.3	14	10.9
7. Prestige and overall image of site	35	50.7	15	25.0	50	38.8
8. Prestige of being linked to the HEI/centre of research	8	11.6	0	0.0	8	6.2
9. Land adjacent to these premises for expansion	1	1.4	1	1.7	2	1.6
10. Availability of additional premises at this location	5	7.2	7	11.7	12	9.3
11. Provision of on-site management and common services	12	17.4	2	3.3	14	10.9
12. Car parking facilities	10	14.5	7	11.7	17	13.2
13. Friendly atmosphere amongst tenants on site	0	0.0	0	0.0	0	0.0
14. Availability of skilled labour in area	3	4.3	2	3.3	5	3.9
15. Good transport and communication links	21	30.4	20	33.3	41	31.8
16. Access to markets	7	10.1	9	15.0	16	12.4
17. Access to materials and components	0	0.0	0	0.0	0	0.0
18. Proximity to firms in similar industrial sectors/using same technology	6	8.7	3	5.0	9	7.0
19. Scope for attracting graduate HEI staff	3	4.3	3	5.0	6	4.7
20. Other	7	10.1	7	11.7	14	10.9
Valid cases	69		60		129	

Note: (a) Some surveyed respondents specified fewer than three factors.

Off-Park firms, however, emphasised different issues. They tended to refer to the "cost of premises" (37.7 per cent compared with 46.7 per cent), the "firm was already based in the area" (26.1 per cent compared with 38.3 per cent), that the "key founder lived locally" (26.1 per cent compared with 38.3 per cent) and the importance of "good transport and communication links" (30.4 per cent compared with 33.3 per cent).

Table 15.5 indicates Science Park firms were more likely to value the contribution which their location played in supplementing the reputation of their business. A significantly larger proportion of Science Park than off-Park firms suggested that, while operating at the current site, they felt the overall reputation and market image of the firm had improved.

Table 15.5   While Operating on this Site Respondents Feel that the Overall Reputation and Market Image of Firm has Changed: 1992 New Sample

Overall reputation and market image of firm	Science Park No.	Science Park %	Off-Park No.	Off-Park %	Total No.	Total %
1. Improved	63	90.0	42	73.7	105	82.7
2. Stayed same	7	10.0	15	26.3	22	17.3
Total	70	100.0	57	100.0	127	100.0

$\chi^2 = 4.78$, d.f. = 1, significance level = 0.0292, reject H_0.

Table 15.6 shows that, for "new sample" firms in leased or licensed accommodation, the majority believed they were paying the full market rent for their premises (65.7 per cent and 52.2 per cent of firms on Science Park and off-Park locations, respectively). Interestingly, more off-Park firms suggested they were paying less than the full market rent (11.9 per cent compared with 21.7 per cent). Hypothesis 5 cannot, therefore, be accepted.

Table 15.6   Firms Paying the Full Market Rent for Premises: 1992 New Sample

Paying full market rent	Science Park		Off-Park		Total	
	No.	%	No.	%	No.	%
1. Yes	44	65.7	24	52.2	68	60.2
2. No – paying less than for other comparable properties in the locality	8	11.9	10	21.7	18	15.9
3. No – paying more than for other comparable properties in the locality	15	22.4	12	26.1	27	23.9
Total	67	100.0	46	100.0	113	100.0

χ^2 = 2.63, d.f. = 2, significance level = 0.2690, accept H_0.

Hypothesis 6 is examined in Tables 15.7 and 15.8. Table 15.7 indicates that half of all firms were considering a move to new or additional premises in the next two years. Consequently, Hypothesis 6 is not supported, since there is no difference between on- and off-Park firms.

Table 15.7   Firms Thinking of Moving to New or Additional Premises in the Next Two Years: 1992 New Sample

Moving to new premises	Science Park		Off-Park		Total	
	No.	%	No.	%	No.	%
1. New premises	25	39.7	21	31.3	46	35.4
2. Additional premises	10	15.9	12	17.9	22	16.9
3. Not moving	28	44.4	34	50.7	62	47.7
Total	63	100.0	67	99.9	130	100.0

χ^2 = 0.99, d.f. = 2, significance level = 0.6101, accept H_0.

Table 15.8 shows that whilst a larger proportion of Science Park firms indicated the new or additional premises would be located on the same site as the surveyed business (30.0 per cent compared with 9.4 per cent) this difference was not statistically significant. It also shows that half of those potential movers anticipated locating less than ten miles away. Therefore, Hypothesis 7 can be accepted.

Table 15.8   Location of New or Additional Premises from the Firm: 1992 New Sample

Location of new or additional premises	Science Park		Off-Park		Total	
	No.	%	No.	%	No.	%
1. This site	9	30.0	3	9.4	12	19.4
2. Less than 10 miles away	16	53.3	19	59.4	35	56.5
3. Elsewhere	5	16.7	10	31.3	15	24.2
Total	30	100.0	32	100.1	62	100.1

χ^2 = 4.86, d.f = 2, significance level = 0.0878, accept H_0.

However, Table 15.9 shows a significantly larger proportion of Science Park firms indicated these new or additional premises would be on a Science Park (39.3 per cent compared with 4.2 per cent). It is important to note here that markedly fewer off-Park firms responded to the question presented in Table 15.9 than the former one detailed in Table 15.8. Even so we conclude based on the evidence presented in Table 15.7 (which explicitly tests Hypothesis 7) that, overall, existing Science Park firms are not statistically more likely to expand on site than off-Park firms and that Hypothesis 7 cannot be accepted.

Table 15.9 New or Additional Premises Located on a Science Park: 1992 New Sample

New premises on a science park	Science Park No.	%	Off-Park No.	%	Total No.	%
1. Yes	11	39.3	1	4.2	12	23.1
2. No	17	60.7	23	95.8	40	76.9
Total	28	100.0	24	100.0	52	100.0

$\chi^2 = 7.11$, d.f. = 1, significance level = 0.0077, reject H_0.

The reasons most frequently given by firms for considering new or additional premises are presented in Table 15.10. It shows that half the reasons given by firms were positive (such as more space required/room for expansion). However, firms currently located on Science Parks are much more likely to be considering alternative premises because of the high cost than is the case for off-Park firms.

Table 15.10 Reasons Given by Firms for Considering New or Additional Premises: 1992 New Sample (number of mentions)

Reasons for move	Science Park No.	%	Off-Park No.	%	Total No.	%
(a) Positive reasons						
1. More space required/ room for expansion	22	46.8	21	53.8	43	50.0
(b) Negative reasons						
2. Cost too great	9	19.1	3	7.7	12	14.0
3. Technical/production	1	2.1	0	0.0	1	1.2
4. Want to own premises/ lease expires	2	4.3	2	5.1	4	4.7
5. Image poor/facilities not to required standard	4	8.5	6	15.4	10	11.6
6. Group decision – parent company	4	8.5	3	7.7	7	8.1
7. Other	5	10.6	4	10.3	9	10.5
Total	47	99.9	39	100.0	86	100.1

15.4 Property needs of follow-on sample respondents

This section tests Hypotheses 5, 6 and 7 in relation to the property characteristics of firms in the follow-on samples. Again, the following discussion relates only to firms based in leased or licensed accommodation.

Table 15.11 shows these firms, even more than those in the "new sample", thought they were paying the full market rent for their premises. As was found in the "new sample" slightly more off-Park firms suggested they were paying less than for other comparable properties in their locality (1.9 per cent compared with 13.2 per cent). This evidence again points to a rejection of Hypothesis 5.

Table 15.11   Firms Paying the Full Market Rent for Premises: 1992 Follow-on Survey

Paying full market rent	Science Park		Off-Park		Total	
	No.	%	No.	%	No.	%
1. Yes	49	92.5	33	86.8	82	90.1
2. No – paying less than for other comparable properties in the locality	1	1.9	5	13.2	6	6.6
3. No – paying more than for other comparable properties in the locality	3	5.7	0	0.0	3	3.3
Total	53	100.1	38	100.0	91	100.0

Table 15.12 indicates significantly more Science Park than off-Park firms were considering new or additional premises in the next two years (52.9 per cent compared with 26.1 per cent). This may have been because of anticipated business growth, lease restrictions and/or for rent reduction purposes. Hypothesis 6, therefore, can be accepted.

Table 15.12   Firms Thinking of Moving to New or Additional Premises in the Next Two Years: 1992 Follow-on Survey

Moving to new premises	Science Park		Off-Park		Total	
	No.	%	No.	%	No.	%
1. New premises	19	37.3	8	17.4	27	27.8
2. Additional premises	8	15.7	4	8.7	12	12.4
3. Not moving	24	47.1	34	73.9	58	59.8
Total	51	100.1	46	100.0	97	100.0

$\chi^2 = 7.30$, d.f. = 2, significance level = 0.0260, reject H_0.

For those firms considering a move, more Science Park than off-Park firms suggested that new or additional premises would be located on the same site as the surveyed business (25.0 per cent compared with 8.3 per cent) (Table 15.13). However, the vast majority of respondents indicated these premises would be located less than ten miles away from the firms' operational premises (58.3 per cent compared with 66.7 per cent). Table 15.14 shows Science Park firms were more likely to suggest those premises would be located on a Science Park (44.4 per cent compared with 22.2 per cent). For these reasons we tentatively accept Hypothesis 7.

Table 15.13   Location of New or Additional Premises from the Firm: 1992 Follow-on Survey

Location of new or additional premises	Science Park		Off-Park		Total	
	No.	%	No.	%	No.	%
1. This site	6	25.0	1	8.3	7	19.4
2. Less than 10 miles away	14	58.3	8	66.7	22	61.1
3. Elsewhere	4	16.7	3	25.0	7	19.4
Total	24	100.0	12	100.0	36	99.9

Table 15.14 New or Additional Premises Located on a Science Park: 1992 Follow-on Survey

New premises on a science park	Science Park		Off-Park		Total	
	No.	%	No.	%	No.	%
1. Yes	8	44.4	2	22.2	10	37.0
2. No	10	55.6	7	77.8	17	63.0
Total	18	100.0	9	100.0	27	100.0

The reasons most frequently given by firms for considering new or additional premises are shown in Table 15.15. As found in the "new sample", virtually half of the reasons given by all firms are positive reasons (such as more space required/room for expansion). A slightly higher proportion of Science Park than off-Park firms gave negative reasons (such as currently high costs).

Table 15.15 Reasons Given by Firms for Considering New or Additional Premises: 1992 Follow-on Survey (Number of Mentions)

Reasons for move	Science Park		Off-Park		Total	
	No.	%	No.	%	No.	%
(a) Positive reasons						
1. More space required/ room for expansion	17	44.7	9	52.9	26	47.3
(b) Negative reasons						
2. Cost too great	9	23.7	1	5.9	10	18.2
3. Technical/production	1	2.6	1	5.9	2	3.6
4. Want to own premises/ lease expires	2	5.3	1	5.9	3	5.5
5. Image poor/facilities not to required standard	5	13.2	1	5.9	6	10.9
6. Other	4	10.5	4	23.5	8	14.5
Total	38	100.0	17	100.0	55	100.0

15.5 Property needs: the combined 1992 sample

Hypotheses 5 to 8 are now tested on the combined sample.

Hypothesis 5 is not supported. No statistically significant difference was recorded between firms located on and off a Science Park with regard to the market rent of leased or licensed premises. More than two-thirds of firms on and off Science Parks indicated they were paying the full market rent for their leased premises. However, a slightly larger proportion of off-Park firms felt they were paying less than for other comparable properties in their locality.

Moreover, confirming the findings of the "new sample" analysis, Table 15.16 indicates that whilst slightly more Science Park firms were thinking of moving (54 per cent compared with 40 per cent) the difference is not statistically significant. Hypothesis 6 cannot be accepted.

Table 15.16 Firms Thinking of Moving to New or Additional Premises in the Next Two Years: Total Sample 1992

Moving to new premises	Science Park		Off-Park		Total	
	No.	%	No.	%	No.	%
1. New premises	44	38.6	29	25.7	73	32.2
2. Additional premises	18	15.8	16	14.2	34	15.0
3. Not moving	52	45.6	68	60.2	120	52.9
Total	114	100.0	113	100.1	227	100.1

$\chi^2 = 5.33$, d.f. = 2, significance level = 0.0696, accept H_0.

Table 15.17 shows that, for the combined sample, Hypothesis 7 is supported. A significantly larger proportion of Science Park firms suggested their new or additional premises would be on the same site as the surveyed business (27.8 per cent compared with 9.1 per cent). Not surprisingly, Science Park firms thinking of moving to new or additional premises were more likely to suggest they would move to a Science Park location.

Table 15.17 Location of New or Additional Premises from the Firm: Total Sample 1992

Location of new or additional premises	Science Park		Off-Park		Total	
	No.	%	No.	%	No.	%
1. This site	15	27.8	4	9.1	19	19.4
2. Less than 10 miles away	30	55.6	27	61.4	57	58.2
3. Elsewhere	9	16.7	13	29.5	22	22.4
Total	54	100.1	44	100.0	98	100.0

$\chi^2 = 6.30$, d.f = 2, significance level = 0.0429, reject H_0.

The combined Science Park sample showed that over 50 per cent of Park firms in the "non-assisted" (50.9 per cent) as well as the "assisted" areas (58.6 per cent) were thinking of moving to new or additional premises in the next two years. However, as hypothesised, a significantly larger proportion of Science Park firms located in the "assisted" areas suggested these new or additional premises would not be on the same site (68.2 per cent compared with 77.4 per cent) as the business but in the same grant-assisted locality as the business (i.e. less than ten miles away) (36.4 per cent compared with 71.0 per cent) (Table 15.18).

Table 15.18 Location of New or Additional Premises from the Firm: Total Science Park Sample by Assisted Area Status

Location of new or additional premises	Non-assisted		Assisted		Total	
	No.	%	No.	%	No.	%
1. This site	7	31.8	7	22.6	14	26.4
2. Less than 10 miles away	8	36.4	22	71.0	30	56.6
3. Elsewhere	7	31.8	2	6.5	9	17.0
Total	22	100.0	31	100.1	53	100.0

$\chi^2 = 8.01$, d.f = 2, significance level = 0.0182, reject H_0.

15.6 Conclusions

This chapter identified nine hypotheses which were tested. We conclude that:

1. Contrary, to the 1986 survey evidence, firms in the 1992 "new sample" were less likely to be new on arrival.

2. However, supporting Hypotheses 2 and 3, Science Park firms in the "new sample" were more likely to be located in small and leased or licensed premises than off-Park firms.

3. Confirming the 1986 results and supporting Hypotheses 4a and 4b, Science Park firms in the 1992 "new sample" were more likely to emphasise the "prestige and image of the site" and to a lesser extent "access to university facilities" as factors influencing their location than off-Park firms.

4. Hypothesis 5 is not confirmed since firms on and off Science Parks in the follow-on, "new" and total combined samples overwhelmingly indicated that they were paying the full market rent for leased or licensed premises.

5. Hypothesis 6 was supported in only the follow-on sample. We conclude that growing Science Park firms, to a greater extent than their more mature off-Park counterparts, are significantly more likely to require new or additional premises within the next two years.

6. Hypothesis 7 was supported in the follow-on and the combined sample. Confirming the evidence from the 1986 survey, Science Park firms were significantly more likely to appreciate the value of their current location and to express a desire to expand on-Park.

7. Finally, the evidence from the combined 1992 Science Park sample suggests firms located in "assisted" areas will seek new or additional premises on-Park but, to a significantly greater extent than their "non-assisted" counterparts, are willing to move locally (less than ten miles away from the surveyed business) to lower cost premises.

Chapter 16

Characteristics of New Technology-Based Firms, Firms Located on Managed Science Parks and Employment Growth Firms

16.1   Introduction

This chapter explores three cross-cutting themes discussed originally in Chapter 7: the characteristics of new technology-based firms (NTBFs); the value of being located on a "managed" Science Park; and, finally, a comparison of the characteristics of firms which have grown rapidly in terms of employment with other less rapidly growing firms. The key hypotheses discussed and explored in earlier chapters are examined for the relevant subsamples of firms.

16.2   New technology-based firms

This discussion compares the characteristics of new technology-based firms located on and off Science Parks in 1992.

16.2.1   Definition of new technology-based firms

We have adopted UKSPA's definition of a NTBF:

> "A 'new technology-based firm' is defined as any organisation exploiting scientific and other knowledge and/or established technology to develop products and/or services which are ultimately intended to be sold at a profit."

Three terms in this definition must be fully appreciated – "new", "technology" and "firm". Each are discussed in detail below:

First, "new" could refer either to the technology or to the firm. For the purposes of this survey "new" refers only to the technology, so it includes long-established firms now based on new technology.

Second, "technology" is defined to be the exploitation and commercial application of scientific and academic knowledge. The underlying knowledge could be chemistry, biology, physics, linguistics, economics, mathematics, computer science, engineering, electronics, etc., and will frequently be derived from more than one source including other forms of technology. "New technology" should therefore be defined as innovative and novel applications of science and knowledge to achieve a practical and commercially useful product, process or service.

Third, a "firm" is defined as a company or a business which is trading for profit. The firm can be of any size (from a one-person business to a multinational company – incorporated or unincorporated) but it must be offering something which can be sold in the market place for a financial return.

The above definition does *not* include university academic departments, charities, learned societies, local and national government departments and professional services such as accountants, lawyers, financial advisers, etc. Retail businesses or offices purely for sales and administration which are not directly related to the "technology" function are excluded. Nor does it cover commercial support bureaux, computer training organisations or businesses merely selling computers and their peripherals (e.g. box movers). The NTBF must genuinely be involved in some form of innovative work which is important to its main line of business. Further, the following organisations are not classified as NTBFs: certain non-commercial laboratory operations such as a R & D laboratories operated by charities, e.g. cancer research or laboratories meant to meet the needs of certain trades, such as research associations. This is because these organisations are not, in themselves, subject to the disciplines of the market-place.

The above definition of NTBFs does not, of course, imply that Science Parks should not provide accommodation for a range of "other" organisations whose presence on the Science Park is considered beneficial to the NTBFs located on-Park, the Science Park itself or to the host organisation. Instead, the purpose of making the distinction is to determine whether the key findings discussed above comparing Science Park tenants with off-Park firms are influenced by removing those firms which are not NTBFs.

16.2.2 Differences between new technology-based firms (NTBFs) located on and off Science Parks: 1992 combined sample

Using the above definition, 77 Science Park NTBFs were identified and compared with 67 off-Park NTBFs. All other firms are, therefore, omitted from analysis in this section.

Based on evidence from the total 1992 sample (the follow-on and "new samples" combined) Table 16.1 shows that only ten statistically significant differences were recorded between NTBFs located on and off Science Parks, of which four relate to the demographics of the two samples.

New technology-based firms on Science Parks were significantly younger than off-Park firms (mean ages of 9.6 and 12.4 years, respectively). A larger proportion of off-Park NTBFs earned income from manufactured products (39.0 per cent compared with 55.2 per cent) and they were also more likely to state that manufactured products were the single most important activity as a source of income. Further, a significantly larger proportion of Science Park NTBFs were located in the "assisted" areas (51.4 per cent compared with 28.4 per cent) and the "north" (68.8 per cent compared with 44.8 per cent).

Statistically significant differences between the two samples were recorded with regard to four input measures of R & D. Table 16.1 shows Science Park NTBFs had significantly higher R & D intensity in terms of QSEs employed than off-Park NTBFs (means of 39.4 per cent and 27.2 per cent recorded by Science Park and off-Park NTBFs, respectively). Second, paralleling the result in Section 11.3, Science Park NTBFs are significantly more likely than off-Park NTBFs to have contacted a HEI (92.2 per cent compared with 75.8 per cent). Third, a significantly larger proportion of Science Park NTBF respondents indicated that an individual from a Science Park had visited them to discuss the HEI's facilities (37.8 per cent compared with 12.5 per cent). Fourth, the development of closer links between Science Park NTBFs and the HEI is reflected in the finding that more Park NTBFs had received copies of the HEI's newsletter than off-Park NTBFs (48.6 per cent compared with 26.7 per cent).

As found in Section 12.5 technology diffusion as reflected in measures of R & D outputs were, however, similar between on- and off-Park NTBFs. Table 16.1 shows that only modest levels of patenting and copyrighting had been undertaken by surveyed NTBFs on as well as off Science Parks. Further, levels of new product/services launches to the existing customer base and to new markets were very similar.

Tabe 16.1 Differences Between Surveyed New Technology-based Firms (NTBFs) Located On and Off Science Parks: Total Sample in 1992 (a) (b)

Variable	Science Park (n = 77)		Off-Park (n = 67)	
1. Current age of the business (years) (c)				
– mean	9.6		12.4	
– median	8		11	
2. Legal status of surveyed business				
– public company quoted in the UK	4	(5.2)	1	(1.5)
– public company quoted abroad	4	(5.2)	0	(0.0)
– non-quoted public company	2	(2.6)	4	(6.0)
– private limited company	60	(77.9)	59	(88.1)
– partnership	4	(5.2)	0	(0.0)
– sole proprietorship	1	(1.3)	3	(0.0)
– other	2	(2.6)	0	(0.0)
3. Business currently earning income from manufactured products (d)	30	(39.0)	37	(55.2)
4. Single most important activity as a source of income				
– manufactured products	21	(27.3)	27	(40.3)
– software (standard packages)	12	(5.6)	5	(7.5)
– bespoke software	7	(9.1)	6	(9.0)
– consultancy work	11	(14.3)	10	(14.9)
– contract research	9	(11.7)	2	(3.0)
– contract design work	6	(7.8)	4	(6.0)
– sub-contract production work	0	(0.0)	2	(3.0)
– testing/analysis	5	(6.5)	4	(6.0)
– licence income	3	(3.9)	3	(4.5)
– training	2	(2.6)	0	(0.0)
– other	1	(1.3)	4	(6.0)
5. Surveyed firm currently located on a government designated "assisted" area (d)	38	(51.4)	19	(28.4)
6. Surveyed firm currently located in the "north" (d)	53	(68.8)	30	(44.8)
7. Percentage of total income that comes from manufactured and/or standard software products (f)				
– mean	66.1		72.7	
– median	70		80	
8. Percentage of total output (by value) that goes to the three largest customers (f)				
– mean	48.5		42.5	
– median	40		35	
9. Percentage of qualified scientists and engineers (QSEs) employed in R & D (g)				
– mean	39.4		27.2	
– median	38.1		20.0	
10. Total R & D expenditure per year (£s) (f)				
– mean	339,730		720,108	
– median	100,000		45,100	
11. R & D expenditure as a percentage of total turnover (f)				
– mean	26.7		18.9	
– median	10		10	
12. Firms recording a "link" with the local university, polytechnic or institute of higher education (HEI) (d, h)	71	(92.2)	50	(75.8)
13. Single most important link with HEI (i)				
– informal contact with academics	13	(22.0)	7	(15.6)
– employment of academics on a part-time consultancy basis	6	(10.2)	4	(8.9)
– sponsor research trials or projects	3	(5.1)	5	(11.1)
– access to specialist equipment	5	(8.5)	3	(6.7)
– test/analysis in HEI	1	(1.7)	1	(2.2)
– student projects	2	(3.4)	3	(6.7)
– employment of recent graduates	8	(13.6)	12	(26.7)
– training by HEI	1	(1.7)	1	(2.2)
– assistance by business in HEI teaching programme	0	(0.0)	1	(2.2)
– other formal links	2	(3.4)	1	(2.2)
– library facilities	8	(13.6)	2	(4.4)
– recreation	1	(1.7)	0	(0.0)
– conferences	1	(1.7)	1	(2.2)
– dining	1	(1.7)	0	(0.0)
– audio-visual	1	(1.7)	0	(0.0)
– university as a customer	5	(8.5)	3	(6.7)
– other	1	(1.7)	1	(2.2)

Variable	Science Park (n = 77)		Off-Park (n = 67)	
14. Has anyone from a Science Park ever visited surveyed NTBFs to discuss the HEI facilities? (e)				
– yes	28	(37.8)	7	(12.5)
15. Respondents in NTBFs received copies of the local HEI's newsletter (d)				
– yes	34	(46.6)	16	(26.7)
16. Number of patents or applications that have been taken out in the last twelve months – surveyed firms whose principal activity is software are excluded (f)				
– mean	1.4		1.1	
– median	0		0	
17. Number of copyrights or applications registered in the last twelve months by software houses (f)				
– mean	0.9		0.3	
– median	0		0	
18. Number of new products/services launched in the last two years to the existing customer base (f)				
– mean	10.2		3.1	
– median	2		2	
19. Number of new products/services launched in the last two years to new markets (f)				
– mean	2.3		2.2	
– median	1		1	
20. Number of sources of finance used in the last twelve months by independent firms (f)				
– mean	2.1		1.8	
– median	2		2	
21. Main source of finance used in the last twelve months by independent firms				
– personal savings	2	(4.7)	1	(2.2)
– profits from business	24	(55.8)	22	(48.9)
– loan/overdraft from clearing bank	8	(18.6)	16	(35.6)
– venture capital from clearing bank	1	(2.3)	0	(0.0)
– venture capital from other source	3	(7.0)	2	(4.4)
– loan from finance company	1	(2.3)	1	(2.2)
– finance from public agency	1	(2.3)	0	(0.0)
– sale of share capital	2	(4.7)	2	(4.4)
– other	1	(2.3)	1	(2.2)
22. Problems with access to finance served to restrict the growth of the independent surveyed firm (as distinct from merely aggravating existing cash-flow difficulties at any stage)				
– yes: in the first year	4	(7.8)	2	(3.8)
– yes: currently	6	(11.8)	3	(5.8)
– yes: at other time	2	(3.9)	5	(9.6)
– yes: continually	18	(35.3)	13	(25.0)
– no	21	(41.2)	29	(55.8)
23. Frequency of corporate planning				
– annual	19	(38.0)	24	(45.3)
– three year	21	(42.0)	13	(24.5)
– five year	4	(8.0)	5	(9.4)
– none	6	(12.0)	11	(20.8)
24. External organisations and individuals formally contacted during the last year (j)				
– central government/government departments	48	(25.8)	26	(24.5)
– local government/local authorities	6	(3.2)	3	(2.8)
– TECs	8	(4.3)	5	(4.7)
– enterprise agencies	6	(3.2)	6	(5.7)
– other public sector	2	(1.1)	1	(0.9)
– universities (HEIs)	16	(8.6)	7	(6.6)
– banks/financial institutions	21	(11.3)	12	(11.3)
– accountants	31	(16.7)	15	(14.2)
– solicitors	16	(8.6)	8	(7.5)
– consultants	12	(6.5)	14	(13.2)
– other private sector	13	(7.0)	6	(5.7)
– other sources	7	(3.8)	3	(2.8)
– **Total Mentions**	186		106	
– **Total Valid Cases**	62		43	

Variable	Science Park (n = 77)		Off-Park (n = 67)	
25. Reason for contacting external organisation and individuals during the last year (j)				
– professional advice	54	(29.0)	29	(27.1)
– advice – unspecified	4	(2.2)	4	(3.7)
– information – technical, technology, overseas trade, etc.	41	(22.0)	18	(16.8)
– training	10	(5.4)	6	(5.6)
– finance and grant application	43	(23.1)	29	(27.1)
– running a business/business and management development	10	(5.4)	12	(11.2)
– premises	5	(2.7)	1	(0.9)
– product design/development	12	(6.5)	5	(4.7)
– other	7	(3.8)	3	(2.8)
– **Total Mentions**	186		107	
– **Total Valid Cases**	62		43	
26. Paying the full market rent for premises (e)				
– yes	57	(78.1)	37	(72.5)
– no: paying less than for other comparable properties in the locality	4	(5.5)	11	(21.6)
– no: paying more than for other comparable properties in the locality	12	(16.4)	3	(5.9)
27. Surveyed firms thinking of moving to new or additional premises in the next two years (k)				
– new premises	28	(40.0)	16	(25.4)
– additional premises	12	(17.1)	10	(15.9)
– not moving	30	(42.9)	37	(58.7)
28. Location of new or additional premises (k)				
– this site	12	(34.3)	3	(12.0)
– less than 10 miles away	19	(54.3)	16	(64.0)
– elsewhere	4	(11.4)	6	(24.0)
29. Location of new or additional premises located on a Science Park (d)				
– yes	13	(43.3)	2	(10.5)

Notes:

(a) Seventy-seven surveyed Science Park firms were classified as new technology-based firms (NTBFs) compared with sixty-seven surveyed off-Park firms.

(b) All percentages in brackets relate to valid responding surveyed firms.

(c) Statistically significant difference was recorded between the two sample means at the 0.1 level of significance (two-tailed "t" test).

(d) Statistically significant difference was recorded between the two samples (χ^2 statistic significant at the 0.05 level of significance).

(e) Statistically significant difference was recorded between the two samples (χ^2 statistic significant at the 0.01 level of significance).

(f) No statistically significant difference was recorded between the two sample means (two-tailed "t" test at the 0.1 level of significance).

(g) Statistically significant difference was recorded between the two sample means at the 0.05 level of significance (two-tailed "t" test).

(h) One surveyed off-Park respondent stated "don't know".

(i) Fifty-nine surveyed Science Park firms identified a single most important link with the HEI compared with 45 off-Park firms.

(j) Percentage of all mentions.

(k) No statistically significant difference was recorded between the two samples (χ^2 statistic not significant at the 0.05 level of significance).

Table 16.1 also shows that NTBFs on and off Science Parks have generally obtained finance from two sources. Whilst a slightly larger proportion of Science Park firms indicated their main current source of finance was profits from the business (55.8 per cent compared with 48.9 per cent) more off-Park than Science Park NTBFs suggested a loan/overdraft from a clearing bank was the most important (18.6 per cent compared with 35.6 per cent). As found in Chapter 13, a larger proportion of Science Park NTBFs had obtained venture capital from a clearing bank (7.0 per cent compared with 4.4 per cent). However, a larger proportion of Science Park NTBFs complained that problems with access to finance had served to restrict their growth (58.8 per cent compared with 44.2 per cent). As noted in Chapter 13, this is a substantially higher figure than that reported in the authoritative study of the financing of United Kingdom small businesses presented by Aston Business School (1991).

Confirming the evidence presented in Chapter 14 the leading external organisation and individuals formally contacted during the last year by NTBFs were central government/government departments, accountants and banks and financial institutions. Similarly, the leading reasons for contacting external organisations and individuals were need of professional advice and finance and grant applications.

Row 26 of Table 16.1 shows significantly more off-Park NTBFs in leased or licensed accommodation felt they were paying less than for other comparable properties in the locality (5.5 per cent compared with 21.6 per cent). Conversely, more Science Park NTBFs felt they were paying more than for other comparable properties in the locality. For those seeking new or additional premises in the next two years a significantly larger proportion of Science Park NTBFs suggested they would be located on site (34.3 per cent compared with 12.0 per cent) as well as on a Science Park (43.3 per cent compared with 10.5 per cent).

With regard to firm performance, Table 16.2 indicates only one statistically significant difference was recorded between NTBFs located on and off Science Parks. It can be inferred from this table that Science Park NTBFs generally employed more males on a part-time basis. However, levels of sales turnover and turnover per total employee were found to be similar between NTBFs on and off Science Parks. Virtually two-thirds of surveyed firms in both groups were in profit, and they had spun out similar numbers of individuals who had established their own business. Finally, the ambitions of respondents were remarkably similar, with the notable exception being that a larger proportion of Science Park NTBFs wanted to "diversify into related areas".

16 CHARACTERISTICS OF NEW TECHNOLOGY-BASED FIRMS, FIRMS LOCATED ON MANAGED SCIENCE PARKS

Table 16.2   Performance and Size Contrasts between Surveyed Independent Single-plant New Technology-based Firms (NTBFs) Located On and Off Science Parks: Total Sample in 1992 (a) (b)

Variable	Science Park (n = 41)		Off-Park (n = 36)	
1. Total male full-time employment size in 1992 (c)				
– mean	12.0		15.9	
– median	6		9	
– sum	480		541	
2. Total male part-time employment size in 1992 (d)				
– mean	1.0		0.2	
– median	0		0	
– sum	24		7	
3. Total female full-time employment size in 1992 (c)				
– mean	6.4		6.7	
– median	2		2	
– sum	229		227	
4. Total female part-time employment size in 1992 (c)				
– mean	1.1		0.9	
– median	1		0	
– sum	33		32	
5. Total employment size in 1992 (c) (e)				
– mean	18.7		23.1	
– median	9		13	
– sum	767		832	
6. Level of sales turnover (£s) in 1990–91 (c)				
– mean	1,250,459		1,315,272	
– median	350,000		700,000	
7. Level of sales turnover (£s) in 1990–91 per total employee in 1992 (c)				
– mean	113,196		71,090	
– median	30,769		40,600	
8. Business made a net profit before tax during the financial year 1990–91 (f)	25	(64.1)	24	(68.6)
9. Employees left surveyed firm to establish their own business (f) (g)	17	(23.0)	25	(39.7)
10. Respondents current ambitions for the surveyed firm				
– maintain the business ownership and structure as at present	18	(45.0)	16	(45.7)
– expand the business by involving equity partners	9	(22.5)	7	(20.0)
– take the business to the USM or obtain a full listing	4	(10.0)	2	(5.7)
– sell out to another business	9	(22.5)	6	(17.1)
– retire from the business	2	(5.0)	5	(14.3)
– drive for acquisition of other businesses	4	(10.0)	6	(17.1)
– diversify into other, unrelated areas	4	(10.0)	5	(14.3)
– diversify into related areas	21	(52.5)	13	(37.1)
– other	6	(15.0)	10	(28.6)

Notes:

(a) Forty-one independent single-plant NTBFs were interviewed of which 36 firms were located on a Science Park and a further 36 firms were located off-Park.

(b) All percentages in brackets relate to valid responding surveyed firms.

(c) No statistically significant difference was recorded between the two sample means (two-tailed "t" test at the 0.1 level of significance).

(d) Statistically significant difference was recorded between the two sample means at the 0.05 level of significance (two-tailed "t" test).

(e) Male and female 1992 employment totals do not sum to the 1992 total employment value because some surveyed firms refused to provide a male/female breakdown.

(f) No statistically significant difference was recorded between the two samples (χ^2 statistic not significant at the 0.05 level of significance).

(g) Relates to the total sample of surveyed NTBFs – 74 surveyed Science Park firms compared with 63 surveyed off-Park firms.

The overall conclusion from the analysis is that an exclusive focus upon NTBFs, on and off Science Parks, adds little extra to our understanding derived from examining all Science Park firms. Perhaps this is only to be expected since the proportion of firms on Science Parks which are not NTBFs is small, and in any event they are "matched" against off-Park firms. Nevertheless, it is reassuring to have conducted the exercise and so be confident that the survey results can be considered relevant to NTBFs generally.

16.3 "Managed" and "non-managed" Science Parks

Monck et al. (1988) recognised that:

"An important distinguishing feature of Science Parks is the emphasis placed in the UK on the existence of a "management function which is actively engaged in the transfer of technology and business skills to the organisation on site" (UKSPA definition of a Science Park). Even so, the way in which this management function is discharged varies considerably between Science Parks. There are wide variations in the level of staffing to support the Science Park, the background of the personnel and the experience and duties which they are expected to perform" (p 186).

16.3.1 Introduction

These differences between Science Parks continue to exist today (Grayson, 1993, p 119). The purpose of this section is to explore the extent and the role of the management function on Science Parks and the impact which it had on firms in 1992. A distinction is made, with the support of UKSPA, between "managed" and "non-managed" Parks – the distinction being that a managed Science Park has a (generally full-time) manager on site whose principal task is to manage the Park. Using this definition the following Science Parks have been agreed by UKSPA as being "non-managed": Aberdeen, Aberystwyth, Cambridge, Highfields (Nottingham), Listerhills (Bradford) and Loughborough. The 1992 total Science Park sample includes 32 firms (27 per cent) located on "non-managed" Parks with a further 86 firms (73 per cent) on "managed" Parks.[9]

16.3.2 Differences between firms on "non-managed" and "managed" Science Parks

The total sample closure rates between "managed" and "non-managed" Science Parks are comparable.[10] Twenty organisations (35 per cent) on "non-managed" Parks had closed compared with 41 (37 per cent) organisations located on "managed" Parks.[11] However, this aggregate closure measure masks a significant difference between the two Park samples. It is interesting to note the total independent organisation closure rate was lower on the "non-managed" Parks (24 per cent compared with 33 per cent) but the subsidiary organisation closure rate was markedly higher on these same Parks (63 per cent compared with 48 per cent).[12,13] The reasons leading to these finer ownership level contrasts remains an area for additional research.

Table 16.3 reports Science Park tenants' responses on their use of facilities. It will be recalled there were approximately three times as many firms on "managed" as on "non-managed" Parks. Examining the total number of facilities mentioned it is clear that firms on "managed" Parks were more likely to mention the use of facilities than those on "non-managed" Parks. Second, the facilities used do seem to differ between the two groups. Those on "managed" Science Parks were much more likely to refer to the use of reception, telephone answering/message-taking and mail services than firms on "non-managed" Parks. The latter were much more likely to be using conference rooms, restaurants/cafeteria and building services.

Table 16.3 Science Park Facilities Made Use of Since Locating Here: Total Science Park Sample by Managed Park

Status use of Science Park facilities	Non-managed			Managed		
	Number of Mentions (a)	%	Mean Score	No of Mentions (a)	%	Mean Score
1. Reception	4	4.3	2.3	55	11.0	2.2
2. Telephone answering/message taking	4	4.3	2.5	34	6.8	2.9
3. Fax/telex	4	4.3	3.5	32	6.4	3.1
4. Photocopying	5	5.3	2.8	37	7.4	2.3
5. Secretarial/word processing	3	3.2	4.3	23	4.6	3.2
6. Mail service	6	6.4	2.3	54	10.8	2.1
7. Conference rooms	18	19.1	3.1	58	11.6	2.6
8. Audio-visual equipment	8	8.5	4.1	35	7.0	3.0(b)
9. Office cleaning	1	1.1	5.0	33	6.6	2.5
10. Restaurant/cafeteria	13	13.8	3.4	38	7.6	2.7
11. Building services: maintenance and installations	12	12.8	4.1	50	10.0	3.2
12. Business advice and planning	4	4.3	3.8	12	2.4	3.2
13. Financial advice	4	4.3	4.0	10	2.0	3.7
14. Finance	2	2.1	5.0	10	2.0	3.5
15. Training	3	3.2	3.3	10	2.0	3.4
16. Book-keeping services	3	3.2	4.3	8	1.6	3.9
Total	94	100.2		499	99.8	

Notes: (a) Importance of Science Park facility on a scale of 1 to 5, where 1 is "extremely important" and 5 is "unimportant".

(b) Statistically significant difference recorded between the two sample mean scores at the 0.05 level of significance (two-tailed "t" test).

More interesting, however, are the findings in Table 16.4. These report the responses of firms relating to the role played by the Science Park manager in the development of surveyed firms. The role played by the Science Park manager was examined with regard to the nine dimensions shown in the rows of the table. Firms were then asked to assess the value of this role.

A scoring system is employed, where a score of one was given when the respondent regarded this role as "essential", and a score of five was given when the respondent regarded this role as being "unimportant". Hence the *lower* the score the *greater* the value placed upon the contribution of the Science Park manager.

The central finding of the table is that the mean scores of managers on "managed" Science Parks were lower, in virtually all dimensions, than those of "non-managed" Science Parks. In this sense the role played by managers was identified, recognised and appreciated by tenant firms.

The table also provides a ranking of the value of the role of the Science Park manager for each of the nine dimensions. On "managed" Science Parks, the Park manager was clearly seen to be approachable and generally thought to run the Park efficiently. Nevertheless, the manager was regarded as being much more effective in responding to the property needs of the business than in either providing signposting facilities to sources of information or in providing a useful route to the HEI services/skills. Indeed, the firms on "managed" Science Parks actually rated this linkage to the HEI provided by the manager as weaker than the perception of firms about the linkage to "non-managed" Parks.

Table 16.4 Role Played by Science Park Manager/Director in the Development of Surveyed Science Park Firms: Total Science Park Sample by Managed Park Status (a)

Role played by Science Park manager in development	Non-managed			Managed		
	Mean Score	Median	Valid Cases	Mean Score	Median	Valid Cases
1. Accessibility: How easy is s/he to get to see?	3.3	3	27	2.0	1	77(b)
2. Approachability: How easy is s/he to talk to in person?	3.1	3	27	1.9	1	76(c)
3. How well informed is s/he on subjects of interest to your firm	3.7	4	27	2.9	3	73(d)
4. Does s/he run the science park efficiently, on the whole?	3.4	3	26	2.3	2	72(c)
5. Does s/he provide a useful route to the HEI's services/skills?	3.5	3	24	3.7	4	64
6. Does s/he provide a useful facility to sources of information?	3.7	4	25	3.2	3	70
7. Does s/he provide a useful range of services for companies on site?	4.2	5	25	2.9	3	72(b)
8. How effective has the management been in responding to your property needs?	3.4	3	28	2.5	2	77(d)
9. How involved has s/he been in discussing aspects of your business other than property requirements (e.g. business planning, research and development, marketing, etc.)	4.4	5	28	4.2	5	69

Notes: (a) Graded on a scale of 1 to 5, where 1 is "essential" and 5 is "unimportant".

(b) Statistically significant difference recorded between the two sample mean scores at the 0.001 level of significance (two-tailed "t" test).

(c) Statistically significant difference recorded between the two sample mean scores at the 0.01 level of significance (two-tailed "t" test).

(d) Statistically significant difference recorded between the two sample mean scores at the 0.05 level of significance (two-tailed "t" test).

Table 16.5 identifies nine aspects of the Science Park which might be important to the tenant firm. It then analyses the extent to which these aspects vary according to whether the business is on a "managed" or a "non-managed" Science Park.

Table 16.5   Which Aspects of Your Current Science Park Location Have Been of Most Use/Importance in Running Your Business?: Total Science Park Sample by Managed Park Status (a)

Aspects of location of most importance in running surveyed businesses	Non-managed Mean score	Median	Valid cases	Managed Mean	Median score	Valid cases
1. Prestige address	2.4	3	31	2.7	3	82
2. Management/business advice	4.6	5	31	4.2	5	75(b)
3. Secretarial/business support services	4.7	5	31	4.1	5	79(c)
4. The unit itself: its facilities and standard of finish	3.1	3	31	2.7	3	81(b)
5. Access to communal space (conference/ meeting rooms, restaurants, etc.)	3.9	4	31	3.1	3	80(d)
6. Access to HEI facilities	3.8	4	31	3.2	3	79(e)
7. Communal atmosphere	4.1	5	31	3.8	4	80
8. Possibilities for intertrading with other science park firms	3.8	4	31	3.5	4	79
9. Possibilities for expansion into additional/adjacent units	3.1	3	31	2.8	3	79

Notes: (a) Graded on a scale of 1 to 5, where 1 is "very good/high level of involvement" and 5 is "very bad/low level of involvement".

(b) Statistically significant difference recorded between the two sample mean scores at the 0.1 level of significance (two-tailed "t" test).

(c) Statistically significant difference recorded between the two sample mean scores at the 0.01 level of significance (two-tailed "t" test).

(d) Statistically significant difference recorded between the two sample mean scores at the 0.001 level of significance (two-tailed "t" test).

(e) Statistically significant difference recorded between the two sample mean scores at the 0.05 level of significance (two-tailed "t" test).

The prime perceived benefit of a Science Park location was seen to be its "prestige address". This is, in fact, of slightly greater importance to the tenant on the "non-managed" than on the "managed" Science Park. In all other aspects, however, the mean scores of firms on "managed" parks suggest they value "management" more highly. For example, firms on "managed" Science Parks are much more likely to value access to communal space and the provision of secretarial and business support services. It is also interesting to note that firms on "managed" Parks regarded the facilities and standard of finish on their own premises as being higher than those firms in "non-managed" Parks. No statistically significant differences emerge, however, in terms of "communal atmosphere", "possibilities for inter-trading with other Science Park firms", or "possibilities for expansion into additional/adjacent units".

Table 16.6 re-emphasises many of these points. It reports the most important benefits which respondents feel they receive from being located on a Science Park; it shows that amongst respondents on "non-managed" Parks the "prestige and overall image of site" was unquestionably the most important aspect, being mentioned on 53 per cent of occasions. Whilst the same benefit was also most frequently mentioned by respondents on "managed" Science Parks it received only 26 per cent of all mentions. It is interesting to note that respondents on "managed" Science Parks were much more likely to mention "friendly atmosphere among tenants/contact with other tenants" than those in "non-managed" Parks.

Moreover, through an open-ended question, respondents were asked to state perceived disbenefits of a Science Park location. Over 45 per cent of firms in "non-managed" and "managed" Parks indicated that their location was associated with a disbenefit (45.2 per cent compared with 50.6 per cent). Not surprisingly, during a period of recession when firms were seeking to cut fixed costs, the most frequently mentioned disbenefit surrounded the cost of premises and the service charge (47.4 per cent and 38.3 per cent of mentions reported by "non-managed" and "managed" Science Park respondents, respectively).

Table 16.6   Most Important Benefits Surveyed Firms Receive from Being Located on a Science Park (Number of Mentions): Total Science Park Sample by Managed Park Status

Science Park benefits	Non-managed		Managed	
	Number of Mentions	%	Number of Mentions	%
1. MD works at local HEI	0	6.0	1	0.6
2. Cost of premises	2	3.4	2	1.1
3. Access to facilities of HEI centre of research	4	6.9	16	9.1
4. Prestige and overall image of site	31	53.4	46	26.3
5. Quality of the property	2	3.4	8	4.6
6. Prestige of being linked to the HEI	0	0.0	5	2.9
7. Land adjacent to these premises available for expansion/flexible accommodation	0	0.0	7	4.0
8. Provision of on-site management and common services	1	1.7	21	12.0
9. Car parking facilities	5	8.6	17	9.7
10. Friendly atmosphere among tenants/contact with other tenants	1	1.7	13	7.4
11. Good transport and communication links	6	10.3	21	12.0
12. Access to markets	0	0.0	5	2.9
13. Proximity to firms in similar industrial sectors	1	1.7	1	0.6
14. Scope for attracting graduate HEI staff	1	1.7	2	1.1
15. Close to city centre	1	1.7	4	2.3
16. Finance available	0	0.0	1	0.6
17. Flexible leases	0	0.0	2	1.1
18. Other	3	5.2	3	1.7
Total	58	99.7	175	100.0

Table 16.7 analyses the performance and size of independent single plant firms according to whether they were located on "managed" or "non-managed" Science Parks. It shows firms on "non-managed" Parks were generally larger in terms of employment than those on "managed" Parks. There is no evidence, however, of statistically significant differences in reported levels of sales turnover or profitability for the two groups of firms during the financial year 1990–91.

Table 16.7 Performance and Size Contrasts between Surveyed Independent Single-plant Science Park Firms by Managed Park Status: Total Sample in 1992 (a) (b)

Variable	Non-Managed (n = 16)		Managed (n = 51)	
1. Total male full-time employment size in 1992 (c)				
– mean	19.5		6.4	
– median	8		4	
– sum	292		314	
2. Total male part-time employment size in 1992 (d)				
– mean	0.3		1.4	
– median	0		1	
– sum	3		37	
3. Total female full-time employment size in 1992 (e)				
– mean	6.5		5.1	
– median	3		1	
– sum	91		204	
4. Total female part-time employment size in 1992 (f)				
– mean	0.6		1.4	
– median	0		1	
– sum	9		47	
5. Total employment size in 1992 (c) (g)				
– mean	30.5		11.8	
– median	12		6	
– sum	488		603	
6. Level of sales turnover (£s) in 1990–91 (e)				
– mean	1,965,067		641,319	
– median	500,000		250,000	
7. Level of sales turnover (£s) in 1990–91 per total employee in 1992 (e)				
– mean	50,091		93,934	
– median	46,875		30,000	
8. Business made a net profit before tax during the financial year 1990–91 (h)	12	(75.0)	30	(61.2)
9. Employees left surveyed firm to establish their own business (h) (i)	11	(36.7)	17	(20.2)
10. Respondents' current ambitions for the surveyed firm				
– maintain the business ownership and structure as at present	8	(50.0)	23	(46.0)
– expand the business by involving equity partners	5	(31.3)	8	(16.0)
– take the business to the USM or obtain a full listing	1	(6.3)	3	(6.0)
– sell out to another business	3	(18.8)	9	(18.0)
– retire from the business	0	(0.0)	3	(6.0)
– drive for acquisition of other businesses	2	(12.5)	5	(10.0)
– diversify into other, unrelated areas	1	(6.3)	5	(10.0)
– diversify into related areas	4	(25.0)	29	(58.0)
– other	0	(0.0)	8	(16.0)

Notes:

(a)   Sixteen independent single-plant firms were interviewed on "non-managed" Science Parks compared with 51 firms interviewed on "managed" Science Parks.

(b)   All percentages in brackets relate to valid responding surveyed firms.

(c)   Statistically significant difference recorded between the two sample means at the 0.1 level of significance (two-tailed "t" test).

(d)   Statistically significant differences recorded between the two sample means at the 0.01 level of significance (two-tailed "t" test).

(e)   No statistically significant difference was recorded between the two sample means (two-tailed "t" test at the 0.1 level of significance).

(f)   Statistically significant difference recorded between the two sample means at the 0.05 level of significance (two-tailed "t" test).

(g)   Male and female 1992 employment totals do not sum to the 1992 total employment value because some surveyed firms refused to provide a male/female breakdown.

(h)   No statistically significant difference was recorded between the two samples (χ^2 statistic not significant at the 0.05 level of significance).

(i)   Relates to the total sample of surveyed firms – 30 surveyed "non-managed" Science Park firms compared with 84 surveyed "managed" Science Park firms.

Very slight differences appear in row 10 of the table, suggesting firms on the "managed" Science Parks were more likely to be seeking diversification than those on the "non-managed" Parks.

More detailed examination of the differences between all surveyed firms on Science Parks is shown in Table 16.8. It compares the 86 firms from "managed" Science Parks with the 32 firms on "non-managed" Parks. Several interesting differences emerge. Analysis of data in row 1 suggests firms on "non-managed" Parks were significantly older than those on "managed" Parks. Row 3 shows firms on "non-managed" Parks were more likely to be currently earning income from manufactured products. This is emphasised in row 4 which shows that 37.5 per cent of firms in "non-managed" Science Parks had manufactured products as their single most important source of income, compared with only 11.6 per cent of firms on "managed" Parks.

Table 16.8   Differences Between Surveyed Science Park Firms by Managed Park Status: Total Sample in 1992 (a) (b) (c)

Variable	Non-Managed (n = 32)		Managed (n = 86)	
1. Current age of the business (years) (d)				
– mean	14.9		9.4	
– median	12		7	
2. Legal status of surveyed business				
– public company quoted in the UK	4	(12.5)	1	(1.2)
– public company quoted abroad	2	(6.3)	4	(4.7)
– non-quoted public company	1	(3.1)	1	(1.2)
– private limited company	22	(68.8)	64	(74.4)
– partnership	2	(6.3)	6	(7.0)
– sole proprietorship	1	(3.1)	3	(3.5)
– other	0	(0.0)	7	(8.1)
3. Business currently earning income from manufactured products (e)	15	(46.9)	17	(19.8)
4. Single most important activity as a source of income				
– manufactured products	12	(37.5)	10	(11.6)
– software (standard packages)	7	(21.9)	11	(12.8)
– bespoke software	2	(6.3)	6	(7.0)
– consultancy work	4	(12.5)	20	(23.3)
– contract research	2	(6.3)	8	(9.3)
– contract design work	0	(0.0)	7	(8.1)
– sub-contract production work	0	(0.0)	0	(0.0)
– testing/analysis	0	(0.0)	5	(5.8)
– licence income	2	(6.3)	2	(2.3)
– training	1	(3.1)	4	(4.7)
– other	2	(6.3)	13	(15.1)
5. Surveyed firm currently located on a government designated "assisted" area (e)	5	(15.6)	54	(65.1)
6. Surveyed firm currently located in the "north" (f)	20	(62.5)	62	(72.1)
7. Percentage of total income that comes from manufactured and/or standard software products (g)				
– mean	71.8		58.3	
– median	75		70	
8. Percentage of total output (by value) that goes to the three largest customers (h)				
– mean	36.5		50.1	
– median	30		50	
9. Uniqueness of any service which the surveyed firms provide (i)				
– based on "leading edge" knowledge	13	(43.3)	46	(56.8)
– knowledge new to the UK	1	(3.3)	9	(11.1)
– not available elsewhere in region	5	(16.7)	16	(19.8)
– standard service	11	(36.7)	10	(12.3)
10. Percentage of qualified scientists and engineers (QSEs) employed in R & D (g)				
– mean	26.4		30.2	
– median	15.8		20.0	
11. Total R & D expenditure per year (£s) (g)				
– mean	418,125		260,626	
– median	95,000		20,000	

Variable	Non-Managed (n = 32)		Managed (n = 86)	
12. R & D expenditure as a percentage of total turnover (g)				
– mean	14.0		20.6	
– median	6		8	
13. Firms recording a "link" with the local university, polytechnic or institute of higher education (HEI) (f)	30	(93.7)	77	(89.5)
14. Single most important link with HEI (j)				
– informal contact with academics	8	(28.6)	9	(14.3)
– employment of academics on a part-time consultancy basis	0	(0.0)	10	(15.9)
– sponsor research trials or projects	2	(7.1)	2	(3.2)
– access to specialist equipment	1	(3.6)	6	(9.5)
– test/analysis in HEI	0	(0.0)	1	(1.6)
– student projects	0	(0.0	3	(4.8)
– employment of recent graduates	5	(17.9)	7	(11.1)
– training by HEI	1	(3.6)	1	(1.6)
– other formal links	1	(3.6)	1	(1.6)
– library facilities	2	(7.1)	11	(17.5)
– recreation	1	(3.6)	0	(0.0)
– conferences	1	(3.6)	2	(3.2)
– dining	1	(3.6)	1	(1.6)
– audio-visual	0	(0.0)	1	(1.6)
– university as a customer	5	(17.9)	7	(11.1)
– other	0	(0.0)	1	(1.6)
15. Respondent attend technical seminars at the local HEI (h)				
– yes	17	(94.4)	32	(64.0)
16. Number of patents or applications that have been taken out in the last twelve months – surveyed firms whose principal activity is software are excluded (g)				
– mean	2.0		0.7	
– median	0		0	
17. Number of copyrights or applications registered in the last twelve months by software houses (g)				
– mean	0.4		0.8	
– median	0		0	
18. Number of new products/services launched in the last two years to the existing customer base (g)				
– mean	6.1		9.3	
– median	2		1	
19. Number of new products/services launched in the last two years to new markets (g)				
– mean	2.8		1.9	
– median	1		1	
20. Number of sources of finance used in the last twelve months by independent firms (g)				
– mean	1.7		2.0	
– median	1		2	
21. Main source of finance used in the last twelve months by independent firms				
– personal savings	0	(0.0)	4	(8.0)
– profits from business	9	(52.9)	29	(58.0)
– loan/overdraft from clearing bank	3	(17.6)	11	(22.0)
– venture capital from clearing bank	0	(0.0)	1	(2.0)
– venture capital from other source	4	(23.5)	0	(0.0)
– finance from public agency	0	(0.0)	1	(2.0)
– sale of share capital	1	(5.9)	1	(2.0)
– other	0	(0.0)	3	(6.0)
22. Problems with access to finance served to restrict the growth of the independent surveyed firm (as distinct from merely aggravating existing cash-flow difficulties at any stage)				
– yes: in the first year	1	(5.3)	4	(6.7)
– yes: currently	5	(26.3)	6	(10.0)
– yes: at other time	0	(0.0)	2	(3.3)
– yes: continually	3	(15.8)	17	(28.3)
– no:	10	(52.6)	31	(51.7)

Variable	Non-Managed (n = 32)		Managed (n = 86)	
23. Frequency of corporate planning				
– annual	7	(36.8)	27	(45.8)
– three year	6	(31.6)	16	(27.1)
– five year	2	(0.0)	6	(10.2)
– none	4	(21.1)	10	(16.9)
24. External organisations and individuals formally contacted during the last year (k)				
– central government/government departments	19	(25.7)	43	(24.3)
– local government/local authorities	3	(4.0)	4	(2.3)
– TECs	3	(4.0)	8	(4.5)
– enterprise agencies	3	(4.0)	4	(2.3)
– other public sector	0	(0.0)	1	(0.6)
– other training organisations	1	(1.4)	0	(0.0)
– universities (HEIs)	9	(12.2)	12	(6.8)
– banks/financial institutions	9	(12.2)	21	(11.9)
– accountants	10	(13.5)	34	(19.2)
– solicitors	5	(6.8)	16	(19.0)
– consultants	4	(5.4)	17	(19.6)
– other private sector	5	(6.8)	9	(5.1)
– other sources	3	(4.0)	8	(4.5)
– **Total Mentions**	74		177	
– **Total Valid Cases**	26		57	
25. Reason for contacting external organisation and individuals during the last year (k)				
– professional advice	22	(29.7)	54	(30.5)
– advice: unspecified	3	(4.1)	4	(2.3)
– information: technical, technology, overseas trade, etc.	20	(27.0)	37	(20.9)
– training	4	(5.4)	11	(6.2)
– finance and grant application	15	(20.3)	50	(28.2)
– running a business/business and management development	4	(5.4)	6	3.4)
– premises	0	(0.0)	4	(2.3)
– product design/development	1	(1.4)	8	(4.5)
– other	5	(6.8)	3	(1.7)
– **Total Mentions**	74		177	
– **Total Valid Cases**	26		67	
26. Paying the full market rent for premises				
– yes	22	(78.6)	63	(75.9)
– no: paying less than for other comparable properties in the locality	3	(10.7)	6	(7.2)
– no: paying more than for the other comparable properties in the locality	3	(10.7)	14	(16.9)
27. Surveyed firms thinking of moving to new or additional premises in the next two years (f)				
– new premises	11	(42.3)	30	(39.0)
– additional premises	1	(3.8)	14	(18.2)
– not moving	14	(53.8)	33	(42.9)
28. Location of new or additional premises				
– this site	1	(9.1)	13	(34.2)
– less than 10 miles away	8	(72.7)	19	(50.0)
– elsewhere	2	(18.2)	6	(15.8)

Notes:

(a) In 1986 firms surveyed on the Bolton and Leeds Science Parks were regarded by UKSPA as being valid Science Park firms. However, in 1992 these two locations were not regarded by UKSPA as being valid Science Parks. The four follow-on interviews conducted in 1992 in Bolton and Leeds were consequently excluded from the following analysis. A further eight interviewed firms which were located on UKSPA defined Science Parks in 1986 (as well as 1992) but had subsequently moved off-Park also excluded.

(b) UKSPA defined a "managed" Science Park as being a Park with a manager on site whose principal task is to manage the Park. Using this definition the following Science Parks were classified by UKSPA as being "non-managed": Aberdeen, Aberystwyth, Cambridge, Highfields (Nottingham), Listerhills (Bradford) and Loughborough. The 1992 total valid Science Park sample includes 32 firms (27 per cent) located on "non-managed" Parks with a further 86 firms (73 per cent) positioned on "managed" Parks.

(c) All percentages in brackets relate to valid responding surveyed firms.

(d) Statistically significant difference was recorded between the two sample means at the 0.1 level of significance (two-tailed "t" test).

(e) Statistically significant difference was recorded between the two samples (χ^2 statistically significant at the 0.01 level of significance).

(f) No statistically significant difference was recorded between the two samples (χ^2 statistic not significant at the 0.05 level of significance).

16 CHARACTERISTICS OF NEW TECHNOLOGY-BASED FIRMS, FIRMS LOCATED ON MANAGED SCIENCE PARKS

(g) No statistically significant difference was recorded between the two sample means (two-tailed "t" test).

(h) Statistically significant difference was recorded between the two means at the 0.05 level of significance (two-tailed "t" test).

(i) Statistically significant difference was recorded between the two samples (χ^2 statistic significant at the 0.05 level of significance).

(j) Twenty-eight surveyed "non-managed" Science Park firms identified a single most important link with the HEI compared with 63 surveyed "managed" Park firms.

(k) Percentage of all mentions.

Interesting differences also emerge on location. Only 15 per cent of firms in "non-managed" Science Parks were in "assisted" areas, with this being significantly less than the 65 per cent which were in "managed" Parks. However, there is no difference between the two groups in terms of whether or not they were located in the "north".

Rows 9–12 of the table do not suggest significant differences between "managed" and "non-managed" Parks in terms of the technological sophistication of firms or their links with their local HEI (rows 13 and 14).

However, the finding on row 15, that firms on "non-managed" Parks were significantly more likely to have attended technical seminars at the local HEI might be thought to be unexpected. We have already observed in Table 16.4 that the aspects in which Science Park managers were deemed to be weakest amongst tenants on "managed" Science Parks was in their ability to foster good links with the local HEI. The result in row 15 of this table, therefore, seems to re-emphasise this point.

Rows 16–20 of the table do not point to any differences in terms of patents, copyrights and new products launched by firms according to whether or not they were located on a "managed" Science Park. It is also difficult to identify differences in forms of financing, contact with external organisations or in premises requirements.

16.4 Fast growing businesses

16.4.1 Introduction

Section 4.5.2 examined employment change recorded in independent single-plant firms in the follow-on study. Tables 4.29 and 4.30 show a small number of firms provided the bulk of employment increases amongst surviving firms between 1986 and 1992. Amongst Science Park firms the five fastest growing firms generated 216 gross new jobs (69 per cent of total gross new jobs), whilst the five fastest growing off-Park firms generated 222 gross new jobs (93 per cent of total gross new jobs).

This section examines the characteristics of these fast growing businesses. The criterion used is that of the largest absolute employment change between 1986 and 1992. The five businesses which grew fastest, according to this criterion, are then compared with two other groups: the first comprises businesses which increased their employment between 1986 and 1992, and the second businesses which experienced either no change or declines in employment.

For descriptive purposes the fastest growing 5 firms are described as "fast growers"; the 27 firms which experienced increases in employment are defined as "growers"; and the remaining 15 firms are defined as "others".

16.4.2 The characteristics of the fast growers

Table 16.9 shows the characteristics of the five independent single-plant firms which grew most rapidly in terms of gross employment between 1986 and 1992. The final column of the table indicates the absolute employment change in the five firms. The fastest growing firm added 170 jobs over this six-year period, and the fifth firm added 22 jobs. The penultimate column shows that, in 1986, all five firms employed between 10 and 20 workers. Their growth over this six-year period varies, therefore, from striking to remarkable.

Turning now to the characteristics of the business, Table 16.9 shows four out of the five firms were, in 1986, located on a Science Park. The businesses were between 8 and 17-years-old at the time of this survey and three out of the five earned income from manufactured products.

Table 16.9 Characteristics of the Five Fastest Employment Growing Surveyed Independent Single-plant Firms: Follow on Survey Coverage

Firm	Location in 1986 on a science park	Currently located on a "managed" science park	Current age of business (years)	Business currently earning income from manufactured products	Single most important activity as a current source of income	Currently located in a government designated "assisted" area	Currently located in the "north"	Total employment size in 1992	Total employment size in 1986	Absolute employment change, 1986–92
A	No	–	8	Yes	Sub-contract production work	No	No	190	20	170
B	Yes	No	–	Yes	Manufactured products	No	No	95	17	78
C	Yes	No	10	Yes	Licence income	No	No	93	18	75
D	Yes	No	9	No	Software (standard packages)	No	Yes	32	10	22
E	Yes	Yes	17	No	Contract design work	No	No	38	16	22

Probably the most striking finding was that none of the five were located in an "assisted" area and four out of the five were located in the "south" of England.

Table 16.10 presents 16 measures of the performance of firms in this survey. These measures are then used to compare the performance of the five "fastest growers" (in terms of employment), the 27 "growing" businesses and the 15 "other" businesses. This information is shown in the three columns of the table.

Rows 1 and 2 of the table indicate that, whilst the total employment size of the "fast growers" in 1986 was not statistically significantly different from all other firms in the survey at that time, the two differ markedly in 1992. The median current employment size of the "fast growers" is 93, that of the "growers" is 12, and that of the "others" is 7.

The significance of the employment growth in the "fast growers" is shown in row 3 of the table where it can be seen that the five "fastest growers" added 367 jobs, the "growers" added 185 jobs and the "others" shed a total of 95 jobs. This serves again to emphasise that employment generation was extremely heavily concentrated, amongst small firms, in a few enterprises.

Table 16.10   Performance and Size Contrasts between Surveyed Independent Single-plant Firms by Absolute Employment Change Categories: Follow-on Survey Coverage (a) (b) (c)

Variable	Five fastest growers (n = 5)	Growers (n = 27)	Other (n = 15)
1. Total employment size in 1992 (d)			
– mean	89.6	17.3	6.5
– median	93	12	7
– sum	448	467	98
2. Total employment size in 1986 (e)			
– mean	16.2	10.4	12.9
– median	17	6	8
– sum	81	282	193
3. Absolute employment change, 1986–92 (d)			
– mean	73.4	6.9	–6.3
– median	75	6	–2
– sum	367	185	–95
4. Total male full-time employment size in 1992 (d)			
– mean	55.0	12.6	3.3
– median	42	8	3
– sum	220	340	50
5. Total male part-time employment size in 1992 (e)			
– mean	0.0	0.8	0.2
– median	0	0	0
– sum	0	21	3
6. Total female full-time employment size in 1992 (d)			
– mean	36.0	3.5	1.5
– median	33	2	1
– sum	144	94	22
7. Total female part-time employment size in 1992 (f)			
– mean	0.3	0.4	1.5
– median	0	0	1
– sum	1	11	23
8. Level of sales turnover (£s) in 1985–86 (e)			
– mean	296,750	350,200	177,929
– median	200,000	125,000	120,000
9. Level of sales turnover (£s) in 1990–91 (g)			
– mean	3,770,000	922,719	266,833
– median	1,550,000	384,971	200,000
10. Absolute sales turnover (£s) change since 1986 (h)			
– mean	1,415,750	613,086	112,364
– median	1,401,500	300,000	80,000
11. Level of sales turnover (£s) in 1990–91 per total employee in 1992 (e)			
– mean	47,024	43,285	70,931
– median	31,597	37,500	34,286
12. Business made a net profit before tax during the financial year 1990–91	3 (60.0)	21 (77.8)	9 (60.0)
13. Employees left surveyed firm to establish their own business	2 (40.0)	5 (19.2)	3 (20.0)
14. Respondents' current ambitions for the surveyed firm – maintain the business ownership and structure as at present	2 (40.0)	15 (55.6)	5 (38.5)
– expand the business by involving equity partners	1 (20.0)	2 (7.4)	3 (23.1)
– take the business to the USM or obtain a full listing	1 (20.0)	0 (0.0)	1 (7.7)
– sell out to another business	1 (20.0)	5 (18.5)	7 (53.8)
– retire from the business	0 (0.0)	0 (0.0)	4 (30.8)
– drive for acquisition of other businesses	1 (20.0)	2 (7.4)	0 (0.0)
– diversify into other, unrelated areas	0 (0.0)	2 (7.4)	1 (7.7)
– diversify into related areas	0 (0.0)	8 (29.6)	4 (30.8)
– other	2 (40.0)	4 (14.8)	1(7.7)
15. Respondents believe that the surveyed business would grow in employment size in the future			
– no change	1 (25.0)	2 (8.3)	4 (28.6)
– increase	3 (75.0)	22 (91.7)	10 (71.4)
16. Respondents believe that the surveyed business would grow its sales turnover in the future			
– no change	0 (0.0)	1 (4.5)	2 (14.3)
– increase	4 (100.0)	21 (95.5)	12 (85.7)

Notes:

(a) Fifty-nine independent single-plant firms were interviewed of which 28 firms were located on a Science Park compared with 31 firms located off-Park. Employment change data was available for 47 surveyed firms (80 per cent). A larger proportion of surveyed Science Park firms provided employment change data (25 firms: 89 per cent compared with 27 firms: 71 per cent.).

(b) All percentages in brackets relate to valid responding surveyed firms.

(c) Male and female 1992 employment totals do not sum to the 1992 total employment value for the "five fastest growers" and "growers" because some surveyed firms refused to provide a male/female breakdown.

(d) Statistically significant difference was recorded between the three samples (analysis of variance – "F" test – 0.001 level of significance).

(e) No statistically significant difference was recorded between the three samples (analysis of variance – "F" test).

(f) Statistically significant difference was recorded between the three samples (analysis of variance – "F" test – 0.1 level of significance).

(g) Statistically significant difference was recorded between the three samples (analysis of variance – "F" test – 0.01 level of significance).

(h) Statistically significant difference was recorded between the three samples (analysis of variance – "F" test – 0.05 level of significance).

An alternative measure of performance is to compare the sales turnovers of these groups of firms. Row 8 of the table shows there was no statistically significant difference in sales turnover between the three groups of firms in 1985–86, but that the median sales turnover of the "fast growers" in 1990–91 was virtually four times that of the "growers", and seven times that of the "others".

However, it is interesting to note in row 11 of the table that the median level of sales turnover per employee in 1990–91 in the "growers" was slightly below that of both the other groups, although no statistically significant difference is identified. This suggests growth in terms of employment was more rapid than sales growth for those firms which we define as "fast growers".

A number of other indicators of performance are shown in the table, but these do not illustrate major differences between the groups.

Since there are relatively few firms which experience rapid employment growth – five in our sample – it is difficult to conduct appropriate statistical tests of the respects in which these types of firm differ from the other firms in the sample. Nevertheless, Table 16.11 presents 30 dimensions or areas of possible difference between the 5 "fastest growers", the 27 "growers" and the 15 "other" firms. Row 1 of the table indicates four of the five "fast growers" were located on a Science Park, compared with only three of the fifteen "other" firms which experienced either no growth in employment or job-shedding. This does provide some "soft" evidence that firms located on Science Parks in 1986 were more likely, if they survived, to experience employment growth than off-Park firms.

A consistent finding from research in this area is that younger small businesses are more likely to grow (and to close) than the older firms. Row 2 of the table, however, shows there is no statistically significant difference between the ages of the firms placed in the three performance categories. Differences in employment growth cannot, therefore, be clearly attributed to firm age, or to legal status as shown in row 3.

Rows 4 and 5 suggest the sectoral composition of the three groups of firms do not differ markedly, but rows 6 and 7 suggest location is an important factor. As was pointed out in Table 16.9, the fast growing businesses are heavily concentrated in the "south" of England and none are located in an "assisted" area.

Table 16.11   Absolute Employment Change Category Characteristics: Follow-on Survey Coverage in Surveyed Independent Single-plant Firms (a) (b)

Variable	Five fastest growers (n = 5)		Growers (n = 27)		Other (n = 15)	
1. Surveyed firm in 1986 on a Science Park	4		18		3	
2. Current age of the business (years) (c)						
– mean	11.0		10.7		12.2	
– median	9.5		10.0		10.0	
3. Legal status of surveyed business						
– public company quoted in the UK	1	(20.0)	1	(3.7)	0	(0.0)
– private limited company	4	(80.0)	22	(81.5)	12	(80.0)
– partnership	0	(0.0)	2	(7.4)	1	(6.7)
– sole proprietorship	0	(0.0)	2	(7.4)	2	(13.3)
4. Business currently earning income from manufactured products	3	(60.0)	12	(44.4)	6	(40.0)
5. Single most important activity as a source of income						
– manufactured products	1	(20.0)	11	(40.7)	4	(26.7)
– software (standard packages)	1	(20.0)	8	(29.6)	0	(0.0)
– bespoke software	0	(0.0)	1	(3.7)	0	(0.0)
– consultancy work	0	(0.0)	3	(11.1)	41	(26.7)
– contract research	0	(0.0)	0	(0.0)	1	(6.7)
– contract design work	1	(20.0)	0	(0.0)	1	(6.7)
– sub-contract production work	1	(20.0)	0	(0.0)	2	(13.3)
– testing/analysis	0	(0.0)	2	(7.4)	1	(6.7)
– licence income	1	(20.0)	0	(0.0)	0	(0.0)
– training	0	(0.0)	0	(0.0)	1	(6.7)
– other	0	(0.0)	2	(7.4)	1	(6.7)
6. Surveyed firm currently located on a government designated "assisted" area	0	(0.0)	9	(33.3)	7	(46.7)
7. Surveyed firm currently located in the "north"	1	(20.0)	17	(63.0)	10	(66.7)
8. For surveyed Science Park firms are they located on a "managed" Science Park (d)	1	(25.0)	9	(56.3)	3	(100.0)
9. Engaged in merger/takeover since 1986 (e)	1	(20.0)	2	(7.4)	0	(0.0)
10. Percentage of total income that comes from manufactured and/or standard software products (c)						
– mean	77.3		69.0		67.7	
– median	85		75		80	
11. Percentage of total output (by value) that goes to the three largest customers (c)						
– mean	41.0		40.3		53.2	
– median	30		33		60	
12. Percentage of qualified scientists and engineers (QSEs) employed in R & D (c)						
– mean	12.3		32.8		19.2	
– median	10.5		28.6		8.3	
13. Total R & D expenditure per year (£s) (f)						
– mean	375,000		98,545		27,875	
– median	250,000		40,000		1,500	
14. R & D expenditure as a percentage of total turnover (c)						
– mean	10.8		17.1		23.6	
– median	7		15		10	
15. Firms recording a "link" with the local university, polytechnic or institute of higher education (HEI)	4	(80.0)	23	(85.2)	12	(80.0)
16. Single most important link with HEI (g)						
– informal contact with academics	0	(0.0)	7	(35.0)	5	(45.5)
– employment of academics on a part-time consultancy basis	0	(0.0)	0	(0.0)	1	(9.1)
– sponsor research trials or projects	1	(33.3)	0	(0.0)	0	(0.0)
– employment of recent graduates	1	(33.3)	4	(20.0)	1	(9.1)
– use of library facilities	0	(0.0)	3	(15.0)	1	(9.1)
– use of conference facilities	0	(0.0)	1	(5.0)	0	(0.0)
– use of dining facilities	0	(0.0)	1	(5.0)	0	(0.0)
– use of audio-visual facilities	0	(0.0)	1	(5.0)	0	(0.0)
– university as a customer	1	(33.3)	1	(5.0)	3	(27.3)
– other	0	(0.0)	2	(10.0)	0	(0.0)

Variable	Five fastest growers (n = 5)		Growers (n = 27)		Other (n = 15)	
17. Number of patents or applications that have been taken out in the last twelve months – surveyed firms whose principal activity is software are excluded (c)						
– mean	1.0		0.4		1.0	
– median	0		0		0	
18. Number of copyrights or applications registered in the last twelve months by software houses (c)						
– mean	0.0		1.1		1.0	
– median	0		0		0	
19. Number of new products/services launched in the last two years to the existing customer base (c)						
– mean	1.8		4.8		1.6	
– median	2		3		2	
20. Number of new products/services launched in the last two years to new markets (h)						
– mean	2.0		3.8		1.1	
– median	1		3		0	
21. Number of sources of finance used in the last twelve months (c)						
– mean	1.8		1.8		2.1	
– median	2		2		2	
22. Main source of finance used in the last twelve months						
– personal savings	0	(0.0)	0	(0.0)	2	(15.4)
– profits from business	2	(50.0)	15	(65.2)	8	(61.5)
– loan/overdraft from clearing bank	1	(25.0)	5	(21.7)	3	(23.1)
– venture capital from other source	1	(25.0)	1	(4.3)	0	(0.0)
– sale of share capital	0	(0.0)	1	(4.3)	0	(0.0)
– other	0	(0.0)	1	(4.3)	0	(0.0)
23. Problems with access to finance served to restrict the growth of the firm (as distinct from merely aggravating existing cash-flow difficulties at any stage)						
– yes: in the first year	0	(0.0)	1	(3.7)	0	(0.0)
– yes: currently	1	(20.0)	2	(7.4)	0	(0.0)
– yes: continually	1	(20.0)	9	(33.3)	7	(46.7)
– no	3	(60.0)	15	(55.6)	8	(53.3)
24. Clearing bank where the main business account is held						
– Bank of Wales	0	(0.0)	1	(4.2)	0	(0.0)
– Barclays	3	(60.0)	7	(29.2)	1	(7.1)
– Lloyds	0	(0.0)	5	(20.8)	3	(21.4)
– Midland	1	(20.0)	4	(16.7)	0	(0.0)
– NatWest	0	(0.0)	7	(29.2)	9	(64.3)
– Royal Bank of Scotland	1	(20.0)	0	(0.0)	0	(0.0)
– Yorkshire	0	(0.0)	0	(0.0)	1	(7.1)
25. Frequency of corporate planning						
– annual	3	(60.0)	12	(44.4)	5	(33.3)
– three year	2	(40.0)	6	(22.2)	0	(0.0)
– five year	0	(0.0)	1	(3.7)	2	(13.3)
– none	0	(0.0)	8	(29.6)	8	(53.3)
26. External organisations and individuals formally contacted during the last year (i)						
– central government/government departments	3	(27.3)	17	(29.8)	11	(35.5)
– local government/local authorities	0	(0.0)	2	(3.5)	3	(9.7)
– TECs	1	(9.1)	1	(1.8)	1	(3.2)
– enterprise agencies	0	(0.0)	0.	(0.0)	3	(9.7)
– universities (HEIs)	1	(9.1)	5	(8.8)	2	(6.5)
– banks/financial institutions	1	(9.1)	8	(14.0)	3	(9.7)
– accountants	4	(36.4)	11	(19.3)	3	(9.7)
– solicitors	1	(9.1)	3	(5.3)	3	(9.7)
– consultants	0	(0.0)	5	(8.8)	2	(6.5)
– other private sector	0	(0.0)	3	(5.3)	0	(0.0)
– other sources	0	(0.0)	2	(3.5)	0	(0.0)
– **Total Mentions**	11		57		31	
– **Total Valid Cases**	4		23		13	

16 CHARACTERISTICS OF NEW TECHNOLOGY-BASED FIRMS,
FIRMS LOCATED ON MANAGED SCIENCE PARKS

Variable	Five fastest growers (n = 5)		Growers (n = 27)		Other (n = 15)	
27. Reason for contacting external organisation and individuals during the last year (i)						
– professional advice	2	(18.2)	19	(33.3)	5	(16.1)
– advice: unspecified	0	(0.0)	5	(8.8)	2	(6.5)
– information: technical, technology, overseas trade, etc.	1	(9.1)	9	(15.8)	9	(29.0)
– training	4	(36.4)	0	(0.0)	0	(0.0)
– finance and grant application	3	(27.3)	15	(26.3)	13	(41.9)
– running a business/business and management development	0	(0.0)	4	(7.0)	1	(3.2)
– premises	0	(0.0)	1	(1.8)	0	(0.0)
– product design/development	0	(0.0)	4	(7.0)	1	(3.2)
– other	1	(9.1)	0	(0.0)	0	(0.0)
– **Total Mentions**	11		57		31	
– **Total Valid Cases**	4		23		13	
28. Paying the full market rent for premises						
– yes	5	(100.0)	23	(92.0)	10	(83.3)
– no – paying less than for other comparable properties in the locality	0	(0.0)	2	(8.0)	2	(16.7)
29. Surveyed firms thinking of moving to new or additional premises in the next two years						
– new premises	2	(66.7)	7	(26.9)	2	(16.7)
– additional premises	0	(0.0)	2	(7.7)	1	(8.3)
– not moving	1	(33.3)	17	(65.4)	9	(75.0)
30. Location of new or additional premises						
– this site	1	(50.0)	3	(37.5)	0	(0.0)
– less than 10 miles away	1	(50.0)	3	(37.5)	3	(100.0)
– elsewhere	0	(0.0)	2	(25.0)	0	(0.0)

Notes:

(a) Fifty-nine independent single-plant firms were interviewed of which 28 firms were located on a Science Park compared with 31 firms located off-Park. Employment change data was available for 47 surveyed firms (80 per cent). A larger proportion of surveyed Science Park firms provided employment change data (25 firms: 89 per cent compared with 22 firms: 71 per cent).

(b) All percentages in brackets relate to valid responding surveyed firms.

(c) No statistically significant difference was recorded between the three samples (analysis of variance – "F" test).

(d) Three Science Park firms in 1986 which had subsequently moved off-Park were excluded.

(c) All three surveyed firms engaged in a merger/take-over since 1986 were located on a Science Park.

(f) Statistically significant difference was recorded between the three samples (analysis of variance "F" test – 0.5 level of significance).

(g) Thirty-four surveyed firms identified a single most important link with the HEI.

(h) Statistically significant difference was recorded between the three samples (analysis of variance – "F" test – 0.1 level of significance).

(i) Percentage of all mentions.

Amongst the other dimensions, it is interesting to note that the median total R & D expenditure per year of the "fast growers" is six times that of the "growers" and 150 times that of the "other" group. However, it does appear that a number of firms in this latter category either undertook no R & D expenditure or invested quite heavily in this area, since there is a huge difference between the mean and the median values. It suggests that there were some firms investing heavily in R & D expenditure, but which were experiencing either no growth or declines in employment. Row 14 of the table confirms this point by showing mean and median R & D expenditure, as a percentage of total turnover, is actually lower for the "fastest growers" than for the 15 "other" firms.

Rows 15 to 19 are unable to isolate any clear differences between the groups according to their links with HEIs or in terms of patents and copyrights.

However, row 20 points to differences in the number of new products/services launched in the last two years. It shows that "other" firms – the no growth or decliners – were introducing fewer new products than either the "growers" or the "fast growers". Indeed, it appears that it was the "growers" which were likely to have introduced more new products than the "fast growers".

Turning now to financing matters, row 23 of the table does not provide any evidence that the "growers" and "fast growers" were likely to report greater problems with access to finance than the "other" firms. Nevertheless, there does seem to be a difference between the groups according to the clearing bank where their main business account was held and, more importantly, the frequency of corporate planning. Row 25 of the table shows over half of the "other" group do not undertake any corporate planning, whereas all of the "fast growers" engage in this exercise.

Of the remaining characteristics the only clear difference between the groups emerges in row 29 of the table where, not surprisingly, more of the "fast growers" were seeking new premises than firms in the other two categories.

16.5 Employment change in independent businesses

In addition to examining employment change in independent single plant firms in the follow-on study (Section 4.5.2), analysis was also conducted exploring employment growth in all surveyed "independent" firms (in 1986) over the six-year period. Employment data for "independent" firms in 1986 is available for two points in time for 46 surviving Science Park firms and a further 31 surviving off-Park firms. In 1986, the mean employment size of the "independent" Science Park firms was 11.3 employees (median = 7 employees) compared with a mean of 21.4 employees in "independent" off-Park firms (median = 11 employees). There was no statistically significant difference between the mean employment sizes of the two groups of firms in 1986 ("t" = −1.47, d.f. = 75, significance = 0.150). However, by 1992–93 the Science Park firms had grown to employ on average 26.8 people (median = 14 employees) whilst the mean employment size of off-Park firms had grown to 37.8 employees (median = 14 employees)[14]. As found in 1986, there is no statistically significant difference between the present mean employ ment sizes of both groups of firms ("t" = −0.82, d.f. = 75, significance = 0.418). Over the six-year period, the mean employment increase in both groups of firms was virtually identical (15.5 employees compared to 16.4 employees) ("t" = −0.09, d.f. = 75, significance = 0.926).

Both groups of "independent" firms in this survey recorded marked increases in employment growth over the six years. The growth recorded is markedly higher than that in a longitudinal study of a representative sample of 298 "independent" small firms in six geographical areas in England and Scotland over the 1985 to 1991 period. In 1991, a follow-up survey was conducted by Jones (1991, p 57) who found that the 130 surviving and interviewed "independent" firms employed on average 8.2 employees per firm in 1991 as opposed to 7.6 employees per firm in 1985. It is apparent from this evidence that the employment growth recorded in Science Park and off-Park firms is markedly higher than that recorded in a group of "independent" small firms in more "conventional" sectors. We believe this is a significant finding.

16.6 Conclusions This chapter has contrasted new technology-based firms (NTBFs) located on and off Science Parks; it has compared firms located on "managed" and "non-managed" Science Parks; finally, it has compared firms which exhibit rapid employment growth with those experiencing slower, zero or negative growth.

1. Although the study made a separate analysis of new technology-based firms (NTBFs) on and off Science Parks the conclusions failed to shed much additional light on differences between Science Park tenants and the off-Park group.

2. Our distinction between firms on "managed", as opposed to "non-managed" Science Parks did yield some interesting differences. First, closure rates on "managed" and "non-managed" Science Parks were comparable. But, at a finer level of analysis, it was found that the independent firm closure rate was lower on the "non-managed" Parks, whilst the closure rates of subsidiaries were markedly higher on these same Parks. Second, firms on "managed" Parks were more likely to utilise facilities and clearly identified the benefits of "management". However, they also recognised they were paying a price premium for these benefits which, in recessionary times, was causing them some concern. A third key finding was that there was no evidence firms on "managed" Parks felt the Science Park manager performed a particularly useful role in linking them to the HEI. In most respects the Science Park manager was clearly viewed as "adding value" but it appears that his/her ability to link firms to the HEI was an aspect which required greater attention.

3. Employment growth in independent single-plant firms in this survey is heavily concentrated in a small number of enterprises. Sixty-nine per cent of total gross new jobs in Science Park firms was concentrated in the five fastest growers. The comparable figure for off-Park firms was 93 per cent.

   An examination of the five fastest growing firms in the total survey showed four out of the five were located on Science Parks; none were in an "assisted" area and only one was in the "north". However, it is not the case they were exclusively concentrated in manufacturing; indeed the sectoral diversity of their single most important activity is striking.

4. Employment change in "independent" Science Park and off-Park firms was markedly higher than that recorded in "independent" firms in more "conventional" industrial sectors.

Chapter 17

Conclusions and Implications

17.1   The background   In 1986 a survey of 183 tenants on United Kingdom Science Parks at that time was carried out. These were "matched" against 101 firms in similar sectors, of similar age, of similar ownership pattern and in similar parts of the United Kingdom. The matching was successful in three out of the four dimensions, the exception being that the off-Park firms tended to be somewhat older than Science Park firms.

The current study identifies two samples of firms:

- Those which were still trading in 1992, having been interviewed in 1986. These firms are called the "follow-on" sample.

- Seventy-one firms which were located on United Kingdom Science Parks in 1992, but which did not exist on Parks in 1986 (and in many cases did not exist at all). These are matched against 71 firms, not located on United Kingdom Science Parks, according to the four criteria of: age, sector, geography and ownership. These 142 firms are called the "new sample". The matching here was again successful in three of the four criteria – the exception being in terms of geography, with more "off-Park" than "Science Park" firms being located in south-east England.

Analyses were then conducted primarily to determine the impact of a Science Park location, on the "follow-on" sample, the "new sample" and for both samples together – referred to as the "combined sample". The purpose of this chapter is to provide an overall summary of the results of each major theme of the research. It then addresses the policy issues emerging from each of the themes.

17.2   Issues   The prime purpose of this research is to estimate the impact or "added value" of the decision by a high technology business to locate on a United Kingdom Science Park. The analysis is conducted at the national level, but specific account is taken of location in government "assisted" areas. This section briefly reviews the nature of any benefits which a technology-based firm might expect to receive by locating on a Science Park. These are placed in five categories:

1. The first is that the Science Park provides a prestige site. Quite simply, location on an HEI Science Park means the business is immediately more credible to its financiers and customers than a more conventional address.

2. Second, the accommodation provided on Science Parks is generally of an extremely high standard. This also is likely to add to the credibility of the business.

3. The third benefit is that the Park is normally very close to, or even part of, an HEI. This means its existence provides an encouragement for academics to commercialise their research activities in a convenient location; it also provides the opportunity for businesses to liaise with academics in a professional and social context. Finally, it provides businesses with the opportunity, should they wish it, to use the facilities of the HEI.

4. The fourth benefit is that Science Parks normally have an individual – a Science Park manager – whose function is not only

to manage the property requirements of the Park, but also to act as a link with the HEI and to provide a networking service for other sources of advice and assistance to tenant firms.

5. Finally, the clustering of high technology firms in a single location can provide benefits in terms of inter-trading between the firms and makes them a more obvious "target" for the provision of government grants, advice, assistance, etc.

For all these reasons it might be expected that the performance of high technology firms located on Science Parks would, in some senses, be better than that of high technology firms located elsewhere. The focus of this research is to determine the extent to which this is the case.

Finally, given that Science Parks are seen as an integral part of regional development, it was deemed to be important to assess the extent to which these benefits varied according to whether or not the Park was located in an "assisted" area.

17.3 Performance/out-turn measures and assessments

In this section four measures of performance/out-turn, comparing Science Park and off-Park firms will be presented. These are:

- closure rates
- performance/out-turn measures
- technological sophistication
- HEI links.

17.3.1 Closure rates

Two relevant comparisons are made in this analysis. The first compares the "closure" rates of firms in this sample as a whole, with those of United Kingdom small businesses more generally, in order to determine whether high technology firms have higher or lower closure rates than comparable businesses in other sectors. The second comparison is between the closure rates of businesses located on and off Science Parks.

There are a number of problems in making both of these comparisons, which are extensively documented in Chapter 2. Nevertheless, several broad conclusions emerge:

- The survival rate in 1992 of firms initially interviewed in the 1986 UKSPA survey is higher than would be expected of a representative sample of United Kingdom businesses. This suggests that high technology businesses have lower closure rates than businesses in other sectors.

- Comparing the total closure rates of businesses located on and off Science Parks in 1986 shows the closure rate on Science Parks was 38 per cent, compared with 32 per cent amongst off-Park firms. This suggests a Science Park location does not lead to overall lower closure rates.

- This difference is attributed to the presence and higher closure rate of subsidiary operations on Science Parks. Comparing only independent firms shows the closure rates on and off Science Parks (32 per cent compared with 33 per cent) are virtually identical. The rates of closure of subsidiary operations is, however, 54 per cent on Science Parks, compared with 22 per cent off-Park.

Our overall conclusion, therefore, is that location on a United Kingdom Science Park for an independent business does not seem to be a factor influencing its survival or non-survival.

| 17.3.2 | *Performance/* | Three performance measures are examined: employment growth, sales
| | *out-turn measures* | growth and profitability. Attention is focused primarily upon employ-

17.3.2 *Performance/ out-turn measures*

Three performance measures are examined: employment growth, sales growth and profitability. Attention is focused primarily upon employment growth which, generally, is strongly associated with sales growth. It is argued that measures of profitability obtained through survey instruments of this type are likely to be subject to greater margins of error. We also favour an emphasis upon employment over sales measures. The two advantages which employment has over sales measures is that employment is in "real" terms, rather than being influenced by inflation so that comparisons over time are more easily undertaken. Second, Science Parks see themselves as having an economic, and ultimately an employment, impact upon their community and therefore employment creation is a highly relevant criteria for judging their success.

It must be emphasised that data on employment is not available for all firms. Also, it is not appropriate, when examining growth, to include employment in subsidiary operations since the factors which influence growth in a major multi-national corporation are unlikely to be influenced by the nature of a Science Park in which one of its establishments is located. Analysis was therefore conducted for independent single-plant firms on employment change between 1986 and 1992 (Section 4.5.2). The results are striking. The arithmetic mean employment gain in employment in Science Park firms was virtually double that of the employment gain in off-Park firms. The mean gain was 12.4 workers for Science Park firms and only 6.7 workers for off-Park firms. Perhaps even more striking is the finding that 88 per cent of independent single-plant Science Park firms reported increased employment between 1986 and 1992, compared with only 46 per cent of independent single-plant off-Park firms.

The second key finding on employment-related matters is the extent to which increases are concentrated in a very few firms. The five fastest growing Science Park firms created 69 per cent of total new jobs on Parks, whilst the fastest growing five off-Park firms generated 93 per cent of gross new jobs in that group. It emphasises again the crucial role which a relatively small number of firms play in employment creation over a period of time.

Not surprisingly, for the reasons outlined earlier, we observe similar patterns in sales turnover with the arithmetic mean increase in sales amongst independent single-plant Science Park firms being markedly higher than that amongst off-Park firms.

We do not observe any significant differences in terms of reported profitability in 1990–91 between independent single-plant firms located on and off Science Parks.

Overall, our conclusion is that, where consistent data exists, high technology, independent, single-plant businesses which were located on Science Parks in 1986 and survived to 1992 on average exhibited faster rates of growth than comparable businesses located elsewhere. Nevertheless, it is the contribution of a relatively small proportion of these firms which is the major influence upon employment growth.

17.3.3 *Technological sophistication*

A third index of the contribution of the Science Park would be whether firms located on it, even though they are in the same sectors as the off-Park firms, were in some senses more innovative or technologically sophisticated. This research formulated a number of indicators of technological sophistication and examined the extent to which these varied between on- and off-Park firms. It also tried to determine whether, for the firms which were interviewed in 1986, there was evidence that over time they became increasingly or decreasingly sophisticated.

The evidence here is mixed. Founders of Science Park businesses are much more likely to have the highest possible educational qualifications than off-Park founders (Chapter 8). Science Park firms appear to employ a higher proportion of individuals classified as qualified scientists and engineers (QSEs) as a proportion of their labour force than off-Park firms (Chapter 10). However, when we ask firms to assess the technological sophistication of the product(s) or service(s) that they provide, the sophistication of the Science Park firms appears no higher than that of off-Park firms (Chapter 9). We also find no evidence of firms as a whole over the six-year period, irrespective of whether or not they are located on a Science Park, becoming increasingly innovative. In general, the self-assessed level of technological sophistication remains fairly static. Finally, we do not find any clear difference in terms of R & D outputs in the form of patenting, licensing, copyrighting, etc. between on- and off-Park firms (Chapter 12).

Our conclusion is that it is only the formal qualifications of the founders, and in their employment of QSEs, that Science Park firms clearly differ from off-Park firms. We also find no evidence that high technology businesses begin life in the "soft" consultancy sector and make a transition towards "hard" manufacturing (Section 4.3). Instead, we are more struck by the lack of change amongst surveyed businesses as a whole. In fact, many firms in the follow-on sample have made the strategic decision to focus their efforts on a wider range of "soft" service-orientated industrial activities.

17.3.4   HEI and other links

One of the key findings in the 1986 survey was that, although closeness to an HEI was seen to be an important factor influencing firms to locate on Science Parks, the extent to which these links existed was less than anticipated. To some extent this was rationalised at that time on the grounds that most of the firms, and many of the Science Parks, were relatively new. It was felt that the building up of links took place only over a lengthy period of time and that, in 1986, it was somewhat premature to assess this matter.

Since firms in the follow-on survey have been on a Science Park for at least six years, this argument is no longer valid. Our current findings suggest Science Park firms generally have increased their links with the local HEI, whereas the off-Park sample have changed little in this respect (Chapter 11). Nevertheless, it would be unwise to assume off-Park firms have little contact with an HEI; for example 45 per cent of off-Park firms claim to have informal contact with academics and 22 per cent claim to have access to specialist equipment. The main difference between the groups tends to be in terms of the use of facilities such as computers, libraries, recreation, etc. where Science Park firms' use is very much higher.

Perhaps the most striking finding which emerges is the evidence of a "latent demand" for contact and liaison with HEIs, both amongst Science Park and off-Park firms. This is illustrated by the strong support for the suggestion that the HEI should make greater efforts to ensure its services and facilities are more accessible to businesses. We also point to the finding that, where respondents have been invited to, and have attended, technical seminars at the local HEI, 88 per cent of the new sample of firms reported they found this useful. Hence, there appears to be, amongst a significant majority of technology-based firms both on and off Science Parks, a feeling that the strengthening of links between themselves and the HEI would be helpful to them.

More disconcerting is the finding that there was no greater likelihood of Science Park firms having received a visit from a representative of an HEI to discuss the facilities available than was the case for off-Park firms. It may be that HEI personnel feel responsibility for Science Park firms in this respect should be left to the Science Park manager. The assumption that Science Park firms are better informed about research in the HEI does not seem to be valid. Technology-based firms in general feel links with HEIs could be improved and that, perhaps by implication, the first move has to be made by the HEIs to set the process in motion.

Chapter 16 distinguished between firms on "managed" and "non-managed" Science Parks. Here, where an assessment was made of the role of the Science Park manager, the aspect in which the opinions of firms on "managed" and "non-managed" Science Parks differed least was in respect of the role of the manager in linking with the HEI. In essence, this suggested that managers on "managed" Parks were comparatively ineffective in linking their tenants to the HEI. Again, this suggests that firms wish these links could be stronger and that the initiative should either be taken by the Science Park manager or by the HEI.

17.4 "Assisted" area status   The closure rate of all surveyed firms located in "assisted" areas is lower (32 per cent) than that of firms in "non-assisted" areas (40 per cent). There are, however, considerable variations according to whether or not these firms are independent or subsidiary organisations and whether or not they are located on a Science Park. The key findings are:

- Firms located on Science Parks in "assisted" areas have a total sample closure rate (37 per cent) which is virtually identical to that of firms on Parks in "non-assisted" areas (38 per cent).

- Firms located off Science Parks in "assisted" areas have much lower total sample closure rates (19 per cent) than those comparable firms in "non-assisted" areas (43 per cent).

- For independent firms only, the most striking difference is that the closure rate of off-Park firms was 43 per cent in "non-assisted" areas, compared with 20 per cent in "assisted" areas.

With regard to the characteristics of Science Park firm founders no statistically significant differences were recorded between the two areas (Chapter 8). The technological level of Park firms in the two areas was also found to be similar (Chapter 9). Similarly, no differences were recorded between Science Park firms in the two environments with regard to R & D expenditures and the proportion of QSEs engaged in R & D (Chapter 10). In Section 11.7 it was found that Science Park firms in "assisted" areas were no better linked to their local HEI than Park firms in "non-assisted" areas. Also, there was no evidence that firms on Science Parks in "assisted" areas have better links with their HEIs than those located elsewhere. Indeed, we found that, in some respects, these links are weaker. However, in relation to R & D outputs no statistically significant differences emerged between Science Park firms located in the "assisted" and "non-assisted" areas (Chapter 12).

Detailed analysis of the financing of Science Parks firms revealed only one difference between firms located in the two areas. Section 13.7 showed that Science Park firms in "assisted" areas were much more likely to report restrictions upon their growth (as distinct from merely aggravating cash-flow difficulties) attributable to problems of obtaining access to finance. This remains an area which is worthy of more detailed investigation.

In Chapter 14 no statistically significant differences were recorded between Science Park firms in the two areas with regard to current sources of formal external advice and assistance.

Also, in Chapter 15 no statistically significant differences were recorded between firms in the two areas with regard to their use of facilities on Science Parks and the perception of the role played by the Science Park manager/director. However, significantly more firms on Science Parks in "assisted" areas suggested there were disadvantages from being located on a Park than those in "non-assisted" areas. In Section 15.5 it was found that significantly more Science Park firms located in "assisted" areas were considering new or additional premises which would not be on the same site as the surveyed business. They were seeking a short distance move (i.e. less than ten miles away).

The performance of Science Park firms between "assisted" and "non-assisted" areas was further explored in relation to employment, levels of sales turnover, profitability and the ability to spin off new firms. On only one of these performance measures was a statistically significant difference recorded between independent single-plant firms in the two environments. Independent single-plant firms in the "non-assisted" areas had markedly higher mean levels of sales (£s) for the financial year 1990–91 (at the 0.1 level of significance).

Overall, the general impression is of strong similarities between firms in the "assisted" and "non-assisted" areas. The closure rates of independent firms on Science Parks in "assisted" areas is similar to those in the "non-assisted" areas (30 per cent compared with 34 per cent). Further, the technological sophistication of the firms looks broadly similar.

17.5 The implications

This section examines the implications of the findings of this research for four groups: government, financial institutions, Science Park managers and HEIs. In many respects the target audience is identical to that in the 1986 survey and, by implication, we shall assess the extent to which our recommendations in 1986 appear to have been acted upon, the extent to which they seem to have been ignored, and the extent to which matters have clearly changed in these respects over the last six years.

17.5.1 Government

Government sees its central role as providing a climate in which different types of businesses can prosper. Elements within that climate are ensuring that firms have access to high-quality business support and a technology network. From this research three key issues emerge which have direct implications for government. The first is that high technology firms in this survey have faster employment growth rates and lower closure rates than businesses in other sectors. The direct and indirect impact upon the economy is high, but the number of such firms is small.

The central issue for government is to stimulate an increase in the size of the high technology sector. Whilst there has been an increase in the number of, for example, NTBFs on Science Parks, over the past six years, further increases are needed.

The problem is that this increase in the quantity must not take place by lowering the quality of such firms, since it is the latter dimension which is at the heart of the competitiveness of high technology firms. What is clear is that the founders of high technology businesses are increasingly those with the highest possible academic qualifications – often a doctorate. Hence it is vital to maintain (and enhance) the output of such highly qualified people. To achieve this requires a wide ranging agenda of policies such as encouraging 14 year olds to study science, to providing attractive Doctoral and post Doctoral positions in science in universities.

The second key finding for government is that the results re-emphasise that, within the small business sector, the vast majority of employment created is in a small number of firms which grow rapidly. If government sees employment creation as an objective of policy, it has to obtain a better understanding of the factors which influence and constrain development of these types of firms.

Thirdly, it is disconcerting to note that the five most rapidly growing firms, which contribute the bulk of employment increases in firms in the survey, were all located outside "assisted" areas and four out of the five were located in the "south" of England (Section 16.4.2.). Given that 55 per cent of firms in the "follow-on" survey were located in "assisted" areas, it suggests that these areas are not generating their "fair share" of growing high-tech firms.

However, we emphasise again that our purpose is not to estimate directly the role which Science Parks play in regional development. Instead, our findings emphasise the importance which high-tech firms play in creating employment and enterprise in all regions of the economy. The focus of policy, in any region, has to be to strengthen, nurture and actively promote links between HEIs and high-tech firms located on as well as off Science Parks. This could be achieved through providing greater incentives to the HEIs to "sell" their services, or to encourage more high-tech firms to be established and developed on and off Science Parks. These policies merit high priority.

17.5.2 Finance   The proportion of independent firms which report their businesses have been constrained in their growth by a shortage of finance is virtually the same as those which report no such constraint (Chapter 13). Evidence from both this survey and elsewhere, suggests the problem is perhaps greater for technology-based businesses, especially in "assisted" areas, than for businesses of comparable sizes in other sectors.

Nevertheless, there has clearly been some improvement in this respect since 1986. First, there has been an increase in the proportion of businesses established in recent years, which have utilised external sources of venture capital, although the number of cases continues to be small. It is also well known that bank lending to small businesses rose very sharply during the late 1980s, although it has fallen back somewhat in the last eighteen months.

In our view the key issue is that of the risk/return relationship between the bank and small businesses. This is particularly true for high technology businesses where the perceived risk is high, if only because the banks have frequently had an imperfect understanding of the technology employed and hence the market place to be served. However, this research shows the closure rates of high technology businesses are below those of businesses in more conventional sectors. Furthermore, where they do survive, these businesses experience rates of growth which are generally substantially faster than those of more typical businesses. The problem from the point of view of the banks is that, since they are not normally equity stake-holders, they do not share in any of the up-side gains if the business is extremely successful. They do, however, share the "down-side" losses in the event of business closure, and it is this which explains why personal guarantees may be sought from the owners of businesses to cover bank lending.

One way to overcome this problem is for the banks and their clients – and high technology businesses would be an ideal group to begin with – to form a much closer and longer term relationship. In essence, this means the firm is prepared to share equity with the financial institution which would benefit from the up-side gains if the business expands and grows. Conversely, the bank would rely less heavily on insisting the personal assets of the directors were secured; funding would move away from an overdependence upon short-term overdrafts which can be removed at short notice, towards a longer term funding package which would include equity.

To achieve this goal requires adjustments on the part of both the bank and the firm. The firm has to recognise that, by offering some equity for sale, it can obtain a longer term funding package which would include equity and other longer term finance.

Other ways of overcoming the risk/return issue for small high technology businesses include the establishment of specialist venture capital funds, incentives for business angels and an extension and development of government funding in the form of SMART-type awards. The evidence from other research such as that by Moore (1990) suggests SMART awards have been very effective in facilitating the development of technology-based firms, but all of these merit some consideration.

17.5.3 *Science Park managers*

Where there is a Science Park manager on site on a full-time basis, the bulk of tenants appreciate the contribution which that individual makes (Section 16.3.2). That contribution, however, is greater in some aspects than in others. For example, the manager is generally seen to be a focus for the property-related problems which a tenant firm experiences, but is much less likely to be seen as a conduit to the facilities of the local HEI or as a source of business information.

Clearly the role which the Science Park manager plays varies markedly from one Park to another depending, at least in part, on the number of personnel working with the manager. We observe a generally higher level of satisfaction expressed by Science Park tenants on "managed", as opposed to "non-managed" Parks. It is our impression, as it was in 1986, that property-based initiatives without a significant managerial function are comparatively ineffective. The problem is that this management has to be paid for. In times of recession, when this survey was being conducted, tenant firms were looking very closely at their own costs and many long-established firms were unsure whether the "premium rents" which they felt themselves to be paying could be justified in terms of the property which they occupied and the management service they received.

It is our view that Science Parks generally need to strengthen their managerial functions, in the sense of being seen to be less of a property-based initiative. Increasing the frequency of contact between managers and tenants is necessary. A more effective way of linking the tenant to the facilities provided at the HEI also needs to be given greater attention by Park managers.

The finding that independent business closure rates are as high on Science Parks as for comparable off-Park firms is surprising. Two reasons for this may be put forward: the first is that they reflect this absence of a close link between manager and tenant Park firms alluded to above. The second is that the relatively high closure rates reflect a lack of selectivity in choosing Science Park tenants which, in itself, stems from a desire to let the highest appropriate proportion of property in order to maximise income flow.

Prior to this research, the closure rates of Science Park firms had not been addressed fully because of the way in which data have been collected. Now that the evidence is available, it suggests this issue be investigated more thoroughly.

17.5.4 *Universities (HEIs)* The most striking finding here is the value which high technology firms place upon their links with HEIs. Where they have attended technical seminars they have, almost without exception, found them to be helpful (Chapter 11). In essence there is a feeling that there is a lot of information within HEIs which would be useful to a business if only it were able to access it appropriately. From the businesses' perspective, however, it finds the "searching out" of information extremely time-consuming and sees it as the responsibility of the HEI to foster better links with the business community. In reality, both parties have a responsibility of ensuring a successful business/academic network.

It suggests the role of industrial liaison officers within HEIs needs to be strengthened. It also suggests these individuals should not assume that firms on their own Science Park are necessarily significantly better informed about what is happening in the local HEI than firms located elsewhere within the locality. In many Science Parks, what is happening in the HEI is not getting through to tenant firms.

The second lesson for the HEI, relating to points made in Section 17.5.3, is that to maximise the contribution which a Science Park makes, it is necessary to have an effective (but not extravagant) managerial structure designed to "add value" to the tenant Park firms. There is a "happy medium" between, on the one hand, a solely property-based initiative which happens to be located adjacent to an HEI and, on the other, what is perceived by tenant firms as an overstaffed bureaucracy which they are funding from their rental payments. The happy medium is a lean central unit which both manages property aspects efficiently and is an effective conduit to the HEI and other sources of business information. This role can only be exercised with regular contact between Science Park management and tenant firms.

The third implication is that HEIs have to demonstrate to government and the general public the importance of maintaining their science research budgets. The ultimate commercialisation of some elements ofthis research should not necessarily be the dominant theme in lobbying government, but should be used as an argument.

Finally, Monck et al. (1986) pointed to the need for HEIs to enter into flexible relationships with members of their staff wishing to commercialise their research ideas. The evidence from this survey is that these arrangements have only developed very modestly and, given the need to increase the number of high technology businesses, this is an area that HEIs should look at more closely.

Notes

1. It is important to appreciate that a larger proportion of surveyed Science Park firms in 1986 were found to be less than ten years of age (63 per cent compared with 34 per cent) (Monck et al., 1988, p 106). Analyses of Value Added Tax (VAT) business deregistrations suggest that small firms have high levels of "infant mortality" and overall generally lower survival rates. In fact, Ganguly (1985) shows that based on VAT returns, 42 per cent of small firms deregister after four years irrespective of macro-economic conditions. Further, Garnsey and Cannon-Brookes (1992, p 11) found an overall trend of lower high technology business failure rates with increasing age.

2. There are a number of problems in making this comparison. The most important of these concerns ownership change. Where, for example, firm X is acquired by firm Y, the latter may or may not choose to include firm X under its VAT registration number. If it chooses to, then firm X is deregistered. This means some firms which are located on Science Parks, but which have changed ownership would be regarded as deregistrations for the VAT data, but not for the Science Park data. Conversely, some firms which have moved off the Park, but which continue to trade under their VAT number would be regarded as losses to the Park, but would not be so identified in the official data. We have no way of definitively resolving these conflicting influences.

3. A recent study of geographical variations in business deregistrations for VAT in the United Kingdom found that environments with high levels of new business entry (for example, areas with high levels of young firms) also have correspondingly high levels of business "failure" (see Westhead and Birley, 1994). This study confirmed the view that "birth" and "death" rates are spatially related (Westhead and Moyes, 1992, p 37).

4. It is important to note here that independent single-plant off-Park firms were significantly older than their Science Park counterparts ("t"= −1.72, d.f.= 39, Reject H_0 at the 0.05 level of significance, one-tailed test).

5. Recorded mean absolute employment increases are comparable to those presented by Oakey (1991b, p 34) in his time series study of new and established independent small firms (with less than 200 employees in 1981) engaged in instruments and electronics. He found for the 114 British firms that were trading in 1981 an additional 354 net jobs had been created by 1985 and on average 11 new jobs per surviving firm was recorded.

6. At the aggregate level of the industrial sector there is evidence suggesting that R & D employment intensive sectors are the best performers. Also, formation and growth rates are higher in R & D employment intensive firms than low-technology firms (Armington et al., 1983). Felsenstein and Shachar (1988) in their study of mainly independent high technology firms in Israel found that a metropolitan location was found to be significantly related to R & D employment intensity but government assistance was not found to be positively related to R & D employment intensity. Moreover, these researchers also indicated that:

" ... smaller firms are not more likely to be engaged in research intensive activity but that the younger firms are more R & D employment oriented" (p 483).

7. It has been pointed out here that:

   "Indeed, Science Parks only represent one particular mechanism to stimulate technology transfers between academia and industry; multiple other mechanisms exist, e.g. research consortia, joint ventures, contract research, etc." (van Dierdonck et al., 1991, p 111).

8. It is important to note here that 9 Science Park respondents compared to 20 off-Park respondents could not categorically identify the single most important link with a HEI. Consequently, these firms were treated as missing cases.

9. In 1986 firms surveyed on the Bolton, East Anglia and Springfield House (Leeds) Science Parks were regarded by UKSPA as no longer conforming to their definition of a Science Park, so in 1992 these three locations are not regarded by UKSPA as being valid Science Parks. The four follow-on interviews conducted in 1992 in Bolton and Leeds were consequently excluded from the subsequent analysis. A further eight interviewed firms which were located on UKSPA defined Science Parks in 1986 (as well as 1992) but had subsequently moved off-Park are also excluded.

10. In 1986, 14 firms surveyed on the Bolton, East Anglia and Leeds Science Parks were regarded by UKSPA as being valid Science Park firms. However, in 1992 these locations are not currently regarded by UKSPA as being valid Science Park locations. These 14 firms were excluded from the subsequent analysis.

11. Total "non-managed" Park sample closure rate (including no telephone listings) = 20/57= 35 per cent.

    Total "managed" Park sample closure rate (including no telephone listings) = 41/112= 37 per cent.

12. Total "non-managed" Park sample independent organisation closure rate (including no telephone listings) = 10/41= 24 per cent.

    Total "managed" Park sample independent organisation closure rate (including no telephone listings) = 28/85= 33 per cent.

13. Total "non-managed" Park sample subsidiary organisation closure rate = 10/16= 63 per cent.

    Total "managed" Park sample subsidiary organisation closure rate = 13/27= 48 per cent.

14. In 1992, 12 Science Park firms had subsequently become subsidiaries, whilst only 2 off-Park firms had made this ownership change.

References

ACOST (1990). *The Enterprise Challenge: Overcoming Barriers to Growth in Small Firms.* London: HMSO.

Aldrich, H. E. (1990). Using an Ecological Perspective to Study Organizational Founding Rates. *Entrepreneurship, Theory and Practice*, 14, pp 7–24.

American Electronics Association (1978). Written Statement before the House Committee on Ways and Means (E. U. W. Zachau, Chairman, Capital Formation Task Force, AEA), 7 March 1978.

Amin, A. and Goddard, J. B. (1986). The Internationalization of Production, Technological Change, Small Firms and Regional Development: An Overview. In A. Amin and J. B. Goddard (eds.). *Technological Change, Industrial Restructuring and Regional Development.* London: Allen & Unwin, pp 1–22.

Angelmar, R. (1984). Market Structure and Research Intensity in High Technological-opportunity Industries. *Journal of Industrial Economics*, 34, pp 69–79.

Appold, S. J. (1991). The Location Process of Industrial Research Laboratories. *Annals of Regional Science*, 25, pp 131–44.

Armington, C., Harris, C. and Odle, M. (1983). *Formation and Growth in High Technology Firms: A Regional Assessment.* Washington DC: Brookings Institution.

Aston Business School (1991). *Constraints on the Growth of Small Firms.* London: HMSO.

Autio, E. and Kauranen, I. (1992). The Effectiveness of Science Parks as a Tool of Technology Policy: Some Empirical Evidence. Helsinki: Institute of Industrial Management, Helsinki University of Technology (Working Paper).

Aydalot, P. and Keeble, D. (eds) (1988). *High Technology Industry and Innovative Environments: The European Experience.* London: Routledge.

Begg, I. G. and Cameron, G. C. (1988). High Technology Location and the Urban Areas of Great Britain. *Urban Studies*, 25, pp 361–79.

Binks, M. R., Ennew, C. T. and Reed, G. V. (1993). *Small Businesses and their Banks.* Knutsford: Forum for Private Business.

Birley, S. and Westhead, P. (1988). *Exit Routes.* Cranfield: Cranfield School of Management.

Birley, S. and Westhead, P. (1990a). 'North–South' Contrasts in the Characteristics and Performance of Small Firms. *Entrepreneurship & Regional Development*, 2, pp 27–48.

Birley, S. and Westhead, P. (1990b). Private Advertised Business Sales in the United Kingdom. *Area*, 22, pp 368–80.

Birley, S. and Westhead, P. (1990c). *Private Advertised Sales in the United Kingdom: Post Stock Market Crash*. London: The Management School, Imperial College.

Birley, S. and Westhead, P. (1992). A Comparison of New Firms in "Assisted" and "Non-Assisted" Areas in Great Britain. *Entrepreneurship & Regional Development*, 4, pp 299–338.

Birley, S. and Westhead, P. (1993a). A Comparison of New Businesses Established by "Novice" and "Habitual" Founders in Great Britain. *International Small Business Journal*, 12, pp 38–60.

Birley, S. and Westhead, P. (1993b). New Venture Environments – The Owner-manager's View. In S. Birley and I. C. MacMillan (eds). *Entrepreneurship Research: Global Perspectives*. Amsterdam: The Netherlands, pp 207–47.

Bishop, P. (1988). Academic–Industry Links and Firm Size in South West England. *Regional Studies*, 22, pp 160–62.

Breheny, M. and McQuaid, W. (1987). High Technology UK: The Development of High Technology Industry. In M. Breheny and W. McQuaid (eds). *The Development of High Technology Industry*. London: Croom Helm, pp 297–354.

Bullock, M. (1983). *Academic Enterprise, Industrial Innovation and the Development of High Technology Financing in the United States*. London: Brand Bros and Co.

Cohen, W. M. and Klepper, S. (1990). *A Reprise of Size and R & D*. Pittsburgh: Carnegie-Mellon University (mimeo).

Covin, J. G. and Slevin, D. P. (1990). New Venture Strategic Posture, and Performance: An Industry Life Cycle Analysis. *Journal of Business Venturing*, 5, pp 123–35.

Covin, J. G., Slevin, D. P. and Covin, T. J. (1990). Content and Performance of Growth-seeking Strategies: A Comparison of Small Firms in High- and Low-Technology Industries. *Journal of Business Venturing*, 5, pp 391–412.

Cressy, R. (1993). *Loan Commitments and Business Starts: An Empirical Investigation on UK Data*. Coventry: Small and Medium Sized Enterprise Centre, Warwick Business School (Working Paper No. 12).

Daly, M. (1991). VAT Registrations and Deregistrations in 1990. *Employment Gazette*, 99, pp 579–88.

Damesick, P. (1987). The Evolution of Spatial Economic Policy. In P. J. Damesick and P. A. Wood (eds). *Regional Problems, Problem Regions and Public Policy in the United Kingdom*. Oxford: Clarendon Press, pp 42–63.

Donckels, R. and Segers, J. P. (1990). New Technology Based Firms and the Creation of Regional Growth Potential. *Small Business Economics*, 2, pp 33–44.

Felsenstein, D. and Shachar, A. (1988). Locational and Organizational Determinants of R & D Employment in High Technology Firms. *Regional Studies*, 22, pp 477–86.

Flamhotz, E. G. (1966). *How to Make the Transition from Entrepreneurship to a Professionally Managed Firm*. San Francisco: Jossey-Bass.

Ganguly, P. (1985). *Small Business Statistics and International Comparisons*. London: Harper and Row.

Garnsey, E. and Cannon-Brookes, A. (1992). *The 'Cambridge Phenomenon' Revisited: Aggregate Change Among Cambridge High Technology Companies Since 1985*. Cambridge: Judge Institute of Management Studies (Working Paper (New Series) No. 3).

Gibb, A. (1992). Can Academe Achieve Quality in Small Firms Policy Research? *Entrepreneurship & Regional Development*, 4, pp 127–44.

Grayson, L. (1993). *Science Parks: An Experiment in High Technology Transfer*. London: The British Library.

Hannan, M. T. and Freeman, J. H. (1977). The Population Ecology of Organisations. *American Journal of Sociology*, 82, pp 929–64.

Hansen, J. A. (1992). Innovation, Firm Size, and Firm Age. *Small Business Economics*, 4, pp 37–44.

Henneberry, J. (1992). Science Parks: A Property-Based Initiative for Urban Regeneration. *Local Economy*, 6, pp 326–35.

Hitchens, D. M. W. N. and O'Farrell, P. N. (1987). The Comparative Performance of Small Manufacturing Firms in Northern Ireland and South East England. *Regional Studies*, 21, pp 543–53.

Jones, M. (1991). *Small Firms Study 1985, 1988 and 1991*. Coventry: University of Warwick (MBA Unpublished Dissertation).

Joseph, R. A. (1989). Technology Parks and their Contribution to the Development of Technology-Oriented Complexes in Australia. *Environment and Planning* C, 7, pp 173–92.

Keasey, K. and Watson, R. (1993). *Investment and Financing Decisions and the Performance of Small Firms*. London: National Westminster Bank.

Keeble, D. and Gould, A. (1984). *New Manufacturing Firms and Entrepreneurship in East Anglia: Final Report to the Economic and Social Research Council*. University of Cambridge: Department of Geography.

Lowe, J. (1985). Science Parks in the UK. *Lloyds Bank Review*, 156, pp 31–42.

MacDonald, S. (1987). British Science Parks: Reflections on the Politics of High Technology. *R & D Management*, 17, pp 25–37.

MacGregor, B. D., Langridge, R. J., Adley, J. and Chapman, B. (1986). The Development of High Technology Industry in Newbury District. *Regional Studies*, 20, pp 433–48.

Maggioni, M. A. (1992). The Economic Analysis of Science and Technology Parks: Theoretical Suggestions and the Italian Experience. Paper Presented at the International Workshop on "The European Experience of Science and Technology Parks", Siena, May 1992.

Mahmood, T. (1992). Does the Hazard Rate for New Plants Vary Between Low- and High-Tech Industries? *Small Business Economics*, 4, pp 201–09.

Markusen., A., Hall, P. and Glasmeier, A. (1986). *High Tech America: The What, How, Where, and Why of the Sunrise Industries.* Boston, Mass.: George Allen and Unwin.

Martin, R. (1985). Monetarism Masquerading as Regional Policy? The Government's New System of Regional Aid. *Regional Studies*, 19, pp 379–88.

Massey, D., Quintas, P. and Wield, D. (1992). High Tech Fantasies: Science Parks in Society, *Science and Space.* London: Routledge.

Miller, R. and Cote, M. (1987). *Growing the Next Silicon Valley.* Lexington, Mass.: Lexington Books.

Monck, C. S. P., Porter, R. B., Quintas, P., Storey, D. J. and Wynarczyk, P. (1988). *Science Parks and the Growth of High Technology Firms.* London: Croom Helm.

Moore, I. (1990). Biotechnology and Scientific Instrument Start-ups in the UK: The Role of Government Policy in Technological Innovation. In N. C. Churchill, W. D. Bygrave, J. A. Hornaday, D. F. Muzyka, K. H. Vesper and W. E. Wetzel, Jnr (eds). *Frontiers of Entrepreneurship Research.* Babson College: Massachusetts, pp 408–21.

Morse, R. S. (1976). *The Role of New Technical Enterprises in the US Economy.* Report of the Commerce Technical Advisory Board to the Secretary of Commerce, January.

Mounfield, P. R., Unwin, D. J. and Guy, K. (1985). The Influence of Size, Siting, Age and Physical Characteristics of Factory Premises on the Survival and Death of Footwear Manufacturing Establishments in the East Midlands, UK. *Environment and Planning* A, 17, pp 777–94.

Nelson, R. R., Peck, M. J. and Kalacek, E. (1967). The Concentration of Research and Development in Large Firms. In E. Mansfield (ed.). *Monopoly Power and Economic Performance.* New York: Norton, 1978.

North, D., Leigh, R. and Smallbone, D. (1992). A Comparison of Surviving and Non-surviving Small and Medium-sized Manufacturing Firms in London During the 1980s. In K. Caley, E. Chell, F. Chittenden, and C. Mason. (eds). *Small Enterprise Development: Policy and Practice in Action.* London: Paul Chapman Publishing Ltd, pp 12–27.

Oakey, R. (1984). High Technology Small Firms. London: Pinter.

Oakey, R. (1985). British University Science Parks and High Technology Small Firms: A Comment on the Potential for Sustained Industrial Growth. *International Small Business Journal*, 4, pp 58–67.

Oakey, R. (1991a). Government Policy Towards High Technology: Small Firms Beyond the Year 2000. In J. Curran and R. A. Blackburn. (eds). *Paths of Enterprise: The Future of the Small Business*. London: Routledge, pp 128–48.

Oakey, R. (1991b). High Technology Small Firms: Their Potential for Rapid Industrial Growth. *International Small Business Journal*, 9, pp 30–42.

Oakey, R. and Cooper, S. Y. (1989). High Technology Industry, Agglomeration and the Potential for Peripherally Sited Small Firms. *Regional Studies*, 23, pp 347–60.

Oakey, R. and Rothwell, R. (1986). High Technology Small Firms and Regional Industrial Growth. In A. Amin and J. B. Goddard. (eds). *Technological Change, Industrial Restructuring and Regional Development*. London: Allen & Unwin, pp 258–83.

O'Farrell, P. N. and Hitchens, D. M. W. N. (1988). The Relative Competitiveness and Performance of Small Manufacturing Firms in Scotland and the Mid-west of Ireland: An Analysis of Matched Pairs. *Regional Studies*, 22, pp 339–415.

Pavitt, K. (1982). R&D, Patenting and Innovative Activities: A Statistical Exploration. *Research Policy*, 13, pp 33–51.

Peck, F. W. (1985). The Use of Matched-pairs Research Design in Industrial Surveys. *Environment and Planning* A, 17, pp 981-89.

Pennings, J. M. (1982). Elaboration on the Entrepreneur and his Environment. In C. A. Kent, D. L. Sexton and K. H. Vesper (eds). *Encyclopedia of Entrepreneurship*. Englewood Cliffs, New Jersey: Prentice Hall, pp 307–15.

Roberts, E. B. (1990). Evolving Toward Product and Market Orientation: The Early Years of Technology-based Firms. *Journal of Product Innovation Management*, 7, pp 274–87.

Rothwell, R. and Zegveld, W. (1982). *Innovation and Small and Medium Sized Firms*. London: Frances Pinter.

Scott, M. G. and Lewis, J. (1984). Re-thinking Entrepreneurial Failure. In J. Lewis, J. Stanworth, and A. Gibb (eds). *Success and Failure in Small Business*. Aldershot: Gower, pp 29-56.

Segal Quince & Partners (1985). *The Cambridge Phenomenon: The Growth of High Technology Industry in a University Town*. Cambridge: Segal Quince & Partners.

Shachar, A. and Felsenstein, D. (1992). Urban Economic Development and High Technology Industry. *Urban Studies*, 29, pp 839-55.

Simmie, J. and James, N. D. (1986). Will Science Parks Generate the Fifth Wave? *Planning Outlook*, 29, pp 54–57.

Smilor, R. W., Gibson, D. V. and Kosmetsky, G. (1988). Creating the Technopolis: High Technology Development in Austin, Texas. *Journal of Business Venturing*, 4, pp 49–67.

Storey, D. J. (1982). *Entrepreneurship and the New Firm*. London: Croom Helm.

Storey, D. J. (1985). Manufacturing Employment Change in Northern England 1965–78: The Role of Small Businesses. In D. J. Storey (ed.). *Small Firms and Regional Economic Development: Britain, Ireland and the United States*. Cambridge: Cambridge University Press, pp 6–42.

Storey, D. J. (1994). *Understanding the Small Business Sector*. London: Routledge.

Storey, D. J. and Strange, A. (1992a). Where Are They Now? Some Changes in Firms Located on UK Science Parks in 1986. *New Technology, Work and Employment*, 7, pp 15–28.

Storey, D. J. and Strange, A. (1992b). *Entrepreneurship in Cleveland 1979–89: A Study of the Effects of the Enterprise Culture*. London: Employment Department (Research Series No. 3).

Storey, D. J., Watson, R. and Wynarczyk, P. (1987a). *Fast Growth Small Businesses: Case Studies of 40 Small Firms in North East England*. London: Department of Employment (Research Paper No. 67).

Storey, D. J., Keasey, K., Watson, R. and Wynarczyk, P. (1987b). *The Performance of Small Firms: Profits, Jobs and Growth*. London: Croom Helm.

Taylor, C. and Silbertson, A. (1973). *The Economic Impact of the Patent System*. Cambridge: Cambridge University Press.

Tsai, W. M-H., MacMillan, I. C. and Low, M. B. (1991). Effects of Strategy and Environment on Corporate Venture Success in Industrial Markets. *Journal of Business Venturing*, 6, pp 9–28.

van Dierdonck, R. V., Debackere, K. and Rappa, M. A. (1991). An Assessment of Science Parks: Towards a Better Understanding of their Role in the Diffusion of Technological Knowledge. *R & D Management*, 21, pp 109–23.

Westhead, P. and Birley, S. (1994). Environments for Business Deregistrations in the United Kingdom, 1987–1990. *Entrepreneurship & Regional Development*, (forthcoming).

Westhead, P. and Moyes, A. (1992). Reflections on Thatcher's Britain: Evidence from New Production Firm Registrations 1980–88. *Entrepreneurship & Regional Development*, 4, pp 21–56.

Printed in the United Kingdom for HMSO.
Dd.297336, 10/94, C10, 3396/4, 5673, 289457.